D0910039

IF THESE STONES COULD TALK

May the sacrifices of the "Greatest Generation" never be forgotten

Calvin G. Lyons

Calvin G. (Jerry) Lyons

If These Stones Could Talk

Calvin G. (Jerry) Lyons

© 2010

ISBN: 978-0-9845166-0-5

No portion of this book may be reproduced
without the written permission
of the author.

www.ifthesestonescouldtalk.com

Warwick House Publishers
720 Court Street
Lynchburg, VA 24504

DEDICATION

This book is dedicated to all of the families whose
loved ones were killed or reported as missing in action
during World War II, and whose remains were never recovered.
Their service to the cause of Freedom should serve as a beacon
to those generations of Americans yet to come.

A special dedication is made to the memory of
Staff Sergeant Wilbur Ward, Company "B,"
21st Infantry Regiment, 24th Infantry Division,
who lost his life while on patrol against the Japanese
on Lubang Island, the Philippines, on 2 March 1945.
I am sure that Wib's broad smile is being reflected
among the clouds in Heaven.

TABLE OF CONTENTS

Chapter Six

Chapter Seven

Chapter Eight

Chapter Nine

Chapter Ten

If These Stones Could Talk

*The Spirit of American Youth bronze statue at the
Normandy American Cemetery and Memorial,
Normandy, France. Photo by author.*

INTRODUCTION

"Older men declare war.
But it is the youth who must fight and die."
Herbert Hoover

Prominent on a bluff overlooking Omaha Beach and the English Channel near the town of St. Laurent-sur-Mer, France, is the beautiful and emotionally draining Normandy American Cemetery and Memorial. The 172 ½ acre cemetery contains 9,387 graves of American military, most of whom died during the D-Day landings and the subsequent fighting in Normandy during the summer of 1944. There is also a memorial wall in the garden area of the cemetery which lists the names of 1,557 missing. As you look over the bluff you see what was designated as "Easy Beach" for the soldiers of the 1st and 29th Infantry Divisions assigned to assault this section of the Normandy Coast on June 6, 1944…D-Day. The action here was anything but "easy."

The Infantry units landing below what is now the cemetery area had to fight their way up the draws leading from the beach to the bluff against a well-hidden and entrenched enemy force. The German defenders poured down a deadly crisscrossing fire from machine guns, 88mm guns, mortars and all the other weapons available to them. More casualties were suffered by the Americans on Omaha Beach that day than at any of the other four main landing beaches (Sword, Juno, Gold and Utah.)

When former President Eisenhower was being interviewed by Walter Cronkite for a television special entitled, *D-Day Plus 20,* Mr. Cronkite asked him what he thought about when he returned to Normandy. In reply, he spoke not of the tanks, the guns, the planes, the ships, the personalities of his commanders and their opponents, or the victory. Instead, he spoke of the families of the men buried in the American cemetery in Normandy. He said he could never come to this spot without thinking of how blessed he and Mamie were to have grandchildren, and how much it saddened him to think of all the couples in America who had never had that blessing because their only son was buried in France. "But it's a wonderful thing to remember what those fellows twenty years ago were fighting for and sacrificing for, what they did to preserve our way of life. Not to conquer any territory, not for any ambitions of our own. But to make sure that Hitler could not destroy freedom in the world. I think it's just overwhelming. To think of the lives that were given for that principle, paying a terrible price on this beach alone on that one day, 2,000 casualties. But they did it so that the world could be free. It just shows what free men will do rather than be slaves." [1]

In the book, *The Victors, Eisenhower and His Boys: The Men of World War II,* the author describes how a young soldier, Fritz Niland, came looking for some buddies in his unit before he returned to the United States. The previous day Fritz had learned that his brother, Bob, had been killed on D-Day. Fritz had then hitched a ride to the 4th Infantry Division area to find another brother, Preston, who was a platoon leader. Preston, too, had been killed. By the time Fritz had returned to his own company, Father Francis Sampson was looking for him to tell him that a third brother, a pilot in the China-Burma-India Theater of Operations, had been killed that same week. Fritz was the sole survivor of the four Niland brothers, and the Army wanted to remove him from the combat zone as soon as possible. Fritz's mother had reportedly received all three telegrams from the War Department on the same day. Father Sampson escorted Fritz to Utah Beach, where a plane flew him to London on the first leg of his return to the States. T/Sgt. Robert Niland and 2LT Preston Niland are buried next to each other in the Normandy American Cemetery. [2]

The story of the Niland brothers is just one of the thousands of stories under the stones of the American Cemeteries where lie the mortal remains of the young men and women who sacrificed their lives during World War II. Many of those buried there were in their teens or very early twenties at the time of their deaths. Brothers are buried side by side. In one cemetery three brothers are buried next to each other. One cemetery has a father and son buried side by side. What could they have become had they not been killed?

The information provided on each headstone is limited: Name, rank, unit, state from which that person entered the service, and the date of death. In addition, Medal of Honor recipients' headstones have a gold star and the words "Medal of Honor" engraved in gold. On the back of each headstone is the serial number for the person buried there. The headstones of the unknown soldiers are engraved with the words, "Here Rests in Honored Glory a Comrade in Arms Known but to God."

Since our first visit to that Normandy cemetery, my wife and I have been able to visit all of the American World War II cemeteries in Europe. We have been unable to visit the cemeteries in Great Britain, Tunisia, North Africa, and Manila, the Philippines. We have also visited the Veteran's Administration cemetery in Honolulu, commonly called "the Punchbowl." Without exception, every cemetery is maintained to the highest standards possible, and each, in its own way, leaves an indelible impression on everyone who visits. For those families who elected to have their loved ones permanently interred overseas following the end of World War II, it should be comforting to know that each grave is cared for with the same degree of dedication and love that they themselves would have provided had their loved ones been returned to the United States for burial. And, further, they should be comforted in knowing that the same care will continue in perpetuity, even after they themselves have passed on.

The purpose of this book is two-fold:

One: To acquaint readers with the overseas cemeteries and memorials, which are administered and maintained by the American Battle Monuments Commission, as well as to provide the readers with an understanding of the process by which our dead were recovered from the battlefields, interred in temporary cemeteries or other initial burial locations, disinterred following the war and either returned to families in the United States or buried in permanent overseas cemeteries.

Two: To introduce readers to a very limited few of the thousands of young men and women buried in the World War II Cemeteries. We will attempt to learn more about their early lives, their families, and their dreams for the future before they became members of the American Armed forces designated to invade Fortress Europe and drive the Japanese from their Pacific conquests. What were their hopes and aspirations? Were they engaged? Were they new husbands, wives or parents? Were they potential All-American athletes or future doctors, lawyers, teachers, scientific researchers, or simply someone's next door neighbor? We may not be able to answer all of these questions, but we will add to the limited information now available on each headstone. We will attempt to determine what might be said *If These Stones Could Talk.*

NOTES

[1] All references to former President Eisenhower and Mr. Cronkite are taken from *The Victors, Eisenhower and His Boys: The Men of World War II*, by Stephen E. Ambrose. New York: Simon and Schuster, 1998.

[2] When the author and his wife visited the Normandy American Cemetery and Memorial in October 2003 as part of a tour group, our guide told us that the third Niland brother had actually been reported as missing in action, not killed, and that he had eventually been found in a Japanese POW camp. He returned home following the end of the war in the Pacific. This information was confirmed during a visit to the American Battle Monuments Commission offices in October 2006. The movie, *Saving Private Ryan*, is loosely based on the story of the Niland brothers.

(Author's Note: The abbreviations used for military rank in this book conform to World War II usage, not current usage.)

Chapter One

WORLD WAR II: A CONCISE SUMMARY

For most Americans, World War II started on 7 December 1941, with the bombing of Pearl Harbor by the Imperial Japanese Navy. That "Day of Infamy" cost the lives of more than 1,300 American Soldiers, Sailors, Airmen and Marines, and seriously wounded another 1,700. An additional 48 civilians were killed and 35 wounded. Almost simultaneously with the attack on Pearl Harbor, the Japanese also attacked other vital American installations in the Pacific such as the Island of Guam and the Philippine Islands. President Franklin Delano Roosevelt, at a joint session of the United States Congress on 8 December 1941, asked Congress to recognize that a state of war already existed due to Japan's sneak attack the day before.

Most Americans have come to believe that we also declared war on Hitler's Germany on the same day that Congress acknowledged the state of war with Japan. That is not correct. In fact, the United States did not declare war on Germany or Italy until after Hitler and Mussolini declared war on the United States on 11 December 1941. Hitler was not compelled to declare war in accordance with provisions of the Tripartite Pact signed by Germany, Italy and Japan in late 1940. That alliance required the other two countries to come to the aid of the third country if that country were attacked. Since the U.S. did not attack Japan, Germany was not required to declare war on the United States. Hitler's senior military and economic advisors argued against the declaration of war against the United States. They recognized that the immense industrial capability of the United States and its huge manpower base would eventually result in the loss of the war. Hitler apparently believed that he could hold off the Allies long enough to defeat Russia and then negotiate a satisfactory end of the war with Great Britain and the United States to Germany's advantage.

Hitler and Nazi Germany had either beaten or forced all of Europe into an alliance. He even had signed a non-aggression pact with Russia. His intelligence agencies were no doubt aware of America's woefully weak military status in mid-1940 after Hitler had already conquered Poland, Holland, Belgium, Luxembourg, and France, annexed Austria and occupied Czechoslovakia. The U.S. had only one supposedly combat-ready division while Germany and Japan had well over 300. The U.S. had less than 500 military planes to more than six times that number for Germany alone. The U.S. was outnumbered over seventeen to one in tanks, and the 200 tanks the U.S. had were inferior to the German tanks in mobility and firepower.

In truth, for the nations of Europe, World War II started at least two years prior to Pearl Harbor when Hitler, without provocation, invaded Poland on 1 September 1939. However, even before that, Japan had initiated hostile action in the Far East with a large scale invasion of the Chinese mainland in 1937, after first invading Manchuria in 1931 and gaining control of that vast area. To help ensure its success in the Far East, Japan had signed a nonaggression pact with the Soviet Union. Japan felt further protected against a threat from the Soviet Union after Hitler launched his attack on Russia in June of 1941. This meant that Russia had to concentrate its forces against the German onslaught, thus freeing Japan from worries of a Russian attack.

Although the United States had not been formally at war with the Axis Powers prior to the bombing of Pearl Harbor, it had been involved in a significant manner. The United States had been providing military equipment and supplies in support of Great Britain after the British forces were ejected from the European mainland by the Germans in 1940. Not only had the United States been selling equipment and supplies to the British, we had also provided Britain with fifty destroyers, badly needed to replace ships they had lost to German and Japanese navy attacks, in exchange for military bases we could use in the Western Hemisphere. President Roosevelt later managed to have Congress pass what became known as the "Lend-Lease Bill." This legislation gave the president the ability to "sell, transfer title to, exchange, lease, lend or otherwise dispose of" defense equipment to "the government of any country whose defense the president deems vital to the defense of the United States."

During the period between Germany's invasion of Poland in September of 1939 and the United States entry into the war, American ships and lives were lost in the Atlantic to the German submarine fleet which was decimating shipping to or from Great Britain and its far-flung empire. One of the first American losses was the USS *Reuben James*, a destroyer sunk by a German torpedo on 31 October 1941, while escorting a supply convoy across the North Atlantic, with a reported loss of 166 lives. A song was later written about the sinking:

The Reuben James

Have you heard of a ship called the good Reuben James,
Manned by hard-fighting men, both of honor and of fame?
She flew the stars and stripes of the land of the free,
But tonight she's in her grave at the bottom of the sea.
  CHORUS:
  Tell me, what were their names,
  Tell me, what were their names?
  Did you have a friend on the good Reuben James?
  What were their names, tell me, what were their names?
  Did you have a friend on the good Reuben James?
One hundred men went down to their dark watery grave;
When that good ship went down, only forty-four were saved.
'Twas the last day of October that they saved forty-four
From the cold icy waters by the cold Iceland shore.
  REPEAT CHORUS
It was there in the dark of that uncertain night
That we watched for the U-boat and waited for a fight.
Then a whine and a rock and a great explosion roared,
And they laid the Reuben James on the cold ocean floor.
  REPEAT CHORUS
Well, many years have passed since those brave men are gone,
And those cold icy waters are still and they're calm.
Many years have passed, but still I wonder why
The worst of men must fight and the best of men must die.

After Hitler broke his secret nonaggression treaty and invaded Russia in the summer of 1941, Roosevelt also authorized military assistance to the Russians. Convoys to Russia were frequently attacked by German subs with disastrous results. One convoy, consisting of thirty-three ships, lost all but eleven ships on what the Navy came to call "the suicide run to Murmansk."

Following the Japanese bombing of Pearl Harbor and Hitler's declaration of war, the United States was faced with a serious strategic decision: how to fight a two-front war in Europe and the Pacific. Although the United States had initiated a buildup of its military strength during 1940, it was not yet on a total war footing. The United States lacked sufficient numbers of trained men to fill the ranks of the Army, Navy, Army Air Corps, Marine, Coast Guard and Merchant Marine forces that would be needed to defeat the Axis Powers. Admiral Ernest J. King of the Navy and the Army's GEN Douglas MacArthur campaigned for a priority aimed at the defeat of Japan first, while Army leaders mostly sided with the British in urging a Europe first strategy while fighting a holding action in the Pacific. The British Prime Minister, Winston Churchill, even though Britain had many holdings in the Far East, urged President Roosevelt to take on the Germans first. Roosevelt agreed with Churchill, so the emphasis on men and equipment was placed on defeating the Germans while doing what we could in the Pacific with limited men and equipment.

Once the decision had been made to place priority on defeating the Germans, the next issue was how to accomplish that. American planners wanted to move men and equipment to Great Britain as quickly as possible in order to invade Fortress Europe in 1942. Churchill and the British military leaders insisted that we could not be ready to invade Europe in 1942, but should not delay offensive action. Instead, Churchill urged the United States to plan for action in North Africa. Great Britain was already involved there in a nasty battle to defend Egypt and the Suez Canal from a major threat by German and Italian forces. Although the Axis forces there were under the overall command of an Italian General, the major threat came from the German Armored Force commanded by GEN Erwin Rommel. Rommel was threatening to run the British out of Egypt and some of the British senior staff members even began to shred and burn documents in their Alexandria headquarters.

Operation Torch, the code name for the U.S. and British invasion of North Africa, was planned under the command of Lieutenant General Eisenhower with MG Mark W. Clark as his deputy. MG. George Patton soon replaced the initial U.S. Corps Commander and MG Terry Allen (Terrible Terry) was the division commander of the First Infantry Division, the Big Red One. Shortly after the Allied landings in North Africa, the Free French forces capitulated to the Allies and the Allied forces then moved to defeat the German and Italian forces from two directions—the Americans from North Africa and the British, under GEN Bernard L. Montgomery, from Egypt.

Once the German and Italian forces were defeated in North Africa, the British argued for an invasion of Sicily in order to establish air bases from which Hitler's positions in Eastern Europe could be bombed, as well as providing bases to bomb Germany's oil supplies in the Caucasus. After the Sicilian Campaign succeeded in forcing the surrender of Italian forces on the island and the evacuation of the German forces to Italy, the next target proposed by the British was Italy itself. Again, the Americans were reluctant to become engaged in a slugging match with the German forces in the rugged Italian terrain, but Churchill prevailed. Allied intelligence had reason to believe that if we invaded Italy, the Italian government would seek terms of surrender and the German forces would be forced to retreat to northern Italy. Based upon this information, the Americans agreed to invade southern Italy. Once the invasion was made and Italy did indeed surrender, Hitler changed his mind and ordered the German forces to defend all of Italy. This resulted in an extended and bloody battle until Rome was occupied in early June, just before D-Day in France. Even after Rome had been taken, the German Army continued to put up a tenacious defense of northern Italy right up until the final German surrender in May of 1945.

While all of this action was taking place in North Africa, Sicily and Italy, and the buildup of forces continued in Great Britain, the U.S. forces in the Pacific had been divided into two major commands and one peripheral command. GEN Douglas MacArthur commanded the forces in the Western Pacific with headquarters in Australia. His initial effort was aimed at clearing Japanese forces from New Guinea with an ultimate aim of retaking the Philippines. The second major command under ADM Chester W. Nimitz began an island hopping campaign using assault forces consisting of both Marine and Army troops aimed at forcing the Japanese back toward the home islands by taking one Japanese-occupied island at a time. Some historians have likened this arrangement to a "compromise between two great feudal lords forcing their own rivalry on a nation under arms." The third U.S. element, under LTG Joseph Stillwell, was fighting in the Burma/China area. All three of these elements competed for the limited resources assigned to the Pacific while the main thrust was aimed at defeating Germany.

The difference between the fighting in the Pacific and the fighting in Europe can best be described as a difference in cultures. German, Italian and Eastern European troops, in general, took a pragmatic approach to fighting. The Germans, in particular, would fight aggressively and employ well-planned defensive tactics in an attempt to defeat or at least delay the advance of the Allies. Once they recognized that a position was untenable they would either retreat, if that was possible, or surrender to the Allied troops. The Japanese, on the other hand, represented a drastically different cultural background. To surrender was to lose face and to be denied the respect of their families and their ancestors. One only has to read accounts of the battles for Guadalcanal, Iwo Jima, Okinawa, or the Philippines to learn that thousands of Japanese committed suicide by placing grenades against their own stomachs, charging our lines with anti-tank mines strapped to their chests, or even beheading their own squads of troops in order to avoid capture. The Japanese also frequently killed all of the local civilians, even when they were Japanese civilians, rather than permit them to come under the control of American forces as the Japanese troops withdrew or also killed themselves. One of the best accounts of fighting in the Pacific, which time and time again depicts this cultural difference, is a book about the 24th Infantry Division's fight to defeat the Japanese forces occupying the Philippine Islands. The book by Jan Valtin is titled *Children of Yesterday*.

Many military historians point to 1942 as the turning point of World War II. It was during 1942 that the Allies invaded North Africa during "Operation Torch" and defeated Rommel's Afrika Korps and the Italian forces operating there. The U.S. Navy destroyed a large part of the Japanese Fleet at the Battle of the Coral Sea in May, followed closely by the even more significant victory at the Battle of Midway in June. The Pacific Island of Guadalcanal was invaded by U.S. Marines in August of 1942, the first major offensive action against Japan, and Hitler sealed the doom of General Paulus's Sixth Army by ordering him in August of 1942 to hold his positions outside of Stalingrad at all cost. Had GEN Friedrich Paulus been authorized to attempt a breakout from the encircling Russian troops, tens of thousands of battle-hardened German troops might have been saved to fight again. Instead, the reinvigorated Russian Army captured General Paulus and most of his command.

The Battle of the Coral Sea not only cost the Japanese Navy at least 77 aircraft and almost 1,100 men, but one light aircraft carrier was sunk and two carriers were damaged to the extent that they and their complement of aircraft were out of action for the subsequent Battle of Midway. Strategically, the Battle of the Coral Sea ended Japanese plans for the invasion of Australia.

The Battle of Midway in June was a key strategic battle in the Pacific Theater of Operation. As a direct result of the extreme losses suffered in that battle, Japan no longer could claim to be the dominant naval force in the Pacific. During this battle, Japan lost over 270 aircraft, at least 4,800 men, four irreplaceable aircraft carriers, two heavy cruisers, three destroyers and three battleships were damaged. Many naval historians compare the U.S. victory at Midway to the British Royal Navy's victory at the Battle of Trafalgar in October of 1805 off the coast of Spain where Britain's Lord Nelson defeated combined naval forces of France and Spain.

With the successful invasion of France by Allied forces on D-Day, 6 June 1944, the ultimate defeat of Hitler and his Nazi forces was sealed, even though bitter fighting continued for another eleven months. Following the U.S. capture of Saint-Lo and the breakout from the hedgerow country of Normandy as part of "Operation Cobra" in July, the American and British forces moved rapidly to liberate Paris and push the German forces back toward Germany's last major defensive barrier, the Rhine River. Many high-ranking allied generals were expecting the collapse of all German forces by Christmas of 1944.

Following the unsuccessful attempt of British General Montgomery's "Operation Market Garden," in an attempt to skirt the German right flank in Holland with a combined airborne and armored thrust to capture the vital industrial area of the Ruhr Valley, General Eisenhower opted for a full frontal advance from the North Sea to the Swiss border. Although General Patton argued vociferously for an armored thrust over the Rhine by his 3rd Army, a serious shortage of fuel and ammunition dictated a virtual halt to aggressive offensive operations all along the Allied front just as the winter of 1944 approached.

It was precisely at that time that Hitler managed to secretly assemble a strong Panzer force in virtually the same area of the Ardennes Forest from which he had launched his surprise attack on the Netherlands, Belgium, Luxembourg and France in the late fall of 1940. In the early morning fog of 16 December 1944, Hitler launched "Operation Wact am Rhein" (Watch on the Rhine) or what the Allies called "the Battle of the Bulge." The attack caught the thinly spread American defenders completely off guard and many units were overrun with heavy losses in both dead and captured troops. It was only as a result of the heroic stand by the 101st U.S. Airborne Division at Bastogne, Belgium, and the determined defense of key road junctions and river-crossing points by scattered and undermanned American units that the German attack was blunted long enough for General Patton to rush armored units into the battle and force the Germans to withdraw from the "Bulge" they had created in the Allied lines. From that point on, it was merely a question of how long Hitler could hold out with the Allies advancing from the west and the Russians from the east.

Meanwhile, in the Pacific Theater, General MacArthur had begun his return to the Philippine Islands when his forces landed on Leyte Island in October of 1944. Many Americans were led to believe that this action by MacArthur's troops and the destruction of much of what remained of the Japanese Navy during the Battle of Leyte Gulf contributed mightily to the ultimate defeat of Japan. However, historians now feel that the severe loss of American lives during the Philippine Campaign was probably not necessary. In fact, objective historians generally acknowledge that the major purpose of invading the Philippines was to stroke General MacArthur's vaunted ego and fulfill the promise to return that he made when forced to evacuate with his family after the Japanese attack in 1941.

One cannot attempt to describe World War II without recognizing the vital importance of the contribution made by the Russians. The American, British and Free French forces had to overcome many problems working with the Russians. The Russians did not trust their Allies, and complained of the lack of a "second front" in Europe to relieve the pressure on Russian forces in the east. President Roosevelt generally felt inclined to trust "Uncle Joe" Stalin while Prime Minister Churchill was more inclined to question Stalin's motives and his actions. However, there can be no question that the Russians absorbed the full land and air power of the Third Reich during the critical period from 1941 until the invasion of France in June of 1944, and suffered the loss of millions of military and civilian personnel as the German forces advanced toward Moscow. The heroic Russian stand at Stalingrad, and the eventual encirclement and destruction of an entire German Field Army there probably was the single most important event of the Allied effort in Europe.

It is impossible to say how long the war in the Pacific would have continued had the United States not dropped two atomic bombs on Japan in August of 1945. However, American planners had predicted that as many as one million Japanese would have died in defense of their home islands and as many as five-hundred thousand Americans would have been killed. One such estimate was developed by U.S. Army COL Andrew Goodpaster based upon his extrapolation of casualty data for both U.S. and Japanese troops during the bloody battle for Okinawa. (Note: Colonel Goodpaster reached the rank of four-star general and served as the Supreme Commander of Europe under NATO, the North Atlantic Treaty Organization. He was generally recognized by his peers as one of the U.S. Army's most intelligent and capable generals of the post-war era.) Although the debate continues to this day as to whether or not President Truman should have authorized the use of the atomic bomb, few, if any, veterans of the Pacific fighting take the position that the invasion of the Japanese homeland by our forces would have been preferable to the use of the "bomb."

Depending upon what source one chooses to use, the numbers of American casualties during World War II will differ somewhat. However, it is generally accepted that 15,000,000 American men and women served on active duty. Millions of others worked in defense plants in support of the war effort. Of the approximately 400,000 young Americans who died during the fighting, roughly 79,000 remains have never been recovered. Even among those remains that were recovered, at least 10,000 could not be positively identified and lie in cemeteries under a white marble cross with an inscription which reads: "Here Lies in Honored Glory a Comrade in Arms Known but to God." Today, over 93,000 young Americans killed during World War II are buried in our overseas cemeteries, and another 13,000 are buried in the National Memorial Cemetery of the Pacific in Hawaii. The names of an additional 79,000 young Americans are inscribed on the memorials to the Missing in Action, both overseas and in the United States.

After Germany had surrendered, but almost six weeks before Japan surrendered, the U.S. Congress passed one of the most important pieces of legislation of the twentieth century; "The Servicemen's Readjustment Act of 1944," passed on 22 June 1944. This act, more commonly known as "the GI Bill of Rights," did much to not only lessen the potentially negative impact of the millions of service men and women who would soon be reentering civilian life, but it provided much-needed monetary support for the veterans to attend college or trade schools, loans for the purchase of a home, and business loans, which facilitated the establishment of thousands of small businesses by the returning veterans. It is estimated that close to eight million veterans took advantage of the educational benefits offered by the bill. If the cost of this single piece of legislation seemed staggering at the time, almost thirty-billion dollars, that cost was recovered several times through the increase in personal and business taxes generated by the recipients. State and local governments also benefited through the generation of additional sales and property taxes.

Thus, while much of Europe and the Pacific areas were slowly recovering from the devastation of World War II, the United States had fully recovered from the Great Depression of the 1930s and had entered a period of economic expansion and social revolution unlike anything it had seen since the end of the Civil War almost one-hundred years earlier.

NOTES

[1] Unless otherwise noted, the reference material for this chapter is available from various U.S Department of the Army publications and publications of the American Battle Monuments Commission.

[2] The National Park Service web site at www.nps.gov/archive/usar/extendweb1.html.

[3] Langsam, Walter Consuelo, *Historic Documents of World War II*, Princeton, NJ. D. Van Nostrand and Company, 1958, pages 76-77.

[4] Ambrose, Stephen E. *Americans at War.* New York, Berkley Books, page 75.

[5] Langsam, Walter Consuelo, *Historic Documents of World War II*, Princeton, NJ. D. Van Nostrand and Company, 1958, pages 67-72.

[6] Ambrose, Stephen E. *Americans at War.* New York, Berkley Books, page 128.

[7] Ibid. pages 179-180.

Chapter Two

MY WORLD WAR II HEROES

"We were that which others did not want to be.
We went where others feared to go, and did what
Others failed to do. We were
AMERICAN SOLDIERS."
(Quoted from memorial outside
the Old Vicksburg Courthouse Museum
Vicksburg, Mississippi)

When the Japanese bombed Pearl Harbor on Sunday, December 7, 1941, I was five days short of being seven and one-half years old. I do not recall where I was or what I was doing when the announcement of the bombing was made on the radio. I don't even have a clear recollection that I was fully aware of that tragic event, although I am sure it must have been discussed in detail by my parents, grandparents and aunt and uncle. I was probably much more interested in playing with my mixed breed dog, Spot, or with my many toys. At that time, we all lived in the same house at 22 Chestnut Street, Jackson, Ohio, a small town in southeastern Ohio. Jackson had a population of roughly 8,000 and served as the county seat of Jackson County. The town had two iron mills, Globe Iron and Steel Company (Globe) and the Jackson Iron and Steel Company (JISCO), with each making a special product needed in the steel industry, Silvery Pig Iron. The town also had at least one brick factory, a nail mill, a railroad cars shop, which repaired railroad cars for the Detroit, Toledo and Ironton Railroad (the DT&I), and numerous mom and pop stores and shops typical of small town USA in the mid-twentieth century.

Early in the war the United States was hard put to claim successes. After Pearl Harbor the Japanese quickly attacked, with devastating success, our very limited and over-matched forces in the Philippine Islands and our other outposts in the Pacific. Many of our fighters and bombers were either destroyed on the ground in those locations or lacked the necessary support and ammunition to even hope to stop Japanese advances. We were, at best, fighting a delaying action while the U.S. Fleet attempted to recover from the Pearl Harbor disaster. Our defense establishment worked feverishly to build the new planes and equipment so badly needed to replace that destroyed by the Japanese in the first few days of the war.

Much like the American people in general, I, as a young boy, was anxious to identify American heroes in the aftermath of those early Japanese successes and our severe losses. Even after over sixty years of intervening events such as the Korean War, the Cold War, the Vietnam War, and most recently our military actions in Iraq and Afghanistan, I can still vividly remember my first heroes of World War II. This chapter will identify those heroes and attempt to provide the reader an insight into why the brave men thus identified properly qualify to be called heroes.

Lieutenant John Pershing Robbins[1]

A few doors up Chestnut Street from where I lived, the Robbins family occupied a large corner house. Mr. Herbert A. Robbins, John's father, had lost an arm while working for the railroad in the nearby village of Hamden, Ohio, and had subsequently moved his family to Jackson. In addition to the parents, Herbert and Elma, the Robbins family consisted of five boys and two girls. A daughter, Lura, was the oldest and another daughter, Tabitha, was the youngest with the five boys (Lance, John, Tom, Steve and Mac) in the middle.

Lieutenant John Pershing Robbins

The Robbins boys left to right: Lance, Tom, Steve, Mac, John

The Robbins boys and their friends frequently played touch football games in their large back yard. Although I was only about five or six years old at the time, I felt that I should be able to play with the big boys. To their credit, they did let me be the "ball boy," which meant that every time the football got away from them and rolled into the street I got to chase it down and throw it back to the real players. What a thrill to be playing with the big boys!

When John was born in 1918, his father named him after Gen. John Joseph "Blackjack" Pershing, the Commanding General of the American Expeditionary Forces in World War I, whose name was on virtually every American's lips as a great American hero of World War I. John grew up in Jackson and attended Jackson City schools. He was a very handsome young man and a good student, as well as a great athlete. John excelled in football, playing three positions (tackle, end and fullback) at various times for the Jackson High School Redmen. He also played varsity basketball and baseball and was on the track team.

After graduating from Jackson High School in 1937, John attended Ohio University in Athens, Ohio, where he was an outstanding member of the Ohio University Bobcats football team and also set a school record for the mile run as a member of the O.U. track team. He was so good on the gridiron at O.U. that the Cleveland Rams professional football team offered him a chance to play for pay. John turned down the Cleveland offer to stay in school. While at O.U., John worked part-time at an Athens business (Beasley's Mill) and held down a job in the student dining hall at Howard Hall to help defray the cost of his education. He was also a member of Delta Tau Delta Fraternity. It was while he was a student at O.U. that John took the first step toward becoming a pilot when he enrolled in a civilian flight training program. He received his pilot's license upon success-fully completing that program.

On November 23, 1940, John traveled from Athens to Fort Hayes in Columbus, Ohio, and enlisted as an Aviation Cadet in the Army Air Corps. Following several weeks training at Albany, Georgia, John was transferred to Maxwell Air Base near Montgomery, Alabama, where he completed his flight training and was awarded his pilot's wings and a commission as Second Lieutenant in the Army Air Corps. During his time at Maxwell, several of John's friends were killed in training accidents, not an unusual event during those early years of World War II. John was then assigned to the 90th Bombardment Squadron stationed at Savannah Air Base near Savannah, Georgia.

One of the planes used for training in those early days of World War II was the PT-17 Stearman "Kaydet." The Stearman Aircraft Company, formed by Lloyd Stearman in 1927, was purchased by the Boeing Airplane Company in 1939, but the Army Air Corps had fol-lowed the Navy's lead and purchased twenty-six of the first versions by Stearman, the PT-13. Both versions, the PT-13 and PT-17, were two-seat biplanes of mixed construction. The wings were made of a wood frame with a cloth covering and the rest of the plane was made of steel tubing with cloth covering. The wheels were non-retracting.

Lieutenant Robbins' first duties consisted of ferrying new light bombers from the manufacturers' plants on the west coast to air fields in the east. He then took part in some of the Army's field maneuvers in the south. John sometimes referred to himself as a "test pilot," but that may not have been technically accurate. He was still sta-tioned at the Savannah Army Air Field on 7 December 1941, when the Japanese attacked Pearl Harbor and President Roosevelt, with the

Stearman PT-13 Aircraft

concurrence of Congress, declared the United States to be in a "state of war" with Japan on 8 December 1941. On Tuesday, 9 December 1941, at about 2:15 p.m., Lieutenant Robbins was on a training flight in PT-17 Aircraft NO. 41-8038 over the Atlantic Ocean just off the Georgia coast with Pfc. Wayne E. Bradley as a passenger in the rear seat. During this training flight, the plane crashed on Skidway Island, a small privately owned island on which the R.C. Roebling family operated a plantation. According to the official accident report:

> "They were performing aerobatics, and at one point the aircraft did a loop, a roll, and then entered a spin. It made three or four turns and came out at about 500. It then did another loop and another spin. After it came out of the second spin it was about 100 feet above the ground. It then continued in a normal glide, straight ahead, descending until it struck the ground about 50 feet from the bank of the Skidway River, about two and one-half miles northeast of the Isle of Hope, near Savannah, Ga. The injured pilot and passenger were placed on a boat for transport to Savannah. They died in the Savannah hospital without regaining consciousness."

Thus, although he did not die in combat, Lt. John Pershing Robbins must have been one of the first Army Air Corps pilots to die after the president addressed Congress on 8 December 1941.

Many years later, one of Lieutenant Robbins' nephews contacted a member of the Roebling family and learned that Mrs. Roebling had kept a diary in which she had noted that the pilot seemed to be trying to avoid hitting a former school building in which one of her young children was sleeping at the time of the crash. Lieutenant Robbins' efforts to avoid crashing into that former school building may have saved the life of the young Roebling child.

I can very vividly recall dressing in my "Sunday best" and walking the few hundred feet from our house to the Robbins' house to pay my respects to one of my first World War II heroes. John's closed casket, covered by the American flag, was immediately inside the front room of the Robbins' house just off their front porch. His family members were present and, as I recall, several of the brothers took special care of the little "ball boy" from down the street and told me that John had died a hero.

In 1950 the Ohio University Air Force ROTC Detachment formed a local Squadron of the Arnold Air Society, a professional, honorary, service organization which was first formed at the University of Cincinnati in 1947. The society was named after World War II Army Air Corps GEN Henry "Hap" Arnold. The Ohio University Squadron was named after Lt. John Pershing Robbins, the first Ohio University student to be killed during World War II. John's parents were made

Mrs. Robbins honored as Ohio University's first Gold Star Mother

honorary members of the squadron and Mrs. Robbins was named the first Gold Star Mother of Ohio University.

Lt. John Pershing Robbins was buried in the family plot in Hamden, Ohio, where he now rests near his mother and father and other family members.

Lt. Robbins grave stone, Hamden, Ohio. Photo by author

CPT Kelly as a West Point Cadet. Photo courtesy of the West Point Association of Graduates

Captain Colin P. Kelly Jr.[2]

The war against the Japanese was only in its third day when CPT Colin P. Kelly Jr., United States Army Air Corps, was killed while on a bombing mission near the Philippine Islands. Captain Kelly was assigned to the 14th Bomb Squadron of the 19th Bomb Group. On 10 December 1941, Captain Kelly and his seven-man crew, manning a B-17C Bomber, attacked what Kelly thought was a Japanese battleship off the coast of Luzon. At that time the American public thought Captain Kelly might have dived his plane into the smoke stacks of the battleship after first ordering his crew to bail out. In April 1942, a comic book, *True Comics*, issue 11, included a two-page version of "the American Eagle – Captain Colin P. Kelly Jr." A small box next to a drawing of Captain Kelly as a West Point Cadet read, "Capt. Colin P. Kelly acclaimed as America's first great hero in the war with Japan!!" The comic strip stated that, "The huge Japanese battleship was in flames and disabled! The young American had played a hero's part in countering Japan's treacherous blow. He lost his life minutes later when attacked by two Jap fighter planes. He stuck to the controls of his ship while he ordered his crew of six to jump to safety." (Note: The crew actually consisted of Captain Kelly and seven other men.)

When the official version of Captain Kelly's action was later released, based upon information provided by surviving crew members, it still supported the presumption that Captain Kelly was indeed a hero, but he met his death in a different manner than first supposed.

The night of 9 December, Captain Kelly, his crew of seven other men, and the crews of five other B-17 aircraft had spent a sleepless night without food in the rain at a remote air strip near San Marcelino on the island of Luzon, the Philippines.[3] Their squadron commander, Maj. Emmett "Rosy" O'Donnell Jr., had flown to Clark Field earlier to get orders for his squadron. (Note: Major O'Donnell himself had a very distinguished career in the Air Force and retired in 1963 as a four-star general in command of all U.S. Air Forces in the Pacific with headquarters at Hickam Air Force Base, Hawaii.) He radioed for all of the B-17 crews to fly to Clark Field at daybreak on the 10th of December for refueling and loading with bombs for an urgent mission. However, only three of the B-17s were actually able to land at Clark, including Captain Kelly's plane.

Because of what was thought to be an imminent attack by the Japanese, the three planes were ordered into the air before they had completed their refueling and loading the plane's normal load of bombs. Captain Kelly's plane, for example, had only three 600-pound bombs aboard. He was ordered to fly to the island of Formosa (now called Taiwan) about 500 miles from Clark Field to attack Japanese airfields there. Kelly and his crew had no fighter escort to accompany them due to the destruction of many of our fighter craft by earlier

Japanese attacks. Today, such a mission would certainly be considered to be suicidal, to say the least. As Kelly and his crew were flying toward Formosa, they saw a Japanese landing force approaching the northern part of Luzon, and thought they saw a battleship among the ships. There had been unconfirmed reports of a Japanese aircraft carrier in those same waters as well.

Captain Kelly radioed back to Clark Field for permission to abort his mission to Formosa and attack the Japanese ships instead. After two attempts to obtain permission, with no response from Clark Field, Captain Kelly took it upon himself to abort the mission to Formosa and attack what he and his crew thought was a Japanese battleship. Because he had only the three 600-pound bombs on board, Kelly advised his crew that he was going to make three passes over the battleship so the bombardier could get lined up for the best possible results. Kelly made two passes at about 20,000 feet and then on the third pass ordered the bombardier to drop the bombs "in train," meaning one after the other instead of all three at once. The crew reported that one bomb hit on each side of the ship and one hit the ship itself. Satisfied that they had inflicted mortal damage to a Japanese battleship, Kelly and his crew turned and started their run back to Clark Field. (Note: It later turned out that the Japanese ship was a cruiser rather than a battleship.) With no fighter protection available, Kelly's plane was an easy target for the Japanese fighters flying cover for the ships in that area. Before Captain Kelly's B-17C could make it back to Clark Field, Japanese fighters attacked the plane and hit it on their first pass, killing one crewman, wounding a second, and destroying the instrument panel. During the second pass the Japanese managed to hit the left wing of Kelly's plane and set it on fire. The blaze rapidly moved to the body of the plane itself causing the flight deck, where Captain Kelly and his co-pilot, 2LT Donald Robins, were trying to maintain control of the plane, to fill with smoke. Captain Kelly immediately ordered his crew to bail out. With the nose of the aircraft now ablaze, Second Lieutenant Robins tried to get through the upper escape hatch, but the plane blew up before he could get free and the blast ejected the badly burned Robins. In addition to Second Lieutenant Robins, five other crew members managed to parachute from the burning aircraft, leaving only the crewman killed on the first pass and Captain Kelly on board. The B-17C crashed within ten miles of Clark Field. Captain Kelly's remains were later found at the site of the crash. There is no record to indicate if Captain Kelly was killed by Japanese machine gun fire or if he was killed in the crash of his plane while attempting to guide it back to Clark Field.

It was initially reported that Captain Kelly would be awarded the Medal of Honor posthumously. In fact, MG Lewis H. Brereton, Commander of all U.S. Far East Air Forces, recommended Captain Kelly for the Medal of Honor and many Congressmen indicated publicly that he would receive the Medal of Honor. However, General MacArthur's headquarters did not approve General Brereton's recommended award of the Medal of Honor for Captain Kelly. Instead, Captain Kelly was recommended for and was awarded the Distinguished Service Cross.

Upon notification of her husband's death, Mrs. Kelly was reported to have said, "Please, when you write, write only of what Captain Kelly has done, not of me, not of Corky. For it is Captain Kelly who deserves all the praise, all the glory."[4] At the time of Captain Kelly's death, his young son was only eighteen months old.

Within a few days of Captain Kelly's death, President Franklin Delano Roosevelt wrote the following letter:[5]

> To the President of the United States in 1956:
> I am writing this letter as an act of faith in the destiny of our country. I desire to make a request which I make in full confidence that we shall achieve a glorious victory in the war we now are waging to preserve our democratic way of life.
> My request is that you consider the merits of a young American youth of goodly heritage—Colin P. Kelly III—for appointment as a Cadet in the United States Military Academy at West Point. I make this appeal in behalf of this youth as a token of the Nation's appreciation of the heroic services of his father, who met death in line of duty at the very outset of the struggle which was thrust upon us by the perfidy of a professed friend. In the conviction that the service and example of Captain Colin P. Kelly Jr. will be long remembered, I ask for this consideration in behalf of Colin P. Kelly III.

Colin P. Kelly Jr. was born in Monticello, Florida, on 11 July 1915, to Colin Purdie Kelly and Mary Mays Kelly. Both parents could brag of military men in their family tree. Each family had men who served in both the Revolutionary War and the Civil War. Colin graduated from the public high school in Madison, Florida, in 1932, and then attended Marion Military Institute at Marion, Alabama, for a year while awaiting an appointment to the United States Military Academy at West Point, New York. Florida Senator Duncan Fletcher offered young Kelly a competitive appointment, which he prepared for while at Marion Institute. He entered West Point in July 1933 and graduated in June 1937. An obituary published in the November 1993 issue of *Assembly* stated that Colin's "academic work was average, his military rating superior, and his interpersonal relations outstanding."

Colin developed an interest in flying while still in high school, and that interest never wavered. One of his West Point classmates stated, "The only thing C.P. didn't laugh at when he was here was aviation. From Plebe Year, he intended to be a bomber pilot and nothing else."

Following graduation in 1937, Second Lieutenant Kelly was assigned to the Infantry Branch and married Marion Wick in the West Point Cadet Chapel on 1 August 1937. Following basic pilot training at Randolph Field, Texas, he received his silver wings and was transferred from Infantry Branch to the Army Air Corps on 13 January 1939.

After a tour of duty at Randolph Field, the Kellys moved to March Field, California, where Second Lieutenant Kelly was assigned to the 19th Bomb Group and where Colin P. Kelly III was born on 6 May 1940. Colin was promoted to first lieutenant on 4 June 1940. The Kellys were next assigned to the 14th Bomber Squadron, 11th Bomb Group at Hickam Field, Hawaii, in April 1941, where Kelly was the Squadron Operations Officer and check pilot for all other pilots. A former B-17 instructor, he was one of the most respected pilots in the 11th Bomb Group.

As the Japanese military actions in Asia became more and more threatening to United States interests in the Pacific, Kelly's squadron was sent to the Philippine Islands. The squadron flew nine aircraft over 10,000 miles from Hawaii to the Philippines with stops at Midway, Wake Island, Port Moresby, and Darwin before finally landing at Clark Field. By November 1941, Kelly was so concerned by the Japanese actions that he advised Marion to take their young son and return to the United States. Marion and "Corky" did as Colin had suggested and lived with her parents in Brooklyn, New York, and with the Kellys in Florida.

It should be noted that "Corky" Kelly did, in fact, enter West Point in 1959, graduated in 1963, and served tours in Germany and at Fort Riley, Kansas. He then left the Army and received a master of divinity degree from the Philadelphia Divinity School, after which he re-entered the Army. During this later service, he had assignments as an assistant chaplain to the Corps of Cadets of the United States Military Academy at West Point, and subsequently as the division chaplain at Fort Carson, Colorado, where he was responsible for the supervision of twenty-one chaplains and spiritual services for over 15,000 troops and their families. After retirement from the Army, the Reverend Kelly became the Rector of Trinity On The Hill Episcopal Church in Los Alamos, Nevada.

The remains of CPT Colin P. Kelly were returned to the United States following the end of the war, and he was buried at Oakridge Cemetery, Madison County, Florida, on 13 October 1948. The American flag from his coffin was presented to his eight-year old son following the burial service. A monument to Captain Kelly was erected at Clark Field, the Philippines, in 2007. The monument, which

Statue of Captain Kelly at Clark Field, the Philippines.
Photo by MSgt. Bert Caloud, USMC (Retired)

stands near the remains of the Colin P. Kelly Jr. Theater, has a plaque on its base, which states in part:[6]

> Capt. Colin P. Kelly Jr. made his last take off from Clark Field on 0700 H on the 10th of December 1941, piloting a four engine Boeing B-17C (Flying Fortress) heavy bomber.
>
> Capt. Kelly and his crew bravely flew to Aparri, north of Luzon Island and credited for attacking and sinking the Japanese light cruiser named Ashigara.
>
> While returning to Clark, Kelly's B-17C was pursued by Japanese fighter aircraft, setting the bomber on fire and one waist gunner was killed. Kelly then ordered the remainder of the crew to bail out and all were saved. Kelly tried to save his bomber by making a "Belly Landing" at the barrio of Bical, Mabalacat, Pampanga, but died in the process.
>
> Subsequently, U.S. President Franklin D. Roosevelt posthumously conferred the "Distinguished Service Cross" on 20th of December 1941 for his sacrifice and was declared as "America's First Hero of World War 2."

The Five Sullivan Brothers[7]

In the early stages of World War II, the Nazi submarine service was successful in sinking thousands of tons of military cargo destined for Great Britain and Russia. Many Merchant Marine crew members, as well as Navy and Coast Guard crew members, were also lost. Later, as the United States began to send military personnel to England for the buildup prior to invading the continent, as well as for the operations in North Africa and Italy, troop ships became a much-prized target for the Nazi wolf packs operating in the Atlantic and the North Atlantic shipping lanes. Although not as extensively equipped with submarines as the Germans, the Japanese Navy was also able to sink many of our ships in the Pacific area of operations. Each sinking brought dreaded telegrams to the families of those young men "lost at sea." One such sinking of an American ship in the Pacific became famous in the annals of the United States Navy, the sinking of a light cruiser, the USS *Juneau* (CL-52) on 13 November 1942.

The *Juneau* had been engaged in a running battle against Japanese ships during the battle of Guadalcanal. A Japanese sub had

The five Sullivan Brothers. Official Navy photo

successfully hit the ship with one torpedo, but had only damaged the *Juneau*. The *Juneau* retired from the battle and was attempting to sail to the closest US Navy repair facility in the New Hebrides Islands when she was again attacked by a Japanese sub, hit by another torpedo, and sank in a very short time. Although about 115 of the *Juneau* crew were thought to have survived the sinking of their ship, rescue efforts were delayed for several days due to uncertainty about the threat by Japanese ships remaining in the area. In the end, only ten men were rescued after being in the water for eight days.

On board the *Juneau* were the five Sullivan brothers, the sons of Thomas and Alleta Sullivan from Waterloo, Iowa; George Thomas (George), Francis Henry (Frank), Joseph Eugene (Red), Madison Abel (Matt), and Albert Leo (Al). The five brothers, their parents, their only sister, Genevieve, and their maternal grandmother, Mae Abel, lived together in a house on Adams Street. The simple fact that the five Sullivan brothers were serving on the same ship was contrary to Navy policy, but the brothers had insisted upon serving together when they had tried to enlist. At first, the Navy turned down their demands, but the brothers persisted and their request was finally approved by the Navy brass in Washington, D.C. The personnel records of the five show that they had "Enlisted in the Navy Reserve on 3 January 1942." In fact, both George and Francis (Frank) Sullivan had previously served four-year enlistments and had been discharged within eleven days of each other in May of 1941.

When the brothers learned of the Japanese bombing of Pearl Harbor on 7 December 1941, and the loss in that attack of a close friend in the sinking of the USS *Arizona*, they were unanimous in their desire to enlist. The five brothers were separated by only seven years from the oldest, George, to the youngest, Albert. They had always done things together, so it was not unexpected that they would now decide to enlist together and serve aboard the same ship. Except for Albert, the brothers were still single. Albert, the youngest brother, had a wife, Katherine Mary, and a son, Jimmy, who was only fifteen months old the last time his father held him. In order to make ends meet on Albert's Navy pay, Katherine Mary and Jimmy lived with the elder Sullivans while Albert was away.

After undergoing training at the Great Lakes Naval Training Station, the five brothers were assigned to the USS *Juneau*, a brand new light cruiser being readied for action in New York. The Navy published publicity photos of the five Sullivan Brothers on board the *Juneau*, and the brothers gained something like celebrity status. Initially, the *Juneau* had one other family of four brothers, the Rogers, as well as seven other pairs of brothers on board. Two of the Rogers brothers later were reassigned to other ships.

In May of 1942, three of the Sullivan brothers, George, Matt and Al, obtained leave and visited Waterloo and their family for the last time. During this last visit, Al was photographed with his little son, Jimmy, his brother, Matt, and his mother and dad. Little Jimmy wore a sailor hat like his dad and uncle.

It has been reported that when the *Juneau* was sunk, four of the brothers went down with the ship and only the oldest, George, managed to survive the sinking. After several days on a raft awaiting rescue, George either died of his wounds or perhaps was attacked by sharks. Some survivors of the *Juneau* stated that they could hear George calling out to his missing brothers immediately after the ship went down.

Although the ship was sunk on the 13th of November, it was not until the 11th of January that a Navy Officer, LCDR Truman Jones, arrived at the Sullivan home in Waterloo with two other men in Navy uniforms.[8] When the three men were inside the Sullivan house, the boys' father, Thomas Sullivan, reportedly asked, "Which one?" Commander Jones could only reply, "I'm sorry. All five." He remarked later that there was no other way to break that kind of news. He then formally advised the Sullivan family that:

> The Navy Department deeply regrets to inform you that your sons, Albert, Francis, George, Joseph and Madison Sullivan are missing in action in the South Pacific.
>
> (NOTE: It seems somewhat ironic that the Navy listed the boys' names in alphabetical order by first name rather than by age or Navy rank. President Roosevelt's letter of condolence, which follows below, lists the boys in order of their age.)

As shocking as that news must have been, it was probably not completely unexpected. The family had not heard from their sons for over a month, and at least one neighbor had received a letter from her own son saying that he had heard that the Sullivan's ship had been sunk.

President Roosevelt sent a personal letter to the Sullivans dated 1 February 1943, which read as follows:[9]

> Dear Mr. and Mrs. Sullivan:
>
> The knowledge that your five gallant sons are missing in action against the enemy inspires me to write you this personal message. I realize full well there is little I can say to assuage your grief.
>
> As Commander-in-Chief of the Army and Navy, I want you to know that the entire nation shares in your sorrow. I offer you the gratitude of our country. We who remain to carry on the fight will maintain a courageous spirit, in the knowledge that such sacrifice is not in vain.
>
> The Navy Department has informed me of the expressed desire of your sons, George Thomas, Francis Henry, Joseph Eugene, Madison Abel, and Albert Leo, to serve in the same ship. I am sure that we all take heart in the knowledge that they fought side by side. As one of your sons wrote, 'We will make a

team together that can't be beat.' It is this spirit which in the end must triumph.

I send you my deepest sympathy in your hour of trial and pray that in Almighty God you will find the comfort and help that only He can bring.

Very sincerely yours,
Franklin D. Roosevelt (signature)

Mr. and Mrs. T. F. Sullivan
98 Adams Street
Waterloo, Iowa

Genevieve Sullivan, sister of the Sullivan brothers, enlisted in the U.S. Naval Reserve as a Specialist Third Class (Recruiter), and she and her parents toured over two-hundred plants and shipyards, urging the workers to do their best to help our forces end the war as soon as possible. Navy records indicate that by January of 1944, Genevieve and her parents had spoken to over a million workers in sixty-five cities as well as other millions of people reached by radio broadcasts.

As a final act of a grateful nation, in February 1943, President Roosevelt informed Mr. and Mrs. Sullivan that a new U.S. Navy destroyer would be launched under the name USS *The Sullivans*. Mr. and Mrs. Sullivan were invited to attend the launching of the new ship near San Francisco, California, and to officially christen the ship. In the closing paragraph of his letter, President Roosevelt stated:[10]

> Your unselfishness and courage serves as a real inspiration for me as I am sure it will for all Americans. Such faith and fortitude in the face of tragedy convinces me of the indomitable spirit and will of our people.

The USS *The Sullivans* remained an active Navy ship until it was decommissioned on 7 January 1965. The destroyer was donated to the city of Buffalo, New York, in 1977, as a memorial in the Buffalo and Erie County Naval and Servicemen's Park. A second USS *The Sullivans*, an Arleigh Burke Class destroyer, the DDG-068, was launched on 12 August 1995. This newest ship was sponsored by Kelly Sullivan Loughren, granddaughter of Albert and Katherine Mary Sullivan.

SULKIS LEONARD S	ENSIGN	USNR	MASSACHUSETTS
SULLIVAN ALBERT LEO	SEAMAN 2C	USNR	IOWA
SULLIVAN CALVIN C	SEAMAN 1C	USNR	MISSOURI
SULLIVAN CHARLES F	LIEUTENANT (JG)	USNR	ILLINOIS
SULLIVAN DAVID J	SEAMAN 2C	USN	ILLINOIS
SULLIVAN DONALD L	SIGNALMAN 2C	USN	MAINE
SULLIVAN EARL P	SEAMAN 1C	USNR	ARKANSAS
SULLIVAN EDWARD F JR	LIEUTENANT (JG)	USNR	WISCONSIN
SULLIVAN EUGENE F	SEAMAN 2C	USNR	NEW JERSEY
SULLIVAN FRANCIS H	COXSWAIN	USNR	IOWA
SULLIVAN FRANCIS M	FIRE CONTROLMAN 3C	USNR	MAINE
SULLIVAN GEORGE B	GUNNER'S MATE 3C	USN	RHODE ISLAND
SULLIVAN GEORGE T	GUNNER'S MATE 2C	USNR	IOWA
SULLIVAN GERALD M JR	LIEUTENANT	USNR	MASSACHUSETTS
SULLIVAN HAROLD W	FIREMAN 1C	USNR	ILLINOIS
SULLIVAN HUGH D	SEAMAN 1C	USNR	GEORGIA
SULLIVAN HUGH E	CHIEF MTR MACHINIST'S MATE	USN	N H
SULLIVAN JAMES P	SEAMAN 2C	USNR	MICHIGAN
SULLIVAN JOHN EDWARD	SEAMAN 1C	USN	MASSACHUSETTS
SULLIVAN JOHN J JR	ELECTRICIAN'S MATE 3C	USNR	MASSACHUSETTS
SULLIVAN JOSEPH E	SEAMAN 2C	USNR	IOWA
SULLIVAN KENNETH J	AVN MACHINIST'S MATE 3C	USNR	MASS
SULLIVAN KENNETH LEE	STOREKEEPER 3C	USN	KENTUCKY
SULLIVAN LEON J	CHIEF GUNNER'S MATE	USN	CALIFORNIA
SULLIVAN MADISON A	SEAMAN 2C	USNR	IOWA
SULLIVAN ROBERT A	FIREMAN 2C	USNR	NEW YORK
SULLIVAN THOMAS J	SIGNALMAN 1C	USN	TEXAS
SULLIVAN WILLIAM D	PAINTER 2C	USNR	NEW YORK
SULLIVAN WILLIAM J	COXSWAIN	USN	OHIO

The Tablets of the Missing, Manila American Cemetery.
Photo by MSgt. Bert Caloud, USMC (Retired)

To this day, no other American family has lost more sons or daughters in wartime than did the Sullivan family of Waterloo, Iowa, on 13 November 1942.

The names of the five Sullivan brothers are inscribed on the Tablets of the Missing at the Manila American Cemetery in the Philippines. Although George was reported to have lived for several days after the sinking of the USS *Juneau*, his inscription, like those of his four brothers, shows his date of death as 13 November 1942.

The Four Chaplains[11]

On the cold morning of 23 January 1943, the USAT *Dorchester* sailed from New York heading for Greenland as part of a convoy of tankers, freighters and other ships escorted by both US Navy and US Coast Guard vessels. The *Dorchester,* a rather old and dilapidated cruise ship launched about sixteen years earlier, had been pressed into service as a troop ship. This was caused by of the lack of shipping in general at that time, and also because of the losses to the Nazi submarine wolf packs that had been operating with deadly efficiency in the Atlantic and North Atlantic areas for over three years. The luxury items that one might expect to find on a cruise ship had been dismantled and cots were crammed in every foot of available space with only inches separating the bottom of one cot from the top of the one below it. The troops using these cots barely had room to turn over at night. The ship was over 360 feet long and weighed slightly over 5,600 tons, a rather light weight for such a large ship. On board the *Dorchester*, in addition to her crew of about 130, were almost 600 military personnel who would be stationed in Greenland and over 150 civilians who would be working for the military in Greenland. Thus, the *Dorchester* had close to 900 personnel on board when it left New York.

Included among the military personnel were four Army chaplains destined for heroic action that none of them could have foreseen, although each had volunteered for duty in a combat zone. The four chaplains were the Reverend George L. Fox, Rabbi Alexander Goode, the Reverend Clark V. Poling, and Father John P. Washington. Each chaplain had a unique personal background, but a common belief in the potential for interaction among the various religious faiths and the good that could accrue to the world from such interfaith action. The four had first met only two months earlier while attending a

The Four Chaplains

George L. Fox, Alexander D. Goode

Clark V. Poling, John P. Washington

The Four Chaplains. Wikipedia photo

new chaplain's orientation program at Harvard University. They had bonded almost at once, and had become close friends who obviously enjoyed each other's company and, more importantly, respected each other's religion. They were frequently seen together at Harvard joking, playing practical jokes and learning about each other's faith.

The Reverend Fox, a Methodist minister, was the oldest of the four at forty-two years old. He had served in World War I and suffered severe wounds while serving as an ambulance driver in the Army's 2d Division. He had won the Silver Star Medal for bravery during a gas attack when he had given his own gas mask to a wounded officer and then carried the man on his back to a safe place. He also received the French Croix de Guerre with Palm, France's highest military award, for saving a French officer. The Reverend Poling, a Dutch Reformed minister and the son of a famous minister, the Reverend Daniel Poling, was the youngest of the four at age thirty. The other two chaplains were within three years of Poling's age. Father Washington was a mild-mannered man with poor eyesight. In fact, he had to "cheat" in order to pass the Army physical exam by using the same eye twice to read the eye chart, an action for which he felt remorse but one that he felt he had to take in order to serve his country in a time of crisis. Rabbi Goode had also followed his father into the ministry. Even before the Japanese bombed Pearl Harbor, Rabbi Goode had attempted to become a Navy chaplain, but he had been turned down. Once war was declared, he again attempted to become a chaplain, and was accepted by the Army. Except for Father Washington, the chaplains were married, and Reverend Fox's son was also on active duty, enlisting in the Marines as soon as he graduated from high school.

The convoy, of which the *Dorchester* was a part, would be moving up the Atlantic coast toward Nova Scotia, then into the Gulf of St. Lawrence, passing through the Belle Isle Strait, which separated Newfoundland from Labrador. The convoy would then be in the open Atlantic at a time of year when the usually cold waters were even more frigid with frequent ice floes, and storms. Even gale force winds were not uncommon at that time of year. However, the greatest threat was the German submarines operating in that particular area of the Atlantic, which had earned the nickname, "Torpedo Junction."

The German subs had been destroying ships at the rate of about 100 per month. To make matters even worse, the convoy had to split after several days at sea since most of the ships were destined for Russia. Only five other ships remained with the *Dorchester* for the rest of the voyage to Greenland: two freighters, the *Lutz* and *Biscaya*, and three Coast Guard cutters, the *Comanche*, the *Escanaba*, and the *Tampa*.

All seemed to be going well in spite of the extremely crowded conditions on the *Dorchester* and a severe storm which had sickened even some of the "old salt" Merchant Marine crew members. The four chaplains had visited every nook and cranny of the ship trying to cheer the men up and keep their minds off of the dangers facing them on the way to Greenland. The chaplains had even planned a talent show for one of the last nights at sea, but they had to call it off due to the rough seas. By the second day of February the little convoy was within 150 miles of Greenland and seemed to have made it through the worst that the Atlantic had to offer. However, that evening one of the Coast Guard cutters reported sonar readings which indicated that at least one enemy submarine was following the ships. The captain of the *Dorchester* ordered all men aboard to put on their shoes (not boots because the heavy boots could weigh you down in the water), their clothes, their heavy jackets, gloves and life jackets, even when they went to bed, in the event that the ship should be torpedoed. As might be expected, many of the men felt that the captain's order was an over-reaction to the perceived threat and didn't even wear their life jackets to bed that night. After all, the ship was almost in Greenland waters, for heaven's sake. No officer or NCO checked on the men to enforce the captain's order.

Shortly before 1:00 a.m. 3 February 1943, the commander of a German submarine, U-223, which had been stalking the little convoy, waiting for an opportunity to attack one of the larger ships, ordered his crew to prepare three torpedoes for firing. He would normally have fired only one torpedo because the German Navy was now short of torpedoes, but he was concerned that if he missed with the first torpedo he would not have time to fire a second before the escort ships would take his sub under attack with their deadly depth charges. One of the torpedoes struck the *Dorchester* with a flash and a roar, tossing men about and collapsing the stacked cots on top of men underneath them, crushing many in their bunks. A second torpedo then hit and killed at least 100 men who were trapped inside the hull of the ship. Some of the crew were probably killed instantly from the high-pressure steam released when the ship's boilers exploded. Power was instantly lost on board and the ship was in total darkness as tons of sea water rushed in from the gaping holes in the ship's hull.

The crew of the *Dorchester* knew from past experience that a man had only about twenty minutes to survive in those ice-cold waters before succumbing to hypothermia and freezing to death. Many of the lifeboats could not be released because their lines were encrusted by thick ice; the explosions and accompanying fires destroyed others. Many of the men had not followed the captain's orders, so found themselves on deck in only their pants and shirts without shoes, coats or life vests. Through all of this chaos, one sight and one action was recalled by many of the lucky few who survived the sinking of the ship...the sight of the four chaplains taking off their own life vests and giving them to soldiers or sailors who had none, after they had carefully handed out the few life vests stored in special lockers on deck. The four acted as guides for numerous men trying to find their way into lifeboats or onto rafts. In several cases, one or more of the chaplains had to order troops into the sea, and, in at least one case, use physical force, rather than permit troops to remain on the deck of the sinking ship and be sucked under when it sank. Several survivors reported that as they were in the water or in a life boat they looked back and saw the four chaplains braced against the slant of the decks, praying, singing, and sharing their fate with their arms linked together. Only twenty-seven minutes after the first torpedo hit the *Dorchester* she sank beneath the waves of the frigid North Atlantic. Hundreds of men were left alive with only their life jackets to keep them afloat in those deathly cold waters, while the few "lucky" ones had managed to find a life boat to climb into or a raft to cling to.

The commander of the convoy refused to order any of the three Coast Guard cutters to attempt rescue operations because of the perceived threat of further enemy submarine attacks. Almost forty-five minutes after the attack, the convoy commander finally authorized one of the three cutters to start picking up survivors, although everyone knew that survival time in those waters had already been exceeded by a factor of two. Later, the commander of a second cutter took matters into his own hands, possibly inviting court martial, and joined the first cutter in rescue operations while also attempting to serve as a screen against further enemy submarine action. Between them, the two cutters managed to pull 226 living men from the freezing waters. Two of those rescued died before reaching land. In all, about 675 men who had boarded the *Dorchester* perished either as a result of the initial explosions or exposure to the frigid temperature while in the water awaiting rescue. How many more might have been saved if the convoy commander had permitted the Coast Guard cutters to begin rescue operations sooner? It is impossible to say, but it is certainly safe to say that many more might have lived. No action was taken against the convoy commander for delaying the rescue operations, but neither was punitive action taken against the cutter captain who elected to commence rescue operations on his own without authority from the convoy commander.

Many Americans felt that the four chaplains were deserving of the Medal of Honor, but the War Department ruled that the Medal of Honor could only be awarded for heroic action during "combat." What might one call the sinking of a ship at sea during wartime by an enemy submarine if not "combat?"

The four chaplains were honored in other ways. The United States Postal Service issued a special stamp on 28 May 1948, in honor of their heroic deeds.

On 14 July 1960, the United States Congress, by Public Law 86-656 of the 86th Congress, authorized

U.S. Postage stamp issued 28 May 1948

the "Four Chaplains Medal." The medal with the Star of David, the Tablets of Moses, and a Christian cross shown in relief on the back of the medal also had the names of all four chaplains inscribed. The Secretary of the Army personally presented the Four Chaplains

Medals to members of their families on 18 January 1961. There is a beautiful stained glass window in the Pentagon Chapel, one in the National Cathedral in Washington, D.C., one in the U.S. Military Academy at West Point, and numerous others honoring the four chaplains. Finally, the Immortal Chaplains Foundation was incorporated in October 1997, in Minnesota, as a non-profit corporation as a result of actions by David Fox, the nephew of Chaplain George Fox, and Rosalie Goode Fried, the daughter of Chaplain Alexander Goode. The foundation's goal is to remind us of the capacity for compassion we all have within us, no matter the differences of race, religion or creed. Among the many notable members of the foundation's board are the First Officer and one crew member of the German U Boat which sank the *Dorchester*.

The names of the four chaplains are inscribed on the Tablets of the Missing at the East Coast Memorial in New York City, stating that they were "Missing in Action or Buried at Sea." Each of the four received the Distinguished Service Cross and the Purple Heart for their actions during the sinking of the *Dorchester*, and the Reverend Fox already had received the Silver Star and Purple Heart in recognition of his World War I service.

ABMC Monument to the missing, Battery Park, New York City. Photo by Ms. Betsy Rombach

Inscribed on the base of the soaring eagle statue are the words:

1941 * * * 1945
Erected by the United States
of America
In proud and grateful remembrance
Of her sons
Who gave their lives in her service
And who sleep in the American
Coast Waters
Of the Atlantic Ocean
Into Thy Hands, O Lord

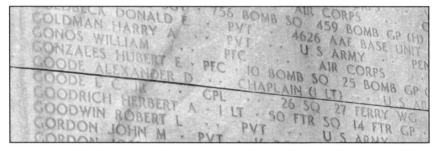

FORRESTER COPELAND A ... SCT · 6 BOMB SQ AIR CORPS ... PENNSYLVAN
FOSTER GEORGE W ... S SCT 29 BOMB GP (VH) · TENNES
FOSTER GLENN E ... 2 LT ... AIR CORPS ... FLOR
FOX GEORGE L ... T SGT ·· AIR CORPS ·· SOUTH CAROL
CHAPLAIN (1 LT) ... U S ARMY ·· VERM
FRANCESCHI GERMANO ·· PVT ·· AIR CORPS ·· MICHI
FRECKLETON HAROLD R · CAPT · INFANTRY CONNECTI
FREE MARTIN E ... S SGT ·· AIR CORPS ·· GEO

Chaplain Fox's name on Tablets of the Missing
Photo by Ms. Betsy Rombach

OLDMAN DONALD F · 756 BOMB SQ AIR CORPS
ONOS HARRY A · PVT · 459 BOMB GP (H)
GONZALES WILLIAM ·· PVT ·· 4626 AAF BASE UNIT
GOODE HUBERT E · PFC ·· U S ARMY
GOODE ALEXANDER D · PFC 10 BOMB SQ AIR CORPS PEN
GOODE L C JR ·· CHAPLAIN (1 LT) 25 BOMB GP
GOODRICH HERBERT ·· CPL ·· 26 SQ U S A
GOODWIN ROBERT A · 1 LT · SO FTR SQ 27 FERRY WG
GORDON JOHN M · PVT PVT 14 FTR GP
U S ARMY

Chaplain Goode's name on Tablets of the Missing
Photo by Ms. Betsy Rombach

PINKHAM ELWIN E ·
PITTMAN ROBERT M ·· PVT ·· U S ARMY ·· PENNSYLVANIA
PLATENAK STEVE J ·· PVT ·· INFANTRY ·· OHIO
PLEMONS GEORGE D · PVT ·· AIR CORPS · NORTH CAROLINA
PLYLEY FREDERICK K · 1 LT · 379 BOMB GP (H) · TENNESSEE
POINTER WAYNE H ·· S SGT ·· AIR CORPS ·· IOWA
POLING CLARK V · CHAPLAIN (1 LT) · U S ARMY · NEW YORK
POMELEK LEO J ·· PVT ·· MEDICAL DEPT ·· NEW YORK

Chaplain Poling's name on Tablets of the Missing
Photo by Ms. Betsy Rombach

WALLACE SACHSE · CAPT · 363 BOMB SQ 304 BOMB GP (H) · OKLA
WALSH MICHAEL P ·· PFC ·· AIR CORPS ·· PENNSYLVANIA
WALTERS LOUIS H · T SGT · 20 TRP CARR SQ · PENNSYLVANIA
WARD IRVING H · CAPT · 6 BOMB SQ 29 BOMB GP (VH) · MASS
WARM LAWRENCE J ·· 1 LT ·· AIR CORPS ·· NEW YORK
WASHINGTON JOHN P · CHAPLAIN (1 LT) · U S ARMY · NEW JERSEY
WATKINS ROBERT A ·· SGT ·· CORPS OF ENGRS ·· VIRGINIA
WATSON GILBERT O · S SGT · 370 BOMB SQ 307 BOMB GP (H) · VA
WEAVER CLAUDE K ·· S SGT ·· AIR CORPS ·· MARYLAND
WEBB ASHER B ·· PVT ·· COAST ARTY CORPS ·· KENTUCKY
WEBB CHARLES F · 1 LT · 756 BOMB SQ 459 BOMB GP (H) · IDAHO

Chaplain Washington's name on Tablets of the Missing
Photo by Ms. Betsy Rombach

The Bedford Boys[12]

When the Allied forces invaded Hitler's Fortress Europe on D-Day, 6 June 1944, many families in cities and towns across the United States waited for news of their loved ones. The long-awaited "Second Front," which Joseph Stalin had been demanding for many months, was finally established, but not without the loss of life of thousands of young men from the United States, Great Britain, Canada, France, and other countries that were a part of the Allied cause. However, one small American town in Virginia was soon to feel the pain of loss of the flower of its youth to a much greater degree than any other town or city. That town was Bedford, Virginia.

Bedford's total population was between 3,200 and 3,400 persons. During the dark days of the Depression, many of Bedford's young men had enlisted in the local Army National Guard unit, Company "A" the 116th Infantry Regiment of the 29th Infantry Division. The Division's units were widely spread among small communities in Virginia, Maryland and Pennsylvania. The men had enlisted for the few dollars a month they would receive for attending scheduled drills at the nearest armory and attending a few weeks of camp each summer, not because they had an intense desire to be a soldier. At that time those few dollars that accrued each month by being a member of Company "A" could mean the difference between making ends meet and doing without. In some ways the Bedford men were better off than their counterparts in larger cities because many of them either lived on farms, where they could raise much of their own foodstuffs, or members of their extended family lived on a farm. They never anticipated being called to active duty or serving in combat. Members of National Guard units might be "called out" to help during emergencies such as floods, blizzards, forest fires, etc., but they did not expect to be fighting in a world war within a few years of "joining up."

The 29th Infantry Division was called to active duty ten months before the Japanese bombed Pearl Harbor.[13] After the bombing, many of the men in the 29th found themselves assigned to coastal defense duties along the Atlantic Seaboard. That relatively benign duty was soon behind them when the United States determined that it needed to provide a major demonstration of support for its British Allies. In September of 1942, only nine months after Pearl Harbor, the 29th Infantry Division, including the men of Company "A," was shipped to England. For the biggest part of two years the division trained, trained, and then trained some more in the British countryside. The 29th was the first American division to complete a rigorous amphibious training program in England in preparation for the anticipated landings in Europe. While the 29th was training for almost two years in England, and enjoying an occasional evening off in a local British pub or at a service club, other American combat units were fighting in North Africa, Sicily and Italy as well as on far-flung islands in the Pacific such as Guadalcanal, Tarawa and Saipan.

Possibly because of all of this training, the 29th was one of the two divisions selected to land on Omaha Beach in Normandy, France, on D-Day. The other division selected to go in alongside the 29th was the combat-tested 1st Infantry Division, the Big Red One. The 1st Division had been bloodied and gained fame for its action in World War I, and had most recently taken part in the invasion of North Africa. Thus, unknown to them at the time, the men from little Bedford, Virginia, would be among the very first to set foot on the rocks and sands of the invasion beaches, and among the first to be targeted by the artillery, mortars, machine guns, rifles and grenades of Hitler's battle-tested divisions manning the defenses along the coast of France.

Much has been written about, and many movies have featured, the terrible slaughter the troops landing on Omaha Beach faced as soon as they stepped off their landing craft. The men of Company "A," 116th Infantry Regiment, 29th Infantry Division were tasked to be in the very first wave of troops to land on Omaha Beach. Of the more than thirty-five Bedford men in Company "A," nineteen were killed on D-Day, two more were killed days later during the battle to enlarge the beachhead and move inland, and two more were killed before the end of the war. Twenty-three men, out of a total Bedford population of 3,400, equals a ratio of one killed for every 148 people. It is doubtful if any other American community suffered such an extreme rate of casualties during the entire war, but little Bedford suffered most of that loss during the first hour, if not the first minutes, of the invasion. It was reported that Company "A" was virtually wiped out as a functioning unit within ten minutes of the first ramp being dropped on the first landing craft to reach Omaha Beach. Of the more than 200 men assigned to Company "A," the after-action reports indicated that only eighteen were left uninjured by nightfall of D-Day, a casualty rate of over 90 percent.

Among the men of Company "A" were brothers, cousins and relatives of various combinations. There was even one set of twin brothers, the Stevens twins, Roy and Ray. The Stevens twins came from a family of fourteen children. Both twins had dropped out of school during the Depression to help support their family. As is the case with many twins, Roy, who was older by merely twenty minutes, and Ray were extremely close. They had managed to scrape up enough money to buy a small farm together, and they had once dated twin sisters. The twins were assigned to different landing craft on D-Day. Roy's landing craft struck an underwater obstacle and sank like a stone, but he managed to stay afloat until rescued and he was returned to England. Ray made it to shore, but he was killed on D-Day. Roy later returned to Normandy and managed to locate Ray's grave in one of the temporary cemeteries near Omaha Beach.

The people of Bedford waited day after day for news of their husbands, sons, brothers and cousins, knowing that thousands of young men had been killed or wounded during the landings. They heard radio broadcasts describing the hard fighting that was still going on as the Allied forces attempted to expand their beachhead and force the Germans back into the French countryside. It was not until a month after D-Day that the *Bedford Bulletin*, the town's newspaper, reported that Company "A" had actually been in the first wave of troops to hit Omaha Beach. Finally, on the morning of 17 July, almost six weeks following D-Day, the Bedford Western Union clerk began receiving the telegrams with those fatal words, "The Secretary of War desires to express his deep regrets..."[14] It is not known how many telegrams poured in that first day, but by the end of July it was known that at least twenty-three of the men from Bedford had given their lives to free Europe from Hitler's grasp.

To perpetuate the memory of the Bedford Boys from Company "A" and all the other young Americans, who lost their lives liberating

D-Day landing recreation at the National D-Day Memorial,
Bedford, Virginia. Photo from Library of Congress
by photographer Carol M. Highsmith

Europe, Congress authorized the establishment of the National D-Day Memorial in Bedford, Virginia. The National D-Day Memorial Foundation was established to administer the funds raised to build the memorial as well as to manage the memorial once it was completed. President George W. Bush attended the formal opening ceremonies for the beautiful memorial on June 6, 2002. The memorial is one of the major tourist attractions on the Piedmont Plateau near the Blue Ridge Mountains and is a fitting memorial to those brave Bedford men who waded ashore on Omaha Beach on June 6, 1944, as well as the thousands of young Americans and men from other nations who landed on Omaha Beach, Utah Beach, Sword Beach, Juno Beach and Gold Beach that same day.

Of the Bedford men killed on D-Day and afterward, eleven of them are buried in the American Cemeteries in France, ten at Normandy and one at Brittany.[15] Roy Stevens returned to Bedford after the war and was one of the founding members of the National D-Day Memorial Foundation. Roy was a frequent, if not daily, visitor to the National D-Day Memorial in Bedford after it was completed, and frequently recounted the story of D-Day to young boys and girls who visited the memorial. Roy died at the age of eighty-seven in January 2007. The funeral home where his last service was held was filled to capacity and they had to arrange for those outside the funeral home to hear the audio portion of the service. The hearse carrying Roy's body, along with more than 100 automobiles, drove through the grounds of the National D-Day Memorial on the way to the cemetery. It seems only fitting that troops from Company "A" of the 116th Infantry Regiment provided the military honors for Roy Stevens at his last roll call.

Major Thomas Dry Howie[16]
The Major of Saint-Lo
3rd Infantry Battlion, 29th Infantry Division

MAJ Thomas Dry Howie, the young commander of the 3rd Infantry Battalion, 116th Infantry Regiment, 29th Infantry Division, was killed outside Saint-Lo, France, at about 1015 hrs. on 17 July 1944. Before he was killed, Major Howie had been discussing the tactical situation with the 29th Division commander, MG Charles H. Gerhardt, over the tactical radio network. Howie's battalion had just relieved the 2d Infantry Battalion, which had been cut off from the rest of the regiment and was running short of rations and ammunition. The official after-action report of the regiment describes this action as follows:

Major Howie in uniform as a Captain. Photo courtesy of The Citadel Archives and Museum

Early on the morning of 16 July 1944, the 3rd Bn was directed to take the Martinville (526640); drive south to occupy objective B (See overlay #3) the highway leading into St. Lo. The 3rd Bn CO, Major Thomas D. Howie, ordered his troops to attack with fixed bayonets and grenades to seize Martinville (528640), reorganized [sic] and move south to Objective B (see overlay #3). This mission was speedily and successfully accomplished. Following contact with the 2[d] Bn, the 3rd Bn began to organize defensive positions and shared rations and ammunition with the 2[d] Bn. (Author's Note: Map coordinates in this after-action report do not seem to agree.)

Howie told General Gerhardt that the 2d Battalion was in no shape to continue the attack toward Saint-Lo. He reportedly told Gerhardt, "They're exhausted. Yes, we can do it. We're in better shape. Yes, if we jump off now. Okay, see you in Saint-Lo." Within minutes of that conversation on the radio Major Howie was struck in the back by a shell fragment from a German mortar round. The battalion executive officer, CPT William Putenny, was nearby and heard Major Howie murmur, "My God, I'm hit." Captain Putenny managed to catch Major Howie as he fell, but the major died at once. The mortar fragment had entered his back and pierced a lung.

Major Howie's last words to General Gerhardt, "See you in Saint-Lo," soon became the battle cry for the battalion. As the general was preparing for the final push to overrun the Germans entrenched in and around Saint-Lo, he recalled Major Howie's last words. According to Hal Boyle, a war correspondent attached to the 116th Infantry Regiment:[17]

> By the general's order, Tom's body, still clad in full combat gear, was placed in an ambulance in the task force column…amid the thunder of guns. The armored column—bearing the dead hero—fought toward Saint-Lo. When the ambulance was needed for the wounded, Tom, lying on a stretcher, was transferred to a leading jeep. After the column entered Saint Lo, Tom's men quickly lifted their dead major from the jeep and ran through enemy sniping to a nearby shell-torn church. There they placed him atop the rubble of the church wall and went back into battle. They had won for him the last goal of his life. He was the "first" into Saint-Lo.

The Major of Saint-Lo
Photo courtesy of The Citadel Archives and Museum

Major Howie's body remained atop the rubble of Saint Croix Church for several days as men from the 29th Infantry Division passed by to pay last respects to a fellow infantryman. Because of wartime censorship, the first photos printed in the United States showing Major Howie's flag-draped body on the pile of rubble were simply labeled "The Major of Saint-Lo." It was sometime later that the nation learned that the "Major of Saint-Lo" was a thirty-six-year-old native of Abbeville, South Carolina, a 1929 graduate of The Citadel, the Military College of South Carolina, and was a peacetime teacher and coach at Staunton Military Academy in Staunton, Virginia.

Thomas Dry Howie was born in Abbeville on 12 April 1908, the oldest child of Torrence V. and Cora Dry Howie, and one of seven Howie children. One of his younger brothers, Franklin (Frank), would tag along after his older brother. Frank could always count on Tom to help out when needed. Frank once said, "Had it not been for him I am sure I would have been a high school dropout." Tom worked as a "printer's devil" for the *Abbeville Press* while in high school and as a laborer at the Abbeville Mills during the summer where he also played on the mill's baseball team.

Tom enrolled at The Citadel in 1925, and excelled in the classroom, on the drill field, and in athletics. An appreciation of the breadth of Cadet Howie's activities at The Citadel can be gained by the entry under his name in the 1929 yearbook:

> 1928-29: First Lieutenant Company C; varsity football; varsity baseball, boxing team; president, Senior Class; president, Epicurean Club; Round Table; Standing Hop Committee; Associate Editor of Bull Dog; Applicant Rhodes Scholarship; president, Abbeville County Club.

Weighing only 150 pounds, Tom played fullback and linebacker for the Bulldog football team. His excellence in both the classroom and on the football field was best exemplified on Homecoming Day of Tom's senior year in 1928. On the day The Citadel was to play the Clemson Tigers, a bitter rival, in Charleston, Tom was also scheduled to take the Rhodes Scholarship exam, one of the most sought-after graduate scholarships. The exam was to be given that same morning in Columbia, South Carolina, over 100 miles from Charleston. The football game started at 2:00 in the afternoon on The Citadel's field in Charleston. Cadet Howie

Thomas Dry Howie in Citadel cadet uniform.
Photo courtesy of The Citadel Archives and Museum

reportedly completed the Rhodes Scholarship exam in less than forty-five minutes and was on his way back to Charleston, with one of the assistant football coaches driving—most likely exceeding posted speed limits. Tom changed from his cadet uniform into his football togs in the car and arrived at the stadium just as the team was ready to take the field. Cadet Howie carried the football for The Citadel on the first play of the game, gained ten yards, and ran over a Clemson

All American. Howie and his Citadel teammates upset the heavily favored Clemson team by a final score of 12 to 7. Howie supposedly missed getting a Rhodes Scholarship by fractions of a point. (Author's questions: Did he lose out on that prestigious scholarship because he had rushed through the exam? If he had become a Rhodes Scholar, would his career and his life have followed a different path? Would there have been a "Major of Saint-Lo?")

Following graduation from The Citadel in 1929, Tom Howie moved to Staunton, Virginia, to teach English and help coach football at the Staunton Military Academy. In 1933 he became head coach as well as Director of Athletics for the academy. During his years as head coach, his teams won four military school championships and were respected by opposing teams for their sportsmanship as well as their basic football skills. Tom later served as academy alumni secretary, in addition to his teaching and athletic duties.

While at Staunton, Tom met, courted, and married Elizabeth Payne in 1932. Their only child, Sally Elizabeth, was born in 1938. Tom also joined the Virginia National Guard as a member of the 29th Infantry Division, known as the Blue and Grey Division because of its majority membership of men from both Virginia and Maryland. The division was one of the first called to active duty as war clouds darkened and the United States began a hurried effort to rearm. Tom served in a number of different positions in the division, rising rapidly in rank until reaching major.

After the D-Day landings, Tom was serving on the 116th Regiment Staff when he was assigned to command the regiment's 3rd Battalion. Shortly after his assumption of command, Tom wrote the following letter to his young daughter:[18]

> Four days ago, I was placed in command of some 850-odd officers and men, a war-strength battalion, with all its weapons, vehicles and equipment; and the responsibility of some day committing them to battle perhaps from which a number may not return is a fearful thought. If that day should ever arrive, I hope I shall be as proud of them as I've always been of you. And I hope they will be well led.
>
> I can't honestly say that I hope I shall never have that privilege and responsibility. It's something like football; somebody has to play the game; somebody has to beat the enemy. And all

my life, I've tried to make the first team in everything. Sitting on the bench when game time comes is no consolation for weeks of bruising drudgery. I know, I did some bench sitting initially in everything I set my heart on. And I've been sitting on the bench and training hard for almost three years now.

Remember what I told you; sit up straight, look people in the eye, and tell the truth.

With all my heart, your Daddy.

The noted CBS television newsman, Andy Rooney, who served as a war correspondent in Europe during World War II, made the following comments during one of the V-E Day anniversaries:[19]

> More American soldiers were killed taking Saint-Lo than were killed on the beaches. A major named Tom Howie was the leader of the battalion that actually captured Saint-Lo. At least he was the leader of it until he was killed just outside town. After he died, his men picked him up, carried him into town and placed him on a pile of stones that used to be the wall of a church. I guess there never was an American soldier more honored by what the people who loved him did for him after he died. There can be no doubt that Thomas Howie was a charismatic leader, a courageous soldier and a man of outstanding character.

The town of Saint-Lo erected a monument to "The Major of Saint-Lo" alongside a busy traffic circle on one of the major highways into town. Each year on 18 July, a wreath is placed at the monument by the people of Saint-Lo in remembrance of the town's liberation from the Germans. There is a brass plaque on the exterior wall of the Saint Croix Church to mark the spot where Major Howie's body lay atop the rubble. There is also a monument to Major Howie in his hometown of Abbeville, South Carolina. The inscription on that monument includes the words, "Dead in France; Deathless in Fame." During ceremonies to unveil that monument, GEN Charles P. Summerall, the eighty-six-year-old president of The Citadel and a famous World War I soldier, stated, "Tom Howie rests in Valhalla."

The noted American poet and author, Joseph Auslander, wrote the following poem about Major Howie. It appeared in the 18 September 1944 issue of *Life* magazine. (Author's Note: Events in the poem are not exact, but the writer's intent was clear.)

They rode him in propped straight and proud and tall
Through St.-Lo's gates. He told the lads he led
That they would be the first in St.-Lo's fall –
But that was yesterday – and he was dead;
Some sniper put a bullet through his head,
And he slumped in a meadow near a wall,
And there was nothing further to be said;
Nothing to say – nothing to say at all.
Into the town they took for you to keep,
Dead Captain of their glory and their pride!
Ride through our hearts forever, through our tears
More splendid than the hero hedged with spears!

Major Howie posthumously received the Silver Star, the Bronze Star, the Purple Heart, and the French *Croix de Guerre*. He is buried at the Normandy American Cemetery and Memorial on the bluffs overlooking Omaha Beach, where the 29th Infantry Division was among the first to hit the beaches on D-Day. He is buried in Plot G, Row 14, Grave 12.

Major Howie's grave site at the Normandy American Cemetery and Memorial. Photo courtesy of the Citadel Archives and Museum

Ernest Taylor (Ernie) Pyle[20]
War Correspondent

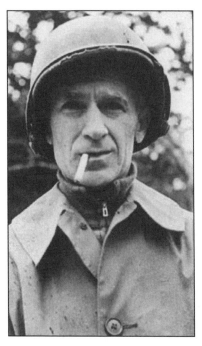

Ernie Pyle
Scripps-Howard War
Correspondent

There were many non-military men and women I could have selected to include among my very short list of heroes. I won't attempt to list all of those persons by name, but most readers would have recognized such names as Edward R. Murrow, Walter Cronkite, William Shirer, Bob Considine and Richard Stout, just to name a few. Each of these reporters or journalists helped to bring the day-to-day events of World War II home to the average American through their radio broadcasts, newspaper or magazine articles and even their photos—when censors permitted. However, the one person who was probably the best known to soldier and civilian alike was Ernest Taylor Pyle, known simply as Ernie Pyle.

Born on a farm in Indiana on 3 August 1900, Ernie joined the Navy when he was about eighteen years old, but World War I ended before he saw action, and he was soon discharged. Ernie then entered Indiana University where he joined a fraternity and edited the student paper, but he left school before he graduated. Between 1921 and the start of World War II, Pyle worked at various newspaper jobs including a three-year stint as editor of the new *Washington Daily News*, a tabloid paper staffed with young reporters and young editors. Following a severe case of the flu, Ernie took time off to recuperate, and he drove from Washington, D.C., to California. Upon his return to D.C., he wrote a series of columns describing what he had seen and heard during the cross-country trip. Those columns led to a job with Scripps-Howard papers writing columns about people and places as Ernie traveled around the United States. It was most likely that experience which influenced his writing style as a war correspondent during World War II.

After the French and British were defeated by the German Blitzkrieg offensive in Holland, Belgium and France in 1940, the Germans concentrated on bringing England to her knees. Hitler's plan called for massive air attacks on England as preparation for a cross-channel invasion to conquer and occupy the British Isles. Ernie Pyle managed to be accredited as a war correspondent and was in London in 1940 when the Luftwaffe fire-bombed the city. Ernie wrote in a column that it was "the most hateful, most beautiful single scene I have ever known." Later, in 1941, his columns written in Great Britain were published as a book titled *Ernie Pyle in England.*

Ernie was in London in October of 1941 when he received word that he would be leaving by train that night with other correspondents to a port where he would board a troop ship. Once at the port, it took two full days to load the ship with all of the troops and their gear. Ernie and his fellow correspondents were assigned four men to a cabin which he described as "better than any of us had expected, and much the same as in peacetime, except for an extra bunk built over each bed. Many officers were in cabins far more crowded than ours." Ernie was on his way to his first actual combat coverage as part of "Operation Torch," the Allied invasion of North Africa.

Once Ernie landed in North Africa he began writing columns which were eagerly read back home. Ernie's dispatches made the readers feel like they were reading a letter from the boy next door. He wrote simply, but with emotion about the infantry, armored, artillery, and engineer troops slugging it out with the Germans and Italians in North Africa, Sicily and the "boot" of Italy. Parents, wives, friends and relatives of the boys overseas hoped to read about their own G.I. in one of Ernie's columns. An example of Ernie's self-deprecating writing style, which included information about one of the boys from home, was an article he wrote about an experience in Tunisia. The article read in part:[21]

> The very first time I ever pitched my pup tent I had to have help, of course, for I didn't even know how to button the thing together. My assistant on that first venture was Sergeant Walter

Hickey, of 401 76th Street, Brooklyn. He was a clerk before the war.

Sergeant Hickey and I picked out a fairly level spot on a sloping mountainside and put up the tent under a fir tree, after pulling out a few shrubs to make a clear space.

When we had the tent finished and staked down, I noticed the ground was crawling with ants. We had unwittingly opened up an enormous ant nest in the loose soil when we pulled up the shrubs. So we had to take the whole tent down and pitch it under another tree.

Ernie was somewhat of a hypochondriac and suffered from bouts of depression. When he was assigned to a combat zone, his health problems seemed to be worse when he was in one of the safer rear areas, and bothered him the least when he was up front with the "grunts" battling the sand, rain, snow, mud, cold and the enemy. Ernie tried to spread himself thin so he could spend time with all elements of the American forces—Army, Navy and Air Corps. Since he had spent most of his time in North Africa with the ground troops or the Air Corps, he elected to stay with the Navy for the invasion of Sicily and write about their part in that campaign. In one of his columns about this experience, he wrote:[22]

> It makes a difference in a man's character. A ship is a home, and the security of home had kept the sailors more like themselves. They didn't cuss as much or as foully as soldiers. They didn't bust loose as riotously when they hit town. They weren't as all-round hard in outlook. They had not drifted as far from normal life as the soldiers – for they had world news every morning in mimeographed sheets, radios, movies nearly every night, ice cream.
>
> Their clothes, their beds were clean. They had walked through the same doors, up the same steps every day for months. They had slept every night in the same spot.
>
> Of course, when sailors die, death for them is just as horrible – and sometimes they die in greater masses than soldiers – but until the enemy comes over the horizon a sailor doesn't have to fight. A front-line soldier has to fight everything all the time.

It is almost an impossibility to select Ernie Pyle's "best" column, but I will make a stab at it. I have read his columns as published in three books: *Ernie Pyle in England, This is Your War*, and *Brave Men*. The one column which most captured the attention of the folks back home at the time, and is my personal choice as Ernie's best, was written while the troops were slogging their way yard by yard up and down the rugged mountains of southern Italy. This column told the story of the death of CPT Henry T. Waskow of Belton, Texas. The full story can be found on Pages 154–156 of the book titled *Brave Men*. Ernie wrote about a night spent in the mountains near a medical unit. The wounded and dead were brought down from the mountain to the medical unit by mules with American soldiers walking beside the mules because the Italian mule skinners were afraid to walk beside the dead. After several other dead men had been brought down the mountain to the medical unit, a soldier came into the shed where Ernie and others were staying warm and quietly said, "This one is Captain Waskow." The following are extracts from Ernie's column:[23]

> In this war I have known a lot of officers who were loved and respected by the soldiers under them. But never have I crossed the trail of any man as beloved as Captain Henry T. Waskow, of Belton, Texas.
>
> Captain Waskow was a company commander in the 36th Division. He had led his company since long before it left the States. He was very young, only in his middle twenties, but he carried in him a sincerity and a gentleness that made people want to be guided by him.
>
> "After my father, he came next," a sergeant told me.
>
> "He always looked after us," a soldier said. "He'd go to bat for us every time."
>
> "I've never known him to do anything unfair," another said.
> After Captain Waskow's body was lifted off a mule it was laid in the shadows beside a stone wall. One soldier came and looked down, and he said out loud, "God damn it!" That's all he said, and then he walked away.
>
> Another man came. I think he was an officer. It was hard to tell officers from men in the dim light, for everybody was bearded and grimy. The man looked down into the dead captain's face and then spoke directly to him, as though he were alive, "I'm sorry, old man."

Then a soldier came and stood beside the officer and bent over, and he, too, spoke to his dead captain, not in a whisper but awfully tenderly, and he said, "I sure am sorry, sir."

Then the first man squatted down and he reached down and took the dead man's hand, and he sat there for a full five minutes holding the dead hand in his own and looking intently into the dead face. And he never uttered a sound all the time he sat there.

Finally he put the hand down. He reached over and gently straightened the points of the captain's shirt collar, and then he sort of rearranged the tattered edges of the uniform around the wound, and then he got up and walked away down the road in the moonlight, all alone.

In the spring of 1944, Pyle returned to England to rest and recover from the rigors of his duties in North Africa, Sicily and Italy. He had suffered from a severe case of anemia and had a close brush with death while covering the Americans' almost disastrous attempt for an end run around the Germans at Anzio. While in England he received word that he had won a Pulitzer Prize for his combat reporting. After the D-Day Invasion of France, Ernie returned to his coverage of front line action as General Bradley's First Army troops tried to fight their way through the stiff German defenses and secure a lodgment area from which to force the Germans back toward the Rhine. Many of his columns during this period were included in his book entitled *Brave Men*. In addition to the Pulitzer Prize and the publication of *Brave Men*, Ernie also received several honorary degrees from American universities.

Worn out after almost four years of covering the war from England, North Africa, Sicily, Italy and northern Europe, Pyle somewhat reluctantly agreed in 1945 to relocate and cover the war in the Pacific. This assignment afforded him a chance to cover Marine and Navy forces as they advanced from island to island on the way to the eventual invasion of the Japanese home islands. By April of 1945, Ernie was with the forward elements of the 77th Infantry Division fighting to clear Japanese troops from the small island of Ie Shima, a short distance from the main island of Okinawa. He was riding in a Jeep with a battalion commander and three other men when a well-concealed Japanese machine gun opened fire from a distance of several hundred yards. The men immediately scrambled out of the Jeep and rolled into a nearby ditch. After the firing ceased, Pyle raised his head to ask if everyone was okay. At that instant the machine gun opened fire again and one bullet struck Ernie on the left side of his head, killing him instantly.

Ernie Pyle was initially buried on Ie Shima among other soldiers. Later his body was moved to a larger temporary cemetery on Okinawa. Near the spot where Ernie was killed on Ie Shima Island, the 77th Infantry Division erected a wooden marker, which was later changed to a permanent stone monument. The wooden marker and the later stone monument were erected as a tribute to their friend and the friend of all "grunts," Ernie Pyle. The wooden marker and the stone monument were inscribed with the same words: "At this spot the 77th Infantry Division lost a buddy ERNIE PYLE 18 April 1945."

When the Japanese government again reclaimed the Okinawa Islands, only three American monuments from World War II were allowed to remain in place. The Ernie Pyle monument erected by the 77th Infantry Division was one of the three. After the end of hostilities his remains were moved to the National Memorial of the Pacific, known as "the Punchbowl," located in an extinct volcano on the Hawaiian Island of Oahu. Ernie's grave marker there is exactly like all of the others but it includes his Navy rank from his service during World War I.

When the soldiers were preparing to bury Ernie on Ie Shima, they found notes in his pocket for a column he appar-

Monument to Ernie Pyle erected on Okinawa by the 77th Infantry Division. Photo purchased on eBay by author.

ently planned to post once the war in Europe ended. In those notes Ernie Pyle had described:

> The unnatural sight of cold dead men scattered over the hillsides and in the ditches along the high rows of hedge throughout the world. Dead men by mass production—in one country after another—month after month and year after year. Dead men in winter and dead men in summer. Dead men in such familiar promiscuity that they become monotonous. Dead men in such monstrous infinity that you come almost to hate them.

How ironic that Ernest Taylor Pyle, renowned war correspondent, author, recipient of a Pulitzer Prize, should end his life as one of those cold dead men in a ditch.

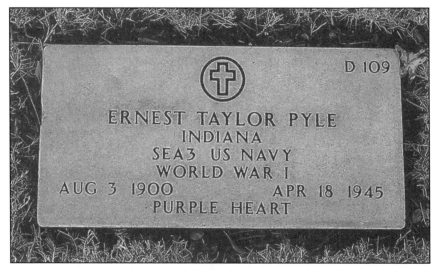

Ernie Pyle grave site at the National Memorial Cemetery of the Pacific, Hawaii. Use of photo authorized by Wikipedia.

NOTES

[1] Family information, Air Force accident investigation report, and photos provided by Ms. Becky Robbins Blystone, Enterprise, Florida, niece of Lieutenant Robbins.

[2] The author is indebted to the West Point Association of Graduates for providing over fifty pages of information, articles, and photos related to Captain Kelly's career as a cadet and as an Army officer.

[3] Article "Valor" by John F. Frisbee, in the U.S. Air Force *Journal of the Air Force Association*, June 1994, Vol. 77, No. 6.

[4] Files of the West Point Association of Graduates.

[5] Archives of the Franklin D. Roosevelt Presidential Library, Hyde Park, N.Y.

[6] Extracted from photo of the plaque on the Kelly statue as provided by MSgt. Bert Caloud USMC (Retired).

[7] General information related to the Sullivan family and the five brothers was extracted from the following on-line sources: www.history.navy. mil; www.iowavetaransmuseum.org; www.homeofheroes.com; www. geocities.com/ww2_remembered/sullivan-bros.html.

[8] Article "The Sullivan Brothers" at www.homeofheroes.com

[9] Archives of the Franklin D. Roosevelt Presidential Library, Hyde Park, N.Y.

[10] Archives of the Franklin D. Roosevelt Presidential Library, Hyde Park, N.Y.

[11] General information related to the Four Chaplains was extracted from the following on-line sources: www.thefourchaplains.com; www. homeofheroes.com; www.immortalchaplains.org; www.fourchaplains. org; http://en.wikipedia.org; and the book by Kurzman, Dan, *No Greater Glory the Four Immortal Chaplains and the Sinking of the Dorchester in World War II,* (N.Y.: Random House, 2004*)*.

[12] General information related to the Bedford Boys was extracted from information in the archives of the National D-Day Memorial Foundation, Bedford, VA; from the following on-line sources: www.findarticles. com; www.historynet.com; and from two excellent books: Kershaw, Alex, *The Bedford Boys,* (Cambridge, MA: DeCapo Press, 2003) and from Morrison, James W., *Bedford Goes to War, The Heroic Story of a Small Virginia Community in World War II,* (Lynchburg, VA; Warwick House Publishing, 2004).

[13] Article titled "The Bedford Boys" by Mr. David Fortuna, June 2004 issue of *World War II Magazine*.

[14] Standard terminology used in World War II telegrams advising families that a loved one had been killed in action.

[15] Information obtained by author by searching American Battle Monuments Commission web site for the names of the 23 Bedford men killed in Normandy.

[16] General information related to Major Howie was obtained from the extensive files in the archives and museum of The Citadel, the Military College of South Carolina, Charleston, SC.

[17] Article on file in the archives and museum of The Citadel, the Military College of South Carolina, Charleston, SC.

[18] Contents of letter from Major Howie to his daughter is on file in the archives and museum of The Citadel, the Military College of South Carolina, Charleston, SC.

[19] Quotation by Andy Rooney, used by The Citadel president, MAJGEN John S. Grinalds, USMC (Retired) at ceremonies for the induction of Major Howie into the South Carolina Hall of Fame on 10 February 2003.

[20] General information related to Ernie Pyle was obtained from the archives of the Indiana Historical Society and from the following on-line sources: www.west-point.org; http://sandiego.edu; www.nytimes.com/learning/general; http://en.wikipedia.org; www.military.com; and from the book *Ermie's War: The Best of Ernie Pyle's World War II Dispatches,* edited by David Nichols, (N.Y.: Random House, 1986).

[21] Ernie Pyle dispatches from North Africa, Scripps-Howard Publishing Co.

[22] Pyle, Ernie, *Brave Men,* (N.Y.: Henry Holt and Company, Inc. 1943) pp. 3-4.

[23] Ibid. pp.154-156.

Chapter Three

GRAVES REGISTRATION SERVICES DURING WORLD WAR II

"I hate war as only a soldier who has lived it can,
only as one who has seen its brutality,
its futility, its stupidity."
Dwight D. Eisenhower,
Supreme Commander Allied Forces, Europe

Prior to the Revolutionary War, protection for villages, towns, cities, and "states" was provided by local militia units. Each male member of the community was expected to possess a weapon and the supporting supplies, such as powder, lead, and cleaning equipment. If the man could not afford such weaponry, it was supposed to be provided by the community or by his employer to be repaid over time. A National Military Force was established at the beginning of the Revolutionary War. The Army, Navy and Marines were each established during that period. Although much was done to formalize the organization and staffing of each service, the critical function of recovery and burial of the dead was accomplished on an ad hoc basis. Where possible, the individual units would deploy teams to recover their own dead and wounded, returning them to the nearest medical team for the wounded or to a designated burial place. In many cases, the nature of the fighting precluded recovery operations. The dead often remained on the battlefields where they fell until their bodies were recovered and buried by local citizens, either in existing cemeteries or in new cemeteries established for that purpose. It was not unusual, especially during the Civil War, for farmers or businessmen to donate a portion of their own property to receive the dead.

During the Civil War, President Lincoln assigned the Army Quartermaster Corps the mission of recovery and burial of the dead of the Federal forces. The cemeteries established following that war were national cemeteries for the burial of Federal troops only. Families with sufficient financial resources paid a mortician to locate the hasty burial place of their loved one and have his remains returned home for burial in the family plot. Confederate soldiers were frequently buried in mass graves near where they fell or in local cemeteries.

During the Spanish-American War, battle casualties were returned to the United States for burial. Some burials were in Arlington Cemetery while others were in local cemeteries throughout the various states. One of the largest burial ceremonies took place at Arlington Cemetery on 6 April 1899, when 336 officers and enlisted men were buried with full military honors in what one newspaper in Canada called "the bivouac of the brave."

World War I was the first major overseas engagement of American forces in which the deceased were initially buried in temporary cemeteries near the battlefields on which they fell. The magnitude of the combat, the numbers of casualties, and the limited transport services dictated the use of overseas cemeteries until the war ended and other provisions could be made.

As early as two days after the Japanese bombed Pearl Harbor, the United States approached British counterparts about obtaining burial sites in Great Britain and Northern Ireland in order to meet the anticipated requirements following an invasion of German-occupied Europe. By mid-1943 at least thirteen locations with a capacity of 230,000 graves had been identified and reserved for use by the United States. This action was based upon initial American plans to return U.S. casualties to Great Britain for temporary burial. In the final analysis, only one location in Great Britain was utilized as a permanent World War II United States site, Cambridge, which was near some U.S. Eighth Air Force bases. By April 1945, more than 9,000 Americans were buried in Great Britain.

Following the invasion of the European Continent, army planners for the provision of Graves Registration Services (now called Mortuary Services) used experience factors from both World War I and the more recent World War II campaigns in North Africa and Italy. It was recognized that designated troops would be needed in the combat areas to locate, recover, identify, evacuate, and bury the remains of those killed in action. One of the early decisions was to ensure that the number of temporary cemeteries should be as limited as feasible and not reach the extreme numbers which had developed during World War I. In excess of 2,200 temporary cemeteries were established in Europe during that conflict. The initial troop list for Operation Overlord (the code name for the planned invasion) called for a total of five Quartermaster (QM) Graves Registration (GR) Companies to be deployed with the U.S. First Army. This allowed one company to be assigned to each of four U.S. Corps with one company remaining under the direct control of First Army. Each QM GR Company could be further segmented, if required, so that one GR Platoon could be attached to each infantry or armored division to bolster the limited GR capability of the divisional QM Company. One GR Platoon was to be attached to each of the two airborne divisions and one GR Platoon was slated for each of the three Engineer Special Brigades assigned to the invasion. The QM Company retained under First Army was designated to establish and operate an Army-level temporary cemetery. By the time Germany surrendered, a total of twenty-four and three-fourths QM GR Companies were deployed in the areas of France, Belgium, the Netherlands, Luxembourg, Germany, Austria, and Czechoslovakia.

Once it was determined that temporary burials would have to be made on the continent, it became the responsibility of each corps commander to select appropriate locations for temporary cemeteries in the assigned geographic area. The corps commanders, in turn, delegated this responsibility to the division commanders. In the final analysis, the divisional GR staff officer or the attached GR Company commander actually selected the temporary cemetery sites. By the end of hostilities, there were more than 30 temporary cemeteries on the Continent with about 140,000 Americans interred. There were also 50 or more temporary cemeteries in the Mediterranean area where nearly 38,000 Americans were buried.

The conflict in the Pacific was spread over much greater distances than in Europe and involved dozens of small and remote islands, which necessitated the use of many more temporary cemeteries. Estimates suggest that over 200 temporary cemeteries were established in the Central and Southwest Pacific areas which held roughly 70,000 Americans. There were probably at least another 40,000 Missing in Action (MIA). Many of the MIA were Navy personnel lost at sea, U.S. Army Air Force crew members shot down at sea or over enemy territory, Prisoners of War who died in captivity and whose remains were not recovered, and men who had been buried hastily under intense combat conditions on the remote battlefields of New Guinea and the Philippines.

By 1947, the U.S. had determined that thirteen permanent cemeteries would be required in Europe, the Mediterranean and North Africa as follows:

France, Five Locations:
> St. James in Brittany
> Colleville/St. Laurent in Normandy
> Epinal southeast of Nancy
> Lorraine near the small town of St. Avold and east of Metz
> Draguignan near Cannes

Belgium, Two Locations:
> Henri-Chapelle northeast of Liege
> Ardennes south of Liege

Italy, Two Locations:
> Sicily-Rome south of Rome
> Florence south of Florence

The Netherlands, One Location:
> Margraten southeast of Maastricht

Luxembourg, One Location:
> Luxembourg City on the outskirts of the city

Great Britain, One Location:
> Cambridge south of the city by the same name

North Africa, One Location:
> Carthage, Tunisia, ten miles from the larger city of Tunis

In addition, twenty-four World War II unknowns are buried in a small plot at the Suresnes American World War I Cemetery on the outskirts of Paris. Most of these troops died in American military hospitals in or near Paris, but their remains could not be positively identified at the time of death.

Only one permanent cemetery under the control of the American Battle Monuments Commission was established in the Pacific. That cemetery was established in the Philippines a few miles southeast of the city of Manila. However, the Manila Cemetery is the largest of all World War II cemeteries containing the remains of over 17,000 troops and the names of more than 36,000 of the missing. The majority of those buried at the Manila Cemetery were killed during the fighting in New Guinea and the Philippines. The large cemetery in Hawaii, the National Memorial Cemetery of the Pacific, called the "Punchbowl," is not an American Battle Monuments Commission permanent cemetery since it is located on American soil. That beautiful cemetery is the responsibility of the Veterans Administration. It was not unusual for U.S. temporary cemeteries to have both Allied troops and enemy troops buried in them, but enemy troops were not buried in the same plots as American or Allied troops. No enemy troops were knowingly buried in the U.S. permanent cemeteries established following the end of hostilities.

The responsibility for the collection and evacuation of the dead was one which was not eagerly accepted by non-GR units. However, the assigned mission of the QM GR units did not include the collection of deceased personnel from front-line units. It was generally accepted, although reluctantly, that it was each combat commander's responsibility to evacuate deceased unit members to the supporting medical aid station. It was also the commander's responsibility to provide as much detail as possible for proper identification of the deceased. This could include individual identification tags, commonly called "Dog Tags," billfolds, watches, rings, clothing (in order to check for laundry marks), and other items of a personal nature that could possibly help to establish positive identification. The deceased were held at the respective aid stations until QM GR personnel could move the bodies to the nearest temporary cemetery. It was not unusual for the removal of the dead to be in quarter-ton trailers towed by a Jeep. In situations where temporary cemeteries were located near aid stations, the remains could be brought directly to the temporary cemetery by the combat unit rather than to aid stations. Of course, many of the wounded died after reaching an aid station. In those cases, the aid station personnel were responsible to assist in the identification of the deceased. The QM GR personnel at the temporary cemeteries attempted to obtain fingerprints, if feasible, as well as prepare dental charts and identify other distinguishing features such as scars, tattoos, healed fractures, etc., which would either confirm the initial identification or assist in ultimate identification at a later time.

An exception to the concept of evacuation of casualties by the combat unit was when conditions were so intense and fluid that it was impossible to evacuate the dead to an aid station. These conditions certainly existed during the early stages of the Battle of the Bulge. Initially, the German forces overran many American front-line positions, and the American units had to leave some or all of their dead behind as they retreated. Once the Americans were able to stop the German advances and counterattack, they began to regain their original positions. At that point the QM GR Companies sent teams to the front lines to search for the dead, many of whom were still in foxholes, bunkers, or in open fields that were covered with snow.

A prime example of this latter case involved the recovery of the Americans who were massacred by members of a German SS division near the village of Malmedy, Belgium. As American units were attempting to retreat from the onrushing Germans on 17 December 1944, several units approached a crossroads near Malmedy. They were attacked by the Germans and a number of soldiers were killed. Those who had not been able to escape into the woods surrendered. An estimated 150 American troops surrendered, were relieved of their weapons, and herded into an open field near the crossroads. For some unknown reason, the Germans opened fire with rifles, pistols and machine guns and slaughtered most of the U.S. prisoners where they stood. Not all sources agree with the actual number killed in this manner versus those who died in the initial, but limited, firefight. The best available figures indicate that at least eighty-two Americans were murdered and left where they had fallen. It was almost a month later, on 13 January 1945, that American QM GR troops were able to enter the area and attempt to remove the frozen bodies and identify them. (An excellent article titled "Mortuary Affairs Operations at Malmedy-Lessons Learned from a Historic Tragedy" detailing this recovery effort was published in the Autumn 1997 issue of the *Quartermaster Professional Bulletin.*)

Another excellent, although morbid, example of the difficulties encountered in attempting to recover remains well after their deaths is that of an American B-24 crew shot down in Germany in August 1944.[1] The plane, named Wham! Bam! Thank You Ma'am, was piloted by 2LT Norman J. Rogers Jr., and had a crew of eight men. All nine men survived the crash landing, but one was badly injured and was taken to a German hospital. As the eight remaining crew members were being taken by train to a POW camp, they encountered a bombed-out section of track. Their German Army guards ordered them to march toward the town of Russelsheim where they expected to board another train. As the eight men were being marched through Russelsheim, the locals started to shout at them, beat them with sticks, and throw rocks, stones and bricks at them. As some of the airmen fell to the ground, they were savagely beaten with shovels and pieces of timber. One townsman, armed with a pistol, started shooting the badly wounded men. The men, some already dead and others severely wounded, were all placed one on top of the other in a small cart and taken to the local cemetery. They were left there for hours when the town air raid siren sounded. During the time the townspeople were gone, two of the injured men managed to extricate themselves from the bodies of their fellow crewmen and escape into the woods. After the all clear was sounded, the townsmen returned and buried the remaining six crewmen, some of whom may still have been alive. About seven months later, after Russelsheim was overrun by the Allies, an American GR team was sent to the town to try to find a British air crew reportedly buried near the town. It was only after the six bodies had been exhumed from the town cemetery that it was discovered they were actually Americans. Even though the bodies had been buried for about seven months, and identification by Quartermaster personnel was very difficult, all six were eventually positively identified.

One last example of the extreme difficulties experienced by GR units involves a group of American Prisoners of War (POWs).[2] These prisoners, most captured during the Battle of the Bulge, were initially sent to a regular POW camp (Stalag IX-B). The Germans either identified or coerced many of the Jewish American POWs into admitting that they were Jewish and then segregated them from the other American POWs. These Jewish prisoners, plus enough other Americans to complete a total of 350, were forced into rail cars and locked in for five days as they were moved to another camp located near the small town of Berga. Berga was in what became known as East Germany following the war. While in Berga the Americans were treated like animals, as were prisoners of other nationalities also housed in Berga. Most of the other prisoners were Eastern European Jews who had been transferred to Berga from other slave labor camps. All of these prisoners were made to work like slaves by the Germans in an attempt to build a synthetic oil factory deep in a mountain near Berga on the banks of the Elster River. They were not properly clothed, were fed starvation rations, were not permitted to receive mail or Red Cross packages, and were forced to perform extremely strenuous physical labor under atrocious conditions. Their German guards frequently beat them with rubber clubs, shovels or rifle butts without cause. After only two months of this slave labor, about two dozen American prisoners died of injuries sustained in the mountain caves or of malnutrition. When the Germans learned that both American and Russian troops were advancing toward the camp, they decided to move all prisoners. The prisoners were ordered out of their shabby barracks into the cruel winter weather without proper clothing, food or medical supplies. During a forced march of roughly 100 miles over a period of eighteen days, it is estimated that at least forty-nine American prisoners either died of malnutrition, illness or were shot by the German guards because they could no longer keep pace with the rest of the prisoners. The dead were either left where they fell, given hasty burials alongside the roads, in the adjoining forests, or, in rare cases, were buried in village cemeteries. No record was kept of these burials by the Germans, and it was only as a result of sketchy diaries kept on scraps of paper by some of the prisoners themselves that QM GR personnel were able to recover some of the bodies after Americans had overrun the area in which the march took place. Those whose remains were not recovered are listed on the various memorials to the Missing in Action in the American cemeteries throughout Europe.

Even in regular military units, there were also many instances in which the dead had to be buried in shallow graves near where they were killed. These "hasty burials" were not always well marked or reported to higher headquarters, thus making it more difficult to recover the bodies once the combat situation had stabilized. QM GR teams searched former battle areas, often under the threat of enemy mortar and artillery fire, for such burial sites once the area was reasonably safe.

Burials in the European Theater of Operations can be assigned to several general classes as follows:

1. Battlefield or Hasty Burials: Usually individual burials in shallow graves or even foxholes by members of the combat unit to which the deceased belonged.

2. Improved Battlefield Burials: Usually small temporary cemeteries established by QM GR teams after the fighting moved forward. In addition to current casualties these small cemeteries might include the deceased initially buried by their own unit personnel as Battlefield or Hasty Burials.

3. Temporary Cemetery Burials: Usually located near hospital areas, these temporary cemeteries were established by QM GR units to support hospitals or aid stations and reduce the distance the deceased had to be transported. Caution was exercised to position these temporary cemeteries to ensure they were not within sight of the hospitals or aid stations, if at all possible.

4. Large Temporary Cemeteries: These cemeteries were established in areas with good road networks, convenient rail lines, and as near ports as possible. These cemeteries received deceased troops from the larger rear area hospitals, as well as the deceased eventually removed from the smaller burial sites as described in 1, 2 and 3 above.

As indicated earlier, it was a much different operating environment in the Pacific, requiring the establishment of many smaller cemeteries, estimated at more than 200. Also, the conditions there were more likely to cause very small burial sites to be utilized. It was not unusual for U.S. units to bypass groups of Japanese troops as the Americans fought to capture specific objectives, such as tactically important hills, river crossings, roadways, etc. Unfortunately, this allowed the bypassed Japanese troops to establish ambush positions in the rear areas to attack American vehicles attempting to supply ammunition and food to the forward troops and transport the dead back to unit cemeteries in the rear. This ambush threat caused units to bury small numbers of their dead along the route of advance to be recovered at a later date, if possible. Due to these tactical conditions, the forces in the Pacific were not able to establish larger temporary cemeteries as in Europe and the Mediterranean areas of operation. Also, because of the fact that the Pacific operation involved many small islands, and both Army and Marine units, the number of temporary cemeteries was significantly greater than in Europe, but most were smaller in size. Only after the end of hostilities were the smaller cemeteries closed and the remains transferred to consolidated cemeteries, especially on Okinawa and in the Philippines.

The first World War II temporary cemeteries in France were established soon after the D-Day airborne drops and amphibious landings in Normandy. Although records are not precise, it appears from information available that the first four temporary cemeteries were established as follows:

1. The first temporary cemetery was most likely established on 7 June 1944, for deceased members of the 82d Airborne Division. This cemetery was at Blosville, France, which is located about six miles north of Carentan, France. At the time it was closed and the remains relocated, it held 5,364 U.S. dead.

2. The second temporary cemetery was probably established on either 7 or 8 June 1944, at St. Laurent, France. Available references differ on the date. It was located about ten miles northwest of Bayeux in the vicinity of Omaha Beach as a First Army cemetery.

3. The third temporary cemetery was established at La Cambe, France, about eighteen miles north of Saint-Lo. Established on 8 or 9 June 1944, it was also a First Army cemetery. After the American dead were removed, the French transferred this location to the Germans. It is now one of the larger German cemeteries in Normandy.

4. The fourth temporary cemetery was located near St.-Mere -Eglise, France, on 9 June 1944, about twenty-one miles south of Cherbourg. Later, another cemetery was opened near St.-Mere-Eglise. This first cemetery was then referred to as St.-Mere-Eglise #1, and the second as St.-Mere-Eglise #2. (Note:

St.-Mere-Eglise was one of the first French towns to be liberated after D-Day.)

In spite of the best efforts of both combat units and QM GR teams, many of the World War II dead were either not recovered at all or the remains could not be positively identified using the techniques available at that time. Approximately 10,000 of the remains buried in U.S. overseas cemeteries are unknowns. The inscription on their grave markers reads "Here Rests in Honored Glory a Comrade in Arms Known but to God." (NOTE: This inscription differs from that used in the World War I Cemeteries. The World War I unknown grave markers are inscribed, "Here Rests in Honored Glory an American Soldier Known but to God.") In addition to the unknown burials, each American World War II cemetery has an area where the names of the Missing In Action (MIA) are inscribed. It is very likely that many MIAs are actually buried as unknowns because there was no means to positively identify the bodies through DNA analysis at that time.

Although it has now been over sixty years since the end of World War II, remains are still being located from time to time either by accident or through the efforts of private citizens who spend much of their free time searching the World War II battlefields, especially those in Europe, for signs of deceased troops. The story of one such group is told in the book, *The Dead of Winter*, by Bill Warnock.[3] Although the men who are the focus of the book initially began hunting for World War II military souvenirs such as helmets, weapons, ammunition, mess kits, etc., they soon became enthralled with the search for remains of Americans who had been declared missing in action and were later classified as Deceased, Body Not Recovered. These men have worked with American veterans to develop information as to the locations where the missing men were last seen alive, where they were thought to have been killed, or where their bodies were buried singly or had to be left on the battlefield as the units either advanced or were forced to retreat. If remains are located, the appropriate American office is notified and the remains are removed for possible identification.

On Sunday, 3 February 2008, the front page of the *New York Times* had an article written by Nina Bernstein titled "Still Trying to

Bring Their Fallen Heroes Home." The article describes the heartbreak of several families who still shelter hope of finding the remains of their loved ones even after more than sixty years. The article states, "The numbers are daunting. Of more than 88,000 American servicemen missing in 20th Century conflicts, some 79,000 are casualties of World War II and though many of them were forever lost at sea, the government still classifies about 35,000 as recoverable."

More recently, an article in the Charleston, South Carolina, *Post and Courier* newspaper, dated Tuesday, 15 July 2008, told of the return of remains of CPT William K. Mauldin who had been reported missing in action during the Korean War. Captain Mauldin, a member of The Citadel Class of 1944, whose education at the Military College of South Carolina had been cut short by the call to duty during World War II, was flying fighter missions during the Korean War when his plane was hit by enemy fire, crashed and burned. Heavy enemy fire precluded a search and recovery effort at the time. Finally, unknown to Captain Mauldin's family, the North Koreans turned over nearly three dozen remains in 1993. In April 2008, almost fifteen years after the North Koreans returned the remains, Captain Mauldin's daughter, Corinne, who was only two years old when her father was reported missing in action, received a call from the military advising that his remains had been positively identified and would be returned to her for burial. Captain Mauldin was buried in Easley, South Carolina, on Friday, 18 July 2008, with full military honors provided by an honor guard from Shaw Air Force Base in South Carolina. The honors included a 21-gun salute and a flyover by two T-6 aircraft from Vance Air Force Base in Oklahoma.

As late as August 2008, Brett Barrouquers, a writer for the Associated Press, reported that the son of a missing airman had been informed that the remains of Lt. Howard Enoch Jr., of Marion, Kentucky, were found in 2006 and had now been identified by the Department of Defense. Lieutenant Enoch, the pilot of a P-51D Mustang, was shot down over Germany on 19 March 1945, and the site of the crash was in what later became the Soviet Zone after Germany surrendered. His son, Howard Enoch III, of Louisville, Kentucky, was born three months after his father was shot down. Now more than sixty-three years old, Howard Enoch III said he never had reason to believe that his father's remains would ever be found. Lieutenant Enoch's remains were buried in Arlington National Cemetery in late September 2008.

Although much less frequent, it is not unheard of that remains of World War I soldiers are located by farmers or construction workers in the areas of some of the heaviest fighting in France and Belgium. Due to the extensive time that has passed since those soldiers were reported missing, and the affects of the soil conditions, climate, and weather, most of those remains, once recovered, will be virtually impossible to identify. Therefore, they will be interred as Unknowns.

Once the permanent World War II cemeteries in Europe opened and were in operation for some time, the American Battle Monuments Commission made the decision to close all but one cemetery to further burials. Only the Ardennes American Cemetery and Memorial near Liege, Belgium, remained open for burials as World War II remains were located and identified. However, that decision was later reconsidered as additional remains were recovered. As an example, when the remains of six veterans of the 99th Infantry Division were recovered and identified, the families of three of them elected to have their remains buried in the Henri-Chapelle American Cemetery in Belgium, in 2002, thus becoming the first burials in that cemetery since 1954.

For more information about World War II Quartermaster Graves Registration operations, the reader is directed to the web site maintained by the U.S. Army Quartermaster Foundation at Fort Lee, Virginia. The web site is http://www.qmfound.com. The following is a partial listing of articles which can be accessed at the QM Foundation web site:

1. "With All Due Honors," by Dr. Steven Anders, first published in the *Quartermaster Professional Bulletin* Autumn/Winter 1994.
2. "Graves Registration," no author shown, first published in the *Quartermaster Review* May/June 1946.
3. *Tell Me About My Boy,* a pamphlet compiled in 1946 by the Technical Branch of the Quartermaster General for distribution to the next of kin of deceased personnel from World War II.

4. "Crosses at Normandy, June 1944," by Colonel Elbert E. Legg (QMC) first published in the *Quartermaster Professional Bulletin* Autumn/Winter 1944.

NOTE: The U.S. Army Quartermaster Museum at Fort Lee, Virginia, has one section dedicated to Graves Registration (now called Mortuary Services) which portrays the advancements in GR services over the years since the Quartermaster Corps was assigned the mission during the latter stages of the Civil War.

NOTES

[1] Madeline E. Teremy, the daughter of Lt. Norman J. Rogers Jr., pilot of the plane, led a successful effort to have a memorial erected in the town of Russelsheim, Germany, in remembrance of the crew and to effect a reconciliation with the residents. She also worked with Helen M. Ruf to prepare an excellent video tribute to her father, his crew and the effort involved to establish a memorial to the crew in Russelsheim. A book titled *Wolfsange: A German City on Trial* by August Nigro published by Brassey's, Inc., Dulles, VA: 2001, provides a detailed description of the events.

[2] Details of this horrific treatment of prisoners of war can be found in the book *Soldiers and Slaves American POWs Trapped by the Nazis' Final Gamble* by Roger Cohen published by Anchor Books, New York, in 2005.

[3] Warnock, Bill, *The Dead of Winter*, New York: Chamberlain Brothers, 2005.

Chapter Four

TEMPORARY CEMETERIES OF WORLD WAR II

"One man with courage makes a majority."
Andrew Jackson

As noted in Chapter Three, **"**Graves Registration Services during World War II," extensive use was made of temporary cemeteries in all areas of operation during World War II. Even though it was decided to attempt to hold the number of temporary cemeteries to a minimum, this objective was easier to achieve in Europe than in the other combat areas, such as India-Burma and the two Pacific areas of operation. There was no specific guide for what qualified as a temporary cemetery. In some instances as few as ten or fifteen remains might be buried in a small area while intense fighting continued in the immediate area. This was especially true during operations against the Japanese in New Guinea and the island-hopping campaigns in the Pacific. In an article titled, "Graves Registration: Graves Registration Search and Recovery Operations After World War II," published in the May/June 1946 issue of *The Quartermaster Review,* it was stated that "as of April 6, 1946, there were a total of 359 American military cemeteries containing the remains of 241,500 World War II dead. Estimated numbers of World War II service dead is 286,959. Of this number 246,492 have already been identified. Of the 40,467 who were unidentified as of March 31, 1946, the remains of 18,641 have been located by graves registration units. The remaining 21,826 were not reported located up to that time. Of those 18,641 remains which have been located, 10,986 now repose in military cemeteries and 7,655 in isolated graves." (Author's Note: Casualty figures here may not agree with figures used elsewhere in this book due to different sources and different dates for the data.)

A summary report of the temporary American cemeteries in Europe published by the American Graves Registration Command,

ETA, titled "United States Temporary Military Cemeteries European Theater Area World War II" (undated) lists the following numbers of temporary cemeteries by country:

France	24
Belgium	4
The Netherlands	3
England	2
Ireland	1
Luxembourg	1
Switzerland	1
TOTAL	36

(Note: The summary report also mentions one cemetery in Sweden and one in the Azores, but no information is provided for those two cemeteries.)

The above summary listing does not reflect that there were temporary cemeteries in Germany, yet it is known that several such cemeteries were established, although the number of burials in each cemetery was small. From the information contained in the summary listing, a table can be constructed showing the temporary cemeteries established from shortly after the D-Day landings in France to the end of the war in Europe. If the reader has access to a good road map of Western Europe the progress of the fighting after D-Day can be followed by plotting the locations and dates of the establishment of each temporary cemetery.

Temporary Cemeteries in Western Europe

Date	Location	Established by	U.S. Burials
7 June '44	Blosville, France	First Army	5,364
8 June '44	La Cambe, France	First Army	4,534
8 June '44	St. Laurent-sur-Mer, France	First Army	3,797
9 June '44	St. Mere Eglise #1, France	First Army	2,172
24 June '44	St. Mere Eglise #2, France	First Army	4,800
30 June '44	Gorron, France	First Army	753
31 July '44	Marigny, France	First Army	3,044
5 Aug '44	St. James, France	Third Army	4,085
7 Aug '44	Le Chen-Guerin, France	First Army	1,202
16 Aug '44	St. Corneille, France	Third Army	521
19 Aug '44	Draguignan, France	Seventh Army	922
24 Aug '44	St. Andre, France	First Army	1,842
25 Aug '44	Villeneuve-sur-Auvers, France	Third Army	534

30 Aug '44	Solers, France	First Army	1,616
1 Sept '44	Champigneul, France	Third Army	1,504
2 Sept '44	Montelimar, France	???	153
8 Sept '44	Fosse, Belgium	First Army	2,200
12 Sept '44	Andilly, France	Third Army	3,424
19 Sept '44	Zon, The Netherlands	First Allied Air Army	416
20 Sept '44	Molenhoek, The Netherlands	First Allied Air Army	795
25 Sept '44	Henri-Chapelle, Belgium	First Army	17,323
28 Sept '44	Margraten, The Netherlands	Ninth Army	15,855
4 Oct '44	Luynes, France	Seventh Army	785
6 Oct '44	Epinal, France	Seventh Army	7,720
6 Nov '44	Limey, France	Third Army	6.012
18 Nov '44	St. Juan, France	Seventh Army	944
18 Nov '44	Varois, France	Seventh Army	169
12 Dec '44	Hochfelden, France	Seventh Army	1,093
18 Dec '44	Neiderbronn, France	???	588
24 Dec '44	Grand Failly, France	Third Army	2,957
29 Dec '44	Hamm, Luxembourg	Third Army	12,300
4 Feb '45	Foy, Belgium	???	2,700
18 Feb '45	Neuville-en-Congroz, Belgium	Communications Zone	937
16 Mar '45	St. Avold, France	Seventh Army	4,221

NOTES:

1. Information is not included for the cemeteries in England, Ireland, Sweden, Switzerland, or the Azores because those cemeteries were established prior to D-Day. Those cemeteries primarily contained the remains of members of air crews and those who died as a result of accidents or disease prior to D-Day.

2. The information in this table reflects known burials as of November 1945.

3. The date each temporary cemetery was established and the number of burials in that cemetery may differ depending upon what reference is used and the date of that reference. The author chose to use this information as the most representative. The table is provided to demonstrate the rather limited use of temporary cemeteries in Western Europe, not to provide definitive information as to each cemetery.

As noted above, the summary report by the American Graves Registration Command, ETA, does not reflect the establishment of temporary cemeteries in Germany. However, another resource, *U.S.*

Army in World War II, the Technical Services, The Quartermaster Corps in the War Against Germany, published by the Office of the Chief of Military History, Department of the Army, on page 689, lists the following temporary cemeteries in Germany: Stromberg, Butzbach, Eisenach, Nuremberg, Ittenbach and Breuna. So there were at least six known temporary cemeteries in Germany. The same reference, on the same page, also states, "none of the U.S. cemeteries in Germany were large, and a priority objective established by General Eisenhower was to remove all U.S. remains buried in Germany as soon as possible following the surrender of Nazi Germany. Those remains were transferred to Epinal, France; St. Avold, France; Henri-Chapelle, Belgium; Hamm, Luxembourg; and Margraten, The Netherlands." The remains thus transferred from temporary cemeteries in Germany remained in the new temporary locations until loved ones were afforded the opportunity to either have the remains returned to the United States for burial or permanently interred in Europe.

In addition to the temporary cemeteries listed, there were numerous burial locations in or near former Prisoner of War camps and concentration camps in enemy territory. Many burials of air crews were made in local cemeteries inside Germany or countries dominated by Germany such as Hungary, Poland, Romania, Yugoslavia and Czechoslovakia. Such burial locations may have contained as few as two or three remains or perhaps dozens, depending upon the location. For example, the burial sites for many U.S. aircrew members were found near the city of Ploesti, Romania. There were at least seven major oil refineries located near Ploesti, and they became primary targets for destruction. Without oil the German war machine would have literally ground to a halt. The entire area was heavily defended by German antiaircraft batteries and Luftwaffe fighter squadrons. The first major American raid on Ploesti took place 1 August 1943, as part of "Operation Tidal Wave" and resulted in a loss of at least fifty-four aircraft and over 400 crewmen. The operation became known as "Black Sunday" to the aircrew members that took part in the raid. Some bodies were never recovered, but those recovered had been buried either in local cemeteries or in special plots established for that purpose by the Romanian people.

There were also a number of temporary cemeteries established in North Africa during the combat operations against Field Marshall Rommel and his Afrika Korps troops. They were eventually consolidated into one permanent cemetery following the end of the war.

By far the largest number of temporary cemeteries was established in the areas that had been occupied by Japanese forces. Unlike Western Europe, the Pacific combat areas generally lacked established highways or rail networks, which would have facilitated consolidation of burials in a few locations. Also, the fighting in these areas generally involved both Army and Marine units, and each service preferred to establish its own temporary cemeteries. A prime example of the geographic area dictating temporary cemetery locations was the campaign against the Japanese in the Philippine Islands. Hasty burials of only a few remains were required time after time as American troops fought under extremely unfavorable conditions after invading Leyte Island. The mountainous terrain was covered by thick jungle-type vegetation and lacked a basic road system. These conditions often required regiments, battalions, and even companies to bury their dead whenever and wherever possible. In addition, the fact that combat operations often took place on numerous islands meant that each island required at least one temporary cemetery. Heavy fighting took place on the Philippine Islands of Leyte, Luzon and Mindanao, while combat operations also took place on many smaller islands.

Even earlier in the war when the Japanese first attacked the Philippines on 8 December 1941, the American forces suffered numerous casualties as they fought first near Manila, then on Corregidor and Bataan. The American dead during this withdrawal operation were buried where possible, sometimes by the local population, and their remains were not recovered until well after the defeat of Japan to end WWII. Not all remains were recovered and the names of those who died during that time frame are listed on one of the walls of the missing either in the Philippines or in Hawaii.

It was not unusual in the Pacific area for the remains of an American fighting man to be buried and reburied several times before being laid to rest in a final grave. An example of this can be found in Chapter Seven, "Jackson County Men." S/Sgt. Wilbur Ward was probably buried initially in a hasty burial site on Lubang Island where he was killed. His remains would later have been moved to a small temporary cemetery before being moved again to either of the two temporary cemeteries located near Manila. Once the decision was made by his family to have his remains interred in the permanent cemetery to be established in Manila, his remains would have been disinterred and kept in a temporary morgue until final burial in the permanent cemetery near Manila.

A final category of "temporary cemeteries" would be the oceans and seas in which many Navy, Coast Guard, Air Force and Merchant Seamen rest either as a result of the sinking of their ship or the downing of their aircraft. Other burials at sea took place under more formal conditions when crewmen were killed in action, died of wounds received, or died of natural causes while at sea. These formal burials at sea followed long-established Naval tradition with a chaplain or senior ship's officer performing the burial service and a complement of the ship's crew present as the remains, usually sewn in a weighted canvas shroud, were slid overboard. When possible, the ship's log would be annotated with the name(s) of the deceased, the date and cause of death, the date of "burial," and the longitude and latitude where the "burial" took place.

U.S. Army Field Manual 10-63 provided guidance for marking burial locations in "official" temporary cemeteries. Graves were to be marked by one of three types of wooden markers:

1. The basic marker in the early stages of fighting consisted of a simple V shaped wooden stake, which was six inches wide at the top, narrowing to a point at the bottom. The stake was to be 41 inches tall so that 18 inches could be buried in the ground and still have 23 inches remaining above ground. An embossed plate

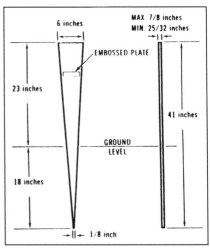

V-Peg temporary grave marker

with information pertaining to the deceased was placed near the top of the stake.

2. When the situation permitted, and in the more "formal" temporary cemeteries, a plain white wooden cross was used to mark the burial site for members of the Christian Faith and for unknowns. The cross was to be 41 inches tall with the cross member being 14 inches long. Like the simple V shaped marker, 18 inches was to be buried in the ground with 23 inches remaining above ground. An embossed plate with information pertaining to the deceased was placed at the center of the cross marker.

3. A wooden Star of David was used for marking the graves of those of the Jewish faith. The Star of David itself was to be 14 inches across and 14 inches high. An embossed plate with the information pertaining to the deceased was placed at the center of the Star of David.

The temporary cemeteries were certainly not uniform in design, appearance or signage. The following photos will

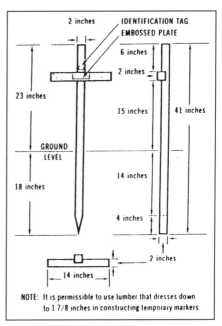

Christian Cross
temporary grave marker

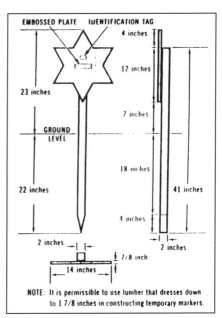

Star of David
temporary grave marker

demonstrate these differences much more dramatically than the written word could hope to do. These photos have been obtained from a wide variety of sources to which the author is deeply appreciative.

Temporary Cemetery, Munda #1, New Georgia, the Pacific. Courtesy of the Quartermaster Museum, Fort Lee, Virginia

Monument marking location of the first American temporary cemetery in Normandy. Photo courtesy of Laurent Le Febure

Army Chaplain Francis Sampson conducts services for paratroopers killed near Saint Marie Dumant, France. Photo courtesy of the Quartermaster Museum, Fort Lee, Virginia

German prisoners working in temporary U.S. cemetery in Normandy, May 1945. A.P. photo by Peter J. Carroll

Temporary cemetery on Guadalcanal Island, the Pacific, 1943.
Photo courtesy of Mr. Andrew Webb, the Robert Hunt Library,
London, Great Britain

U.S. Marines fire rifle salute over graves at New Georgia, the
Pacific, 1943. Photo courtesy of the Julia S. Tutwiler Library,
University of Western Alabama

The 5ᵗʰ Marine Division cemetery on Iwo Jima. Photo by Jerry Schoenbert as shown at http://picasaweb.google.com/7thfighter

The 3ʳᵈ Marine Division cemetery (right) and the 4ᵗʰ Marine Division cemetery (left) on Iwo Jima as shown at www.grunt.com.images

Burial at Sea. Courtesy www.thewarpage.com

Burial at Sea for two casualties from the USS Liscome Bay *air-craft carrier. Services conducted on board a Coast Guard Assault Transport. Government Archives photo 26-G-3182*

*Two Coast Guardsmen
pay respects to a buddy
killed in the Ryukyu
Islands, the Pacific, 1945.
Government Archives
photo 26-G-4739*

*U.S. temporary cemetery Manila #1 opened February 1945.
Photo courtesy MSgt. Bert Caloud USMC (Retired)*

U.S. temporary cemetery Saarebourg, Germany, 1945.
One of only a few U.S. temporary cemeteries in Germany.
Original photo purchased by author on eBay

The German Army seems to have permitted burials in individual graves, small unit cemeteries, or larger temporary cemeteries. This may be explained by the operational conditions, which the German forces faced during the early stages of their rapid advance in Western Europe in 1940 and later in the early stages of the invasion of Russia. The Germans advanced over long distances in a very short period of time, making the establishment of large temporary cemeteries difficult at best. When the Germans were forced to retreat on both fronts during the last two years of the war, they faced much the same conditions, only in reverse.

As the reader looks at the photos of German graves that follow, he or she may wonder what became of those graves, which were so well tended in some of the photos. Germany has an organization that functions somewhat as our own American Battle Monuments Commission. Germany has established six World War II cemeteries in the Normandy/Brittany area of France and others across France, Belgium and Germany. One of the largest German WWII cemeteries is located in Normandy near the city of Bayeux at La Cambe. This location first served as one of the largest U.S. temporary cemeteries. After all U.S. remains were either returned to the U.S. or reinterred in one of the new permanent cemeteries, the French Government allocated the La Cambe site to the Germans.

The photos which follow were all purchased by the author from the extensive listings of German war photos available on eBay. In many cases, the original German photo was very small, some as small as 2 1/4 by 2 1/4 inches. In such cases, the author has enlarged the photo for use in this chapter by using a scanner and computer.

German soldiers honor fallen comrade, probably in Russia.
Photo purchased by author on eBay

Lonely German burial site, probably in Russia.
Photo purchased by author on eBay

Solitary German grave in ruins of Berlin, 1945.
Photo purchased by author on eBay

Decorated German grave near Stablehelm, Russia.
Photo purchased by author on eBay

German soldier buried along roadside. Note horse-drawn wagons. Photo purchased by author on eBay

Carefully maintained German grave, probably in Russia. Note at least 3 other graves in background. Photo purchased by author on eBay

*Neatly maintained German cemetery, probably in Russia. Note un-
usually shaped markers. Photo purchased by author on eBay*

*German cemetery somewhere in Russia.
Photo purchased by author on eBay*

Chapter Five

LEST THEY BE FORGOTTEN

"The soldier, above all other people, prays for peace,
for he must suffer and bear the deepest
wounds and scars of war."
General Douglas MacArthur

One of the stated purposes of the American World War II Orphans
Network (AWON) is to preserve the memory of their fathers who
died during World War II. (See chapter six for more information
about AWON.) Most of the vignettes in this chapter were written in
coordination with AWON members. They provided as much information as was available about the veteran's life before entering the
military service as well as photos, letters, telegrams and copies of
newspaper articles which they had accumulated and treasured over
the past sixty years or more. Contact with the AWON members was
facilitated through an article published in the AWON newsletter, *The
Star*, and through a notice posted on the AWON web server. In each
instance, preliminary information was provided by the family member and then draft vignettes were exchanged until the most complete
vignette possible was finalized. Although the general format is the
same for each vignette, the reader will note differences in the depth
of information provided, as well as the length of the vignettes. These
differences are caused by the fact that it has been over sixty years
since the death of the person in each vignette. Also, in some cases,
the family background information and information about the person's youth was simply not available.

The vignettes in this chapter are arranged in chronological order
by date of death. No attempt was made to focus on officers, non-
commissioned officers, or enlisted men. Likewise, no attempt was
made to focus on one military service over another. Also, no attempt
was made to provide broad geographical representation. The reader

will find states represented in this chapter based solely upon the locality the person in question called "home."

It may come as a shock to some readers that two of the vignettes in this chapter were made possible as a result of information provided by children whose fathers died before they could marry the mother, what current readers might call "Love Children." Those two daughters volunteered to participate in this project, and cooperated fully with the author to provide as much information as possible about the life of their father prior to his meeting their mother. Their own young lives were not easy without a father. However, the pride that each feels about her father was very clear to this author through the many exchanges of letters and e-mails during the drafting process and in the effort each woman devoted to providing as much background information as possible and such photos as were available.

What comes across vividly when one communicates with each child or close relative of a deceased veteran of World War II is their fervent wish that the memory of their loved one be perpetuated so that generations as yet unborn may be aware of the ultimate sacrifice made by their ancestor. Without exception, the sense of pride felt in their deceased parent or loved one is a very deep and caring one, even though they may never have personally known the deceased. Some of the children were born after the father was already overseas or even after the father's death. In those cases where the child was not old enough that his or her father had held them or actually played with them, memories of their father most likely derived from stories told by their mother, a grandparent, or an aunt or uncle. We might describe that as either assisted memory or enhanced memory.

Information for the vignettes in this chapter also came from sources other than AWON members. In one case, I was having blood drawn for an annual physical when the medical technician mentioned that her grandfather was killed in WWII and was buried overseas. The technician provided a phone number for her father, who, it turned out, lived less than three miles from my home. Regardless of how contact was established, each person was eager to help present and preserve their father's or relative's story for their own children and grandchildren.

Several of the vignettes in this chapter relate to men whose remains have not been recovered or identified. The families of these men listed on the Walls of the Missing in our cemeteries and memorials, even after all these years, still maintain hope that some day their loved one's remains will be located and given a proper burial. These hopes are sustained when one reads in a local paper or sees on national television where the remains of a long-lost soldier, sailor, airman or marine have been located in some farmer's field or on some faraway beach and subsequently identified. It must be a bittersweet occasion for the family when those remains are returned for burial in a family plot or are interred in one of the overseas cemeteries. Their loved one is home at last.

A number of families have never been able to visit the overseas cemetery where their loved one is buried or is memorialized on the Walls of the Missing. In several cases, the author was able to provide a photo of the grave site or a photo of the name on a Wall of the Missing to the family for the first time, or was able to provide new details about the action in which the loved one was killed. Those were rewarding experiences for both the author and the family of the deceased.

The author and publisher have elected to include available photos within each vignette rather than show a collection of all photos on several consecutive pages. We feel that this lets the reader feel closer to the person about whom he or she is reading. The available photos almost without exception seem to convey the love that the individual felt for his wife, child or family members, as well as respect for the uniform of his service. The reader should keep in mind that most of the photos, other than photos of grave sites, were taken over sixty years ago, so the quality may not be as good as one would wish. Also, some of the photos were provided in color which then had to be converted to black and white, thus losing some of the sharpness that even an old color photo may have contained.

Private First Class
Milous McEntyre[1]
22[d] Infantry Regiment
4th Infantry Division

Pfc. Milous (Buck) McEntyre was killed on 15 July 1944, somewhere between Saint-Lo and Cherbourg, France. Although no specific details are available as to how Pfc. McEntyre was killed, it is known that his unit had to negotiate the swampy areas, which the Germans previously flooded in an attempt to delay Allied forces in the event of a landing in that

Pfc. McEntyre in uniform

area. Private First Class McEntyre landed with the rest of the 4th Infantry Division[2] at Utah Beach on D-Day, 6 June 1944, and had been in almost continuous combat for the five weeks since landing in France. The 4th Infantry Division landed some 2,000 yards south of its intended landing areas on Utah Beach, but the assistant division commander, BG Theodore Roosevelt Jr., son of former President Theodore Roosevelt, made the decision to initiate the attack where the division had landed. This "accidental landing" south of the planned landing area may have helped keep the division's initial losses to a minimum since the strongest German defenses were in the planned landing area. After making excellent progress inland on the first day, and capturing the town of St.-Mere-Eglise on the second day, the division soon found itself in the very difficult hedgerow country, which caused progress to be measured in yards rather than kilometers. Further, the division's next objective was a narrow isthmus of land that led through a naturally formed swampy area known as Prairies Marecageuses de Gorges. The swampy terrain, made even worse by recent heavy rains, significantly aided in the defense of the isthmus, which was already heavily defended by the Germans. Capture of this isthmus was necessary in order to cut the essential roadway between

Lessay and Periers. According to the U.S. Army's Center of Military History, the most difficult of the 4th Division's missions was assigned to the 22nd Infantry Regiment, as it assaulted along the division's right flank, consequently involving Private First Class McEntyre's unit in some of the heaviest fighting in that sector.

Just about the time the division commander, Major General Barton, received orders to regroup and attack toward the critical port city of Cherbourg, Pfc. Milous McEntyre became one of the division's many casualties. In fact, it was reported that the 4th Infantry Division suffered well over 2,000 casualties in its first ten days of fighting. Although his wife, Pauline, was not officially notified by the Adjutant General of the Army that her husband was missing in action until she received a telegram dated 3 August, Private First Class McEntyre had actually been missing since 15 July. It was not until days later that Pauline received confirmation that her husband had, in fact, been killed on 15 July. For many years the family believed that McEntyre had been the victim of "friendly fire." His daughter, son and grandson visited Normandy in 2007 and learned the approximate location where their father was killed, and that he was not killed by "friendly fire" but by enemy fire.

A few letters retained by Pauline and excerpts from other letters published in the local paper and in a church memorial bulletin provide insight into Pfc. Milous McEntyre's final days prior to his death. One of his last letters home was dated 16 June 1944 and reads as follows:

Dear Loved Ones:

Here I am again, guess you are wondering why you haven't heard from me in quite a while. But I suppose you have already guessed why. So far I am all together [*sic*], but don't know for how long. But I am praying that everything works out all right. Honey I got those pictures after so long. I am sending all three to you and you can send Myrtle one for me. I don't have time... this is worse than Hell. Sweetheart when I get a chance I will tell you more about it. Up until now I will say pray for me and may God be with you and the children until we meet again. So look to the bright side and everything will be alright [*sic*]. With all my love to you and the kids.

                                                        Buck

Private First Class McEntyre's wife's last letter to him was written on 15 and 16 July 1944, but was returned to her unopened. He had been killed on 15 July, possibly even while his wife was writing to him.

Pfc. Milous McEntyre was a member of the Knoxville Baptist Tabernacle Church. The church newsletter, "Tabernacle News," Volume I, No. 3, published in September 1944, advised the congregation that Buck had been killed in France in July. Private First Class McEntyre was the first Gold Star member of the church. The newsletter included excerpts from four of McEntyre's letters home. His letter of 4 July 1944, was quoted in part as follows: "Yes, I put my trust in the Lord all the time and I am sure he is watching over you and the kids as well as myself. I'm praying for him to send me safely back to you and the kids."

Milous McEntyre was born on 15 May 1908, the fifth of eight children born to Manuel Irvin McEntyre and Elizabeth Newton McEntyre. Typical of many residents of that era in Kennesaw, Georgia, his parents worked at farming for a livelihood. However, his father also made and sold chenille bedspreads to vacationers heading through Georgia on their way to Florida. It was not unusual at that time to see brightly colored and extensively decorated bedspreads for sale along major highways in the south. In what may have been an attempt to escape the difficult life his father and mother lived, Buck lied about his age and at age sixteen enlisted in the Army after only seven years of school. He served in the Army for several years, including service in the Pacific, returned to Kennesaw, and went into the furniture upholstery business with his older brother, Tom.

When Tom moved to Knoxville, Tennessee, in the early 1930s, Buck soon followed. Through mutual friends in the Knoxville area, Buck met his future wife, Pauline (Pat) Baker. After dating for about a year, Buck and Pauline were married in the Knox County Courthouse on 31 March 1934, and the following year their first child, Lois, was born. About five years later a son, Ronnie, was born. After several more attempts at the furniture business, Buck found work with the Southern Railway and was trained to become a brakeman/flagman. In that capacity, he was responsible for reading the signals along the railway lines, which were so critical to the safe operation of the trains. Although it was probably due in large part to the war that Buck was hired by the Southern Railway, it became evident that he would soon be drafted. In January 1944, he reenlisted in the Army from his home state of Georgia and reported to Fort Oglethorpe for training. Probably because of his previous service, Buck received only three weeks of training at Fort Oglethorpe before he was shipped to England with the 4th Infantry Division. The division then began intensive training in England for about five months before the D-Day Invasion on 6 June 1944.

Pauline McEntyre's struggles as a war widow must have mirrored those of thousands of other wives who suddenly found themselves single parents raising children who might not even remember their father. Four years after his death, the Army advised Pauline in 1948 that she had the option of having Buck's body returned to the United States for burial or having him buried in one of the new permanent cemeteries being established in Europe. She chose to have him buried with his buddies in Europe. Her children feel that the mere thought of having to relive the agony of his death four years after he was killed in action must have weighed heavily upon her decision. His remains were re-interred in the American Cemetery and Memorial near Collieville-sur-Mer, France. Pat worked for a couple of years following Buck's death. Fortunately, she learned that she was eligible for Southern Railroad retirement benefits earned by Buck and elected to stay at home to raise her young children. Although her life was a simple one, and rather Spartan, she managed to provide a comfortable life for herself and the two children.

Buck's daughter, Lois McEntyre Harbin, his son, Ron McEntyre, and Michael McEntyre, Ron's son, visited the American Cemetery and Memorial in Normandy, France, in 2007. Lois and Ron agree that their visit was extremely gratifying in major part due to the very warm welcome given them by the staff at the Cemetery. Following the visit to the cemetery, and at the suggestion of the staff, they visited the Utah Beach Museum and Saineny, the location of the 22[d] Infantry Regiment when Pfc. Milous McEntyre was killed in action. Ron McEntyre stated that merely being near the soil where his father was killed was very meaningful to him, his sister and the family. He added that the simple fact that many of the structures in that area remained much the same as they had been in 1944 was almost like being able to go back in time. This helped Ron to enhance the connection between himself and his father. As a result of these visits and the fact that they could actually see and touch their father's white marble cross, the two war orphans felt in some measure reunited with the father they had really never known. They now speak of gaining a new respect, honor, and pride in their father's sacrifice.

Pfc. Milous (Buck) McEntyre is buried in the Normandy American Cemetery and Memorial near Collieville-sur-Mer, France, in Plot C, Row 21, Grave 3.

Lois McEntyre Harbin and Ron McEntyre
at their father's grave site

Private Harry Victor Graber[3]
9th Infantry Regiment
2d Infantry Division

Pvt. Harry Victor Graber was wounded on 2 September 1944, near Fourneuf, France, during the battle to take the heavily fortified and strongly defended port city of Brest, France, on the Brittany Peninsula. Private Graber was operating a machine gun to provide harassing fire on German positions when he was hit by enemy fire. Taken to the 100th Evacuation Hospital, he had to have an operation for a gunshot wound to the abdomen. Although he survived the surgery, Harry died on 4 September of complications from the severe wound. He was thirty-six years old at the time of

Pvt. Graber in uniform

his death. Private Graber was posthumously awarded the Bronze Star and the Purple Heart for his heroic action and was also the recipient of the Expert Infantrymans Badge and the Combat Infantrymans Badge.

Three American divisions had been assigned the mission to capture Brest—the 2d Infantry Division, the 29th Infantry Division, and the 8th Infantry Division. The battle to take Brest was one of the most difficult battles fought during the Allied breakout from the hedgerow countryside in Normandy, France. The breakout had been given the code name "Operation Cobra" and was intended to permit General Patton's tank-heavy Third Army room to attack over better suited terrain. Brest was an important objective for two primary reasons: it was the second largest port in France, and it was home port for German submarines that were attacking Allied shipping responsible for bringing supplies, equipment, and replacement troops into France. It was estimated that 50,000 German troops were defending Brest and the port area.

Harry Graber was born in Wayne Township, Tuscarawas County, Ohio, on 26 June 1908. He was the oldest of four children born to Ratio and Jenny Klingle Graber. His siblings were Joseph, born in 1909, Ruth, born in 1911, and Ruby, born in 1912. Harry liked the outdoors and he went hunting and fishing at every opportunity. He had to drop out of school at age sixteen when his father died of pneumonia at age forty in 1925. Harry followed in the footsteps of other men in the family and obtained work on the Wheeling and Lake Erie Railroad as a member of a bridge repair and maintenance team.

Pvt. Graber with son, Larry

Harry married Helen Shutt on 30 March 1931. A son, Larry, was born on 19 May 1943. After their marriage, Harry and Helen lived in Wayne Township until moving to Dundee, Ohio, also in Tuscarawas County, where they stayed until Harry was drafted.

Since Harry was working in an essential industry—the railroads—he was not drafted during the early stages of the war. However, he was drafted on 26 October 1943, at age thirty-five, five months after the birth of his son. After first

Helen and Harry Graber with the family dog

reporting to the Army Induction Center at Fort Hayes in Columbus, Ohio, he was assigned to the Infantry Training Center at Fort Benning, Georgia, for basic training.

Following his infantry training, he was shipped out on board the *Queen Elizabeth* ocean liner, which had been converted to use as a troop carrier, and he arrived in England in June 1944. Harry was soon assigned to "H" Company (Heavy Weapons) of the 9th Infantry Regiment, of the 2d Infantry Division,[4] "The Indian Head Division." Although the exact date is not known, Harry joined the division in France. The 9th Regiment landed on Omaha Beach on D-Day +1, 7 June 1944. The regiment was immediately committed to heavy fighting in Normandy and within three days had crossed the main railroad line running between Paris and Cherbourg. The division advanced through the Carisy Forest area and was given a short rest period. It then returned to the front lines and captured the town of St. Germane d'Elle.

As a "reward" for their hard fighting, the Indian Head Division was ordered to the Brittany Peninsula to take part in the attack on the heavily defended city of Brest with its critical port area. Hitler had refused permission for his forces to evacuate Brest, and ordered it held at all costs. The 9th Regiment succeeded in capturing two of the strong points around Brest on 4 September, the same day Pvt. Harry V. Graber succumbed to his injuries. The enemy garrison in Brest finally surrendered on the evening of 19 September, and American forces took control of the city.

Private Graber was initially buried in a temporary cemetery at St. James, in the Brittany area of France, and he was reburied in that same cemetery when it was designated to become a permanent cemetery following the end of the war. Mrs. Graber elected to have her husband's remains buried with the other fallen members of his unit rather than have them returned to the United States for burial. Mrs. Graber never remarried. She supported herself and Larry with the income received from her husband's military insurance, his Railroad Retirement Pension, and by cleaning houses. She also supplemented their income by baking pies for restaurants in the area.

Larry Graber has been able to visit his father's burial location two times, once in 1990 and again in 1992. Larry contacted the American

Battle Monuments Commission in 1994 to request that his father's remains be returned to the United States for burial closer to home so the family could visit the grave more often. His request was denied.

Private Graber is buried in Plot I, Row 10, Grave 6 of the St. James American Cemetery and Memorial in Brittany, France.

(Author's Note: Following the end of WWII, the military offered parents or spouses the opportunity to have the remains of their loved ones returned to the United States or other location of choice or they could elect to have them buried in one of the permanent cemeteries to be established overseas. The next of kin were cautioned that if they elected to have their loved ones buried overseas, that decision was irrevocable.)

Pvt. Graber's grave site

Staff Sergeant
Sherwood Hallman[5]
Medal of Honor Recipient
75th Infantry Regiment
29th Infantry Division

S/Sgt. Sherwood Hallman was one of the thousands of infantrymen who landed on Omaha Beach on 6 June 1944, as a member of the 29th Infantry Division. He survived the murderous German crossfire on the beach, only to be wounded on 7 June 1944, when he was hit by pieces of shrapnel from Allied aircraft attempting to bomb and strafe

Then Pfc. Hallman in England, 1943

enemy positions in front of Hallman's unit. Suffering from wounds to the right side of his body, face, torso, arm and leg, he was evacuated to England where he was treated for his wounds and returned to his unit in France within three weeks. By September 1944, the 29th Division[6] had advanced down the Brittany Peninsula and was ordered to attack the vital port city of Brest, where German U-boats were operating to attack Allied shipping carrying vital supplies to the forces ashore in France. The Germans encircled Brest with a chain of strongly fortified defensive positions, which seemed to be virtually impenetrable. One of the strongest German defense positions was called Fort Keranroux, and it was this fort that Staff Sergeant Hallman's unit was ordered to capture.

By 13 September, the American attack on Fort Keranroux was halted by withering fire from a number of enemy positions situated to provide interlocking fire on the attacking American troops. Staff Sergeant Hallman ordered his men to cover him with their fire so he could personally attack the main enemy position. His assigned weapon was the Browning Automatic Rifle (BAR) which weighed about eighteen and a half pounds. For his attack, Staff Sergeant Hallman swapped his BAR for the smaller, lighter M1 Carbine which weighed just over five pounds. He then charged an enemy machine gun position while tossing hand grenades and firing his carbine. By the time he actually reached the enemy lines, he was out of ammunition and grenades. He pointed his empty carbine at the enemy troops and shouted for them to surrender. His bluff worked!

Staff Sergeant Hallman was posthumously awarded the Medal of Honor for his action. The citation for the Medal of Honor reads in part:[7]

> Without hesitating, S/Sgt. Hallman leaped over a hedgerow into a sunken road, the central point of the German defenses which was known to contain an enemy machinegun position and at least 30 enemy riflemen. Firing his carbine and hurling grenades, S/Sgt. Hallman, unassisted, killed or wounded 4 of the enemy, then ordered the remainder to surrender. Immediately, 12 of the enemy surrendered and the position was shortly secured by the remainder of his company. Seeing the surrender of this position, about 75 of the enemy in the vicinity surrendered, yielding a defensive organization which the battalion, with heavy supporting fires, had been unable to take. This single heroic act on the part of S/Sgt. Hallman resulted in the immediate advance of the entire battalion for a distance of 2,000 yards to a position from which Fort Keranroux was captured later the same day. S/Sgt. Hallman's fighting determination and intrepidity in battle exemplify the highest tradition of the U.S. Armed Forces.

The very next day, 14 September 1944, Staff Sergeant Hallman was hit by a German sniper's bullet and killed. Almost eight and one half months later, BG Malcolm F. Lindsey, the Commanding General of Indiantown Gap Military Reservation in Pennsylvania, presented Staff Sergeant Hallman's Medal of Honor to his widow, Virginia, and his two-year-old son, Sherwood Hallman II. Sherwood Hallman II was only seven months old when his father left the United States for England.

Sherwood Henry Hallman was born on 20 October 1913. One of five children born to Henry Harrison Hallman and Emma Poinsett Hallman, Sherwood had two brothers, Raymond and Lester, and two sisters, Marion and Elaine. Sherwood's father was a mail carrier and his mother was a housewife and seamstress. The family lived on Queen Street in Spring City, Pennsylvania, near Pottstown, where

Sherwood grew up. He attended Spring City High School, played on the football team, enjoyed going camping with friends, and loved horses. He was a member of the Zion Evangelical Lutheran Church in Spring City. Sherwood had to drop out of high school before graduation during the Depression so he could help the family. He found work grooming horses at the Spring City Race Track. Once the racing season ended, he managed to get a job at Stauffer's market where Mr. Stauffer took a liking to Sherwood and trained him to become a butcher.

Although Sherwood was a handsome young man, 5 feet 10 inches tall, with dark brown hair and beautiful blue eyes, it was probably his warm personality and ready smile that people noticed the most. He was also very outgoing and generous.

By 1939, Sherwood managed to save enough money to open his own business. Purchasing an old truck, he converted it to a grocery on wheels and called his business "Sherry's Modern Market." He provided doorstep service, selling canned and packaged food, fresh produce, dairy products, and even meat and poultry. He referred to his business as a "Store to Door Market." (Author's Note: My hometown of Jackson, Ohio, had about a dozen of these "rolling stores" operating in the rural areas of southeastern Ohio during the '40s, '50s and '60s. My uncle, Arthur (Art) Butts, operated one such store.)

Henry Harrison Hallman died in 1941, and Sherwood, a bachelor, was given a draft classification of 3-A because he was the sole support for his mother and siblings, thereby keeping him out of the military service.

Also in 1941, a young high school student, Virginia Dieter, was working part-time at a local meat packing company while still attending high school. Sherwood came to the plant one day to deliver a rush order for meat and Virginia waited on him. One of Virginia's close friends lived on Sherwood's delivery route. After learning that Sherwood and Virginia had met at the meat packing company, the friend's mother invited Virginia to lunch on the day she knew Sherwood would be making his rounds. Virginia and Sherwood were introduced and he asked her for a date. Their first date was to go to the midget race car track at Frankford.

Virginia and Sherwood Hallman, summer 1941

That first date led to more dates, and on 4 January 1942, Sherwood and Virginia were married in the Zion Evangelical Lutheran Church. They lived with Sherwood's mother and his siblings after the wedding. On 25 October 1942, Virginia gave birth to a son, Sherwood Hallman II. Two weeks after his son's birth, Sherwood's draft status was reclassified to 1-A, a sure indicator that he would soon be in the military. After he received his draft notice, Sherwood entered the Army on 8 January 1943, and was sent to Fort McClellan, Alabama, for Infantry Replacement Training. Although most draftees were young men in their late teens or very early twenties, Sherwood was twenty-nine years old when he started basic training. Because of his age, his fellow trainees usually called him "Pops."

After barely four months in the Army, Sherwood's unit was shipped to England in May 1943. The entire 29th Infantry Division spent a year undergoing intensive training for the long-anticipated assault on Hitler's "Fortress Europe." Sherwood was assigned to Company "F," 2d Battalion, 175th Infantry Regiment of the 29th Infantry Division. The 29th was primarily composed of Maryland and Virginia National Guard Troops. The division had seen combat during World War I where it participated in the Meuse-Argonne Offensive action in October 1918. After the Armistice of 11 November 1918, the division was returned to the United States and demobilized at Fort Dix, New Jersey, on 30 May 1919. For the next two decades the divisional units trained as part of the National Guard until the threat of war caused the War Department to reactivate the 29th Infantry Division on 3 February 1941.

Following the D-Day landings on Omaha Beach, the 29th Division fought through Normandy including the battle to capture the French city of Saint-Lo with its strategically important road network. The Germans defended Saint-Lo with all the strength they could muster, resulting in heavy U.S. casualties and the virtual destruction of Saint-Lo. Staff Sergeant Hallman managed to make it through the Saint-Lo fighting with no further injuries, although the 29th Division did take numerous casualties. After the capture of Saint-Lo, the 29th Division shifted its attack to focus on Brest, where Staff Sergeant Hallman earned his Medal of Honor.

Sherwood Hallman II and Virginia
at S/Sgt. Hallman's grave site, 1997

S/Sgt. Sherwood H. Hallman is buried at the Brittany American Cemetery and Memorial located near the town of St. James (Manche), France, in Plot M, Row 5, Grave 11.

Fifty years after D-Day, in 1994, Virginia Hallman and her son, Sherwood II, were invited to the Brittany Cemetery, totally unaware that a local Frenchman, Yanneck Creac'h, had been the driving force behind a local effort to raise funds to erect a memorial to Staff Sergeant Hallman. With Virginia, Sherwood II, and an Honor Guard from the French Navy present, the S/Sgt. Sherwood H. Hallman Memorial was unveiled.

Before the 60th D-Day Anniversary Commemoration activities in 2004, soldiers and veterans of the 29th Infantry Division visited the Brittany Cemetery to pay tribute to Staff Sergeant Hallman at his grave site. During a very emotional wreath-laying service, Pfc. John K. Pace, a member of the 29th Infantry Division Band, played taps and D-Day veteran Don Miller read Staff Sergeant Hallman's Medal of Honor citation.

Virginia Hallman is currently researching and writing a book on the life and heroic actions of her husband.

Second Lieutenant
John Charles Eisenhauer[8]
60th Infantry Regiment
9th Infantry Division

2LT John Charles Eisenhauer was reportedly hit by enemy fire on 27 September 1944, while attempting to silence an enemy pillbox that was delaying his unit's advance. At the time of his death, his unit was engaged in heavy fighting in the Huertgen Forest area. Due to the intense action at the time, an attempt to recover his body was not made until the next day, but his remains could not be found. It took another three and a half years before his remains were recovered and properly identified. One can only imagine the terrible toll this long delay must have taken on his wife and family.

2LT Eisenhauer in uniform

John Charles Eisenhauer was born in New York City on 23 March 1917, the first child of Charles and Helen Gustafson Eisenhauer. A younger brother, Allen, was born six years later. The family moved to Queens when John was about eight years old. John's father was a salesman for a company that sold surgical knives. Charles's parents lived in an apartment above them, so John and Allen had virtually daily contact with their grandparents. John enjoyed stamp collecting and reportedly had an excellent collection. An avid sports enthusiast, he was a loyal New York Giants baseball team fan and sometimes got to attend games in the old Polo Grounds with friends. He liked to watch basketball games and play board games, especially the game of Battleship, which he played frequently with one of his cousins. John and his close friend, Chet Sheldon, enjoyed just hanging out together to talk and listen to their favorite radio shows including "The Shadow," "Jack Benny," "Bob Hope," and "Ed Sullivan." John also liked to sail model sailboats on Jackson Pond in Richmond Hill. His daughter, Gail, still has one of his model boats, which he named Comet.

Following graduation from Richmond Hill High School in 1935, John found a job in an office in Manhattan, and also worked in some capacity at the New York Worlds' Fair in Flushing Meadows in 1939. He met his future wife, Dorothy (Dottie) Krumm, on a blind date in 1937 or 1938 while visiting friends in upstate New York. Dorothy was a nursing student at the Flower 5th Avenue Hospital in New York City, so they were able to see each other frequently.

Allen (left) and John (right) with their father

Among some of the first young men to be drafted, John was inducted on 16 January 1941. This was almost a full year before the Japanese bombed Pearl Harbor, but almost sixteen months after Hitler attacked Poland, and about six months after the British Expeditionary Forces (BEF) had been forced to evacuate the European Continent at Dunkirk, France. John was sent to Fort Bragg, North Carolina, for training as a part of the 9th Infantry Division. While at Fort Bragg, Dorothy joined him and they were married at Dillon, South Carolina, on 7 February 1942. John remained at Fort Bragg until 23 October 1942, when he sailed on the *Susan B. Anthony* for North Africa. Dorothy then returned

John and Dottie Eisenhauer

to New York to work at Horton Hospital in Middletown, New York, and await the birth of their first child. John landed near Port Lyautey, Morocco, as part of Operation Torch on 8 November 1942; the following day Dorothy gave birth to their daughter, Gail.

The 9th Infantry Division[9] fought its way from Algeria to Tunisia, took part in the subsequent invasion of Sicily in late summer of 1943, and then sailed for England to begin training for the invasion of Fortress Europe. Arriving in England on Thanksgiving Day 1943, John spent the next six months in the rigorous training required for troops who would take part in the invasion. His unit landed on Utah Beach along the Normandy Coast of France on D-Day + 4, 10 June 1944, and was assigned the mission of splitting the German forces defending the area known as the Cotinten Peninsula.

The division then fought across France and Belgium into  Germany. Toward the end of July 1944, John Eisenhauer was recognized for his combat skills and leadership qualities and received a battlefield commission promoting him from his NCO rank of technical sergeant to second lieutenant. John also earned the highly prized and respected Combat Infantrymans Badge.

2LT John Charles Eisenhauer is buried in the Ardennes American Cemetery and Memorial located near Neupre, Belgium. His grave is in Plot B, Row 32, Grave 21. His daughter, Gail, first visited her father's grave site in 1981 and was able to show photos to John's mother who was still alive at that time. In May 2007, Gail returned to the Ardennes Cemetery for the annual Memorial Day service held at each of the American overseas cemeteries.

Gail Eisenhauer at her father's grave site

Pfc. Baker in uniform

**Private First Class
Norman Baker[10]
315th Infantry Regiment
79th Infantry Division**

Pfc. Norman Baker was killed by enemy small arms fire that hit him in the chest. According to Army records, Norman was reported as Missing in Action (MIA) from about 29 September to 8 October, at which time his body was recovered by the 3041st Quartermaster Graves Registration Company.

Private First Class Baker was serving as a unit sniper when he was killed. At the time of his death, the 79th Infantry Division[11] was engaged in a severely contested fight to take the area called the Foret-de-Parroy located near the Moselle and Meurthe Rivers. This area is in the Alsace-Lorraine area of France near borders with Belgium and Germany. The 315th Regiment had been isolated in fighting to take and hold a key road junction in the Foret-de-Parroy on 5 October. An attack by the entire division finally forced the German forces to withdraw from the forest area on 9 October. Even the German enemy apparently respected the fighting spirit of the 79th Infantry Division, as noted in an intelligence report prepared on 26 October 1944, by the Nazi 361st Volksgrenadier Division: "The 79th Division is said to have fought particularly well in Normandy, and is considered as one of the best attack divisions in the U.S. Army."[12]

Norman Baker, born in 1925, was the second child of Joseph and Mazal Camhi Baker. His brother, Albert, was five years older. Norman and Albert's parents were Sephardic Jewish immigrants from Jerusalem. The boys were born into what has been described as a very loving, extended family. The two boys were expected to clean after themselves, and their mother always told them she was not their maid. One cross look from their mother served as well as a

Norman Baker's family. He is in the middle.

slap on the face, but she was equally adept with her many displays of affection.

During the early years of the Great Depression, the family lived in a "flophouse," owned by a relative, in the Coney Island area of New York. When Joseph was not able to find work in New York, the family moved to Virginia, reportedly near Lynchburg, where other members of the family already lived. During those difficult Depression years, the two Baker boys often had to attend school barefooted, and their parents sometimes had to deny themselves food in order to feed Albert and Norman.

The family later moved back to New York where Norman attended Lincoln High School in Brooklyn. Norman loved baseball, especially the New York Yankees. He also enjoyed playing punch ball, pool, and listening to the many swing bands of that era. His favorite song was one made famous by the great Benny Goodman Band, "In the Mood." A graduate of Lincoln High in June of 1942, Norman was inducted into the Army on 4 March 1943. Available family records do not reveal what Norman did for approximately nine months between high school graduation and his induction into the Army, but limited records made available by the Army would seem to indicate that he was a "packer" for high explosives, most likely in an ammunition plant. Norman had a girlfriend named Claire, who married one of his cousins after the war.

Although Norman was right-handed, he played baseball left-handed, earning him the nickname "Lefty." Another nickname for Norman was "Blackie" because of his thick, wavy, black hair. He was described as "wise beyond his years" and was a very outgoing and kind young man. In addition to an infectious sense of humor, Norman also had a strong sense of family values and individual responsibility. When he was fourteen years old, an age at which most boys frown at displays of affection from or for their mothers, Norman included a typed letter in a Mother's Day card thanking his mother for the many sacrifices she had made for him.

As was the case of most troops killed in action, Norman was initially buried in a temporary American Military Cemetery near the village of St. Avold, France. After the war, Norman's parents decided to permit the Army to bury his remains in one of the permanent cemeteries to be established overseas rather than have his remains returned to the United States. His niece, Ms. Merrill Baker, wrote an article submitted to *Chicken Soup* in December 2005, in which she noted, "My best guess was that it was such a heartbreaking and difficult time for them that they just chose to deal with his burial from a distance."

Norman's parents managed to make one visit to his burial site at Epinal, France, and his niece visited the cemetery for the first time in 1994, fifty years after Norman was killed in action. No other family member has visited the cemetery. In her *Chicken Soup* article, Merrill wrote, "Aside from my grandparents' one visit, no family member or friend had been there. I felt his presence in a rainbow which appeared over his grave. I sensed he had led me there to see the beautiful place where he rests."

Merrill visited Epinal American Cemetery and Memorial again during Memorial Day ceremonies in 2005. Again, quoting from her *Chicken Soup* article, Merrill said, "There was an offering of wreaths, then a 21-gun salute was sounded and Taps played. The local children placed flowers on the soldiers' graves, which were already decorated with French and American Flags. Wrapping up the event was the U.S. Air Force flying overhead in the missing man formation. What a tribute! These fallen men were certainly not forgotten."

Pfc. Norman Baker is buried in the Epinal American Cemetery and Memorial, located near Metz, France, in Plot A, Row 38, Grave 9.

(Author's Note: So long as our honored dead have extended family members such as Merrill Baker to research and write about them, they, indeed, will not be forgotten. Rest in peace, Norman.)

Pfc. Baker's grave site.

Second Lieutenant
Theodore Rowman[13]
106th Reconnaissance Squadron
8th Armored Division

2LT Theodore Rowman was killed in action on 15 October 1944, while serving with "C" Troop of the 106th Cavalry Reconnaissance Squadron of the 8th Armored Division during heavy fighting in the Foret-de-Parroy area of eastern France. This region, which is near the French borders with Germany and Belgium, was defended by a strong German force and the battle

2LT Rowman in uniform

for the Foret-de-Parroy turned out to be one of the hardest since the Allied forces had broken out of Normandy and driven the Germans out of Paris. Information obtained by Lieutenant Rowman's daughter, Jo Anne Rowman Morrissey, indicates that Lieutenant Rowman's unit was on patrol when they observed a mined area covered by dug-in enemy troops. Lieutenant Rowman was killed instantly by shrapnel from an enemy shell that exploded near his position.

Theodore Rowman was born in Hudson, New Hampshire, on 4 June 1919, to Lewis and Maria Krasnowsky Romanczuk. His father was originally from the Ukraine and his mother was from Austria. The family never legally changed their surname, but simply became known as Rowman. Theodore was the youngest of four children with an older sister and two older brothers. About the time he graduated from high school in Nashua, New Hampshire, his father died. Theodore then enlisted in the Army at age eighteen in 1937. After completing basic training, he was stationed in Hawaii for two years and reached the rank of corporal in the small peacetime army. After his enlistment, he returned to Nashua, New Hampshire, where he operated a window washing business with his brother. The business had been established by their father before his death.

2LT Rowman with wife, Marjorie and daughter Jo Anne

Theodore and Marjorie Louise Goodale had grown up in the same town and always felt that they were a couple. They were married on 2 September 1940, and a daughter, Jo Anne, was born on 3 July 1941. Theodore was six feet tall and very thin. He was known as a fun-loving person with many friends. He loved children and animals. He wanted very much to become a pilot, but the urgent need for ground forces dictated his induction into the Army on 9 September 1942. His prior volunteer enlistment and service did not exclude him from the draft during wartime. He was selected for Officer's Candidate School (OCS) at Fort Knox, Kentucky, probably due in large part to the evaluation reports he had received as an enlisted man, which referred to his "outstanding leadership qualities." Marjorie and Jo Anne accompanied Theodore to Fort Knox while he was in OCS from December 1942 until March of 1943. Lieutenant Rowman was then assigned to Camp Polk in Louisiana, where he was involved in advanced unit training and various field maneuvers until he shipped out for England in 1944. Jo Anne says that she has vague memories of uniforms, parades, traveling on trains, and staying with her grandparents when her mother went to Fort Knox to find a place for them to stay while Theodore was in OCS. She also recalls that her father called her from London on her third birthday in July of 1944, but she heard loud background noises caused by the poor cross-Atlantic telephone connection and started to cry.

Theodore joined his unit in France as a replacement officer shortly after the invasion and took part in the intense fighting as the Germans were forced eastward from Normandy toward Paris and then back toward the heavily fortified German border area where he was killed on 15 October 1944. The roster of officers assigned to the 106th Cavalry Reconnaissance Squadron shows a total of eighty-two officers served with the unit during combat. Of that number, fourteen, or 17 percent, were killed in action.[14] Reconnaissance units were frequently the first to make contact with enemy forces, so their casualty rate was usually higher than other units.

It appears from the records available to Jo Anne that the decision to bury Theodore overseas was made by his mother. Jo Anne also indicates that her mother, Theodore's wife, had remarried about seven months after Theodore was killed, which would have been about mid-1945. The next of kin of troops temporarily buried overseas were not contacted by the military until the 1946-47 time frame to determine if their loved ones should be returned to the United States for burial or should be buried in one of the new permanent cemeteries to be established overseas. Since Jo Anne's mother had already remarried by the time that decision had to be made, the military would have relied on Theodore's mother as his next of kin to make that decision.

Jo Anne indicates that she had little connection with her grandmother Rowman because her mother and stepfather moved to another state and soon had two children of their own. If Jo Anne asked questions about her father she was told to, "Stop asking questions." Jo Anne did not get along well with her "new" family and she left home at age seventeen knowing very little about her father. She did finally manage to locate a cousin in 2000 and learned more about her father's family. After her mother's death in 2001, Jo Anne found that almost all of the photos of her father showed her in his arms. It was only after Jo Anne learned about the American World War II Orphan's Network (AWON) that she found she was not alone in trying to deal with a lack of information about her father and his extended family.

Although Jo Anne has not been able to visit her father's burial site in France, she does have photos of the cemetery and his grave site. 2LT Theodore Rowman is buried in the Epinal American Cemetery and Memorial located in Epinal, France. His gravesite is in Plot B, Row 17, Grave 37.

2LT Rowman's grave site

Pvt. Farris in uniform

Private Fred C. Farris[15]
120th Infantry Regiment
30th Infantry Division

Pvt. Fred C. Farris was killed in action on 22 October 1944, during a patrol conducted by his infantry platoon in Germany near Wurselen. The unit had successfully completed a mission to clear enemy troops from its assigned sector and had taken about forty prisoners. While wrapping up the patrol the platoon ran into a German ambush and Private Farris was killed. Initially reported as Missing in Action by the Army, his wife later learned from a good buddy that Fred died in his arms and should have been reported as Killed in Action at once. About five months after his death, Mrs. Farris finally received official word in March 1944 that her husband was dead. Captain Hill, the battalion S-3 (operations officer) of Private Farris's unit, commented, "This was the first time I saw our troops engaged in bayonet fighting with the enemy, and it was one of the hottest fights I ever saw."

Fred Farris was born on 3 October1913, in Lebanon, which was then part of Syria and under the rule of the Turkish Ottoman Empire. His father was Attallah Farris Maroun and his mother was Budrah Rizk Maroun. Fred's given name was Farris Attallah Farris Maroun. (The name Farris in Arabic means "knight.") Fred had a younger sister named Linda Rizk, also born in Lebanon, but the two never saw each other. Fred's mother, Budrah, would not leave Lebanon so his father made trips back and forth from the United States. At age thirteen, Fred immigrated to the United States in 1926 to join his father and didn't speak a word of English. After arriving in the United States, Fred's name was changed to Fred Charles Farris. With the considerable guidance and attention of the Sisters at St. Francis Xavier Parish in St. Joseph, Missouri, young Fred completed eight years of grammar school in only four years and attained Eagle Scout rank in the Boy Scouts of America. He attended the Christian Brothers High School in St. Joseph, Missouri, where he played football.

Fred and his father lived with his father's brother, Abdullah (who took the name Albert), in the part of St. Joseph where most of the "Syrians" lived. Fred's future wife, Louise Dawaliby, whose parents had also immigrated to the United States from Lebanon, lived in the same section of town just a few doors from Fred. Fred and Louise were married in 1938 and had three children: Linda Frances, born in October 1939; Charles J., born in July 1941; and Phillip F., born in January 1944.

Fred started his own restaurant called "the Midway Buffet" in St. Joseph, Missouri, after having worked in his father's restaurant. His customers often included men from Rosecrans Field, an Army Air Corps base, who would stop in for a cold beer and sandwich.

Louise and Fred Farris with their three children

Even though Fred had been exempted from the draft, probably because he was married with three children, he closed the tavern one afternoon in March 1944, walked to the post office, and volunteered for duty in the Infantry. He then went home to tell Louise what he had just done. When Louise asked why he did that, Fred responded, "I want to fight for my country." Following his basic training at Camp Fannin, Texas, Fred was assigned to the 120th Infantry Regiment and shipped to England as part of the 30th Infantry Division. The 30th Division took part in the Allied sweep across France, Belgium, and Holland, fighting its way into Germany where Fred was killed.

Pvt. Fred C. Farris is buried in Plot A, Row 5, Grave 9, at the Netherlands American Cemetery and Memorial near Margraten, the Netherlands. Fred's widow and three children have each been able to visit his grave. In 2000, Fred's oldest son, Joe, visited his father's grave site and realized he hadn't been this close to his father since 1944 when he was only three years old.

Pvt. Farris' grave site

Second Lieutenant
David Baird Finch[16]
17th Infantry Regiment
7th Infantry Division

2LT Finch in uniform

2LT David Baird Finch was killed on Leyte in the Philippine Islands on 13 November 1944, while leading a reconnaissance patrol in the foothills of Guinarona. The patrol's assigned mission was to locate and determine the strength of the opposing Japanese forces. The ground in that area was densely covered by tall grass and bamboo thickets. As the patrol approached a high ridge, it was hit by enemy machine gun and mortar fire from close range. With the realization that he was greatly outnumbered, 2LT Finch decided it was necessary to withdraw in order to save the lives of the men with him on the patrol. While exposing himself to enemy fire so that his men could withdraw, 2LT Finch was hit by enemy sniper fire and died at once. The men in his patrol risked their own lives to recover his body and carry him back to their base camp.

David Baird Finch was born on 5 June 1912, at Atkinson, Illinois, the last of eight children of James Madison Finch and Kate Nichol Finch. His father was a Congregational minister, a farmer, and, at times, a county judge. The oldest child, Robert, was killed in France during World War I and another older brother, Durell, suffered permanent injury from a German gas attack during World War I. David graduated from high school at Bellwood, Nebraska, where he was a member of the basketball team and, most likely, also played baseball since he later played semi-pro baseball. He was considered to be a charming person and was admired greatly. He attended Wayne College in Wayne, Nebraska, but did not graduate.

Like many young men during the Great Depression of the 1930s, David found work where and when he could. At various times he worked for the Civilian Conservation Corps (CCC) on a survey crew and for the Bureau of Reclamation. In 1937, he joined the 116th Cavalry of the Idaho National Guard. Although called to active duty with his guard unit, he was given a discharge from the National Guard in order to enter Officer's Candidate School (OCS) at Fort Benning, Georgia. Graduating from OCS on 12 November 1942, David spent several months at Camp Wolters, Texas, until being assigned to Fort Lewis, Washington, in July 1943. While at Fort

Zelpha and David Baird Finch

Lewis he met Zelpha Galloway Hawkins, a young divorcee who was living in Seattle with her five-year-old son, Ed. They "fell for each other pretty hard" and were married in the chapel at Fort Lawton, Washington. When Zelpha became pregnant, she and David talked about how excited they would be to have a little girl. Consequently, they were not prepared for the birth of their son and didn't even have a boy's name in mind, and had to scramble before deciding on the name of Baird. David managed to be at the hospital when Baird was born on 27 March 1944, but he was not allowed to hold his new baby. David even tried to bribe the nurses to let him hold his son, but his attempt was to no avail. In a letter to one of his sisters, David told her how proud he was of his family.

Soon after the birth of his son, David was shipped to the Pacific where plans were already being prepared for the invasion of the Philippine Islands to make good on General MacArthur's famous promise, "I shall return." On 20 October 1944, the initial landings took place on Leyte Island, one of the larger islands of the Philippine archipelago. The Sixth U.S. Army, commanded by Lt. Gen. Walter Krueger, consisting of two corps plus supporting troops, made the landings following heavy bombardment by both Navy ships and aircraft. Although the initial landings went smoothly, the Japanese defense stiffened and defended the area with all its ability. Following his death, 2LT Finch's company commander wrote that, "David had won the admiration of officers and the respect and affection of his men by his sincerity, his courage, and cheerfulness." Another of David's friends wrote, "His loss to the company was a great blow, as the men liked and admired him so much. He was well liked and thought of by his fellow officers too."[17]

2LT David Baird Finch is buried in the Manila American Cemetery and Memorial located southeast of the city of Manila. His grave site is in plot D, Row 7, Grave 69. David's son, Baird, was able to visit his father's grave site in 2007 as part of a group sponsored by the American World War II Orphan's Network (AWON). He took the following photo while at the cemetery.

2LT Finch's grave site

1LT Bert Stiles in uniform
Courtesy of Tutt Library,
Colorado College,
Colorado Springs.

First Lieutenant Bert Stiles[18]
505th Fighter Squadron
339th Fighter Group
Also
401st Bomber Squadron
91st Bomb Group

(Author's Note: In August 2007, I was shopping for good books about World War II in the largest used bookstore in Knoxville, Tennessee, when I found a small, paperback book titled, *Serenade to the Big Bird* published by Bantam Books in 1984. The cost of the book was five cents! The author was 1LT Bert Stiles. The paperback version totaled 206 pages and took only three evenings to read–it was that good. When I finished reading the book, I noticed in the "About the Author" page at the end of the book that Bert Stiles had been killed when his P-51 Mustang fighter plane crashed near Hanover, Germany, on 26 November 1944. I then checked the American Battle Monuments Commission web site and found that Bert Stiles was buried in the Ardennes American Cemetery and Memorial near Neupre, Belgium. Next, I Googled "Bert Stiles" and found articles about him at www.acmedepot.com, http://en.wikipedia.org, and at www.coloradocollege.edu. There are probably more web sites and many other references with information about Bert Stiles, but those three sites provided much of the information needed to prepare the vignette that follows. I was also able to obtain information and photos of Bert from the Tutt Library at Colorado College in Colorado Springs. All I can say to further introduce this vignette about Bert Stiles is, "Bert, I am saddened that a life with so much promise was cut so short at such a young age.

However, the fact that it was supports the premise behind my desire to write this book. You were one of the many thousands of young men and women who were cut down in the very early stage of life. We will never know what you or they might have contributed to society had you lived."

1LT Bert Stiles flew the required thirty-five missions as a copilot of a B-17 Bomber crew in the 401st Bomber Squadron of the 91st Bomb Group flying out of England. His crew flew missions over France, Belgium, and Germany, experiencing numerous close calls caused by enemy flak from antiaircraft guns on the ground and from attacks by German fighter planes. Many of his friends were either killed, missing, or captured. Hardly a mission was flown during which his crew did not see other planes from their own squadron or bomb group spiral to earth, trailing flames and smoke, or simply disintegrating in the air. After Stiles completed the required thirty-five missions, he was due for reassignment to the United States and most likely would have been assigned as a flight instructor—a relatively safe way to finish the war. However, Bert's passion, in addition to writing, was flying fighters, so he volunteered to remain in England and took the necessary transition training to become a P-51 Mustang fighter pilot.

In September 1944, Bert was assigned to the 505th Squadron of the 339th Fighter Group. During his sixteenth mission as a fighter pilot, Bert recorded his first kill when he shot down a German FW-190 while on a bomber escort mission near Hanover, Germany. Bert may have become disoriented during the dogfight with the FW-190 or he may have become fixated on the crashing enemy plane and forgot to pull up. Regardless of the cause, his P-51 Mustang crashed, killing Stiles. 1LT Bert Stiles was awarded the Distinguished Flying Cross and the Air Medal with five clusters for his service as a bomber copilot and as a fighter pilot. He also received the Purple Heart.

Bert Stiles was born in Denver, Colorado, on 30 August 1920, the son of Bert Stiles Sr. and Elizabeth Huddleston Stiles. Bert's father was an electrician and a contractor and his mother was a music teacher. Bert graduated from Denver's South High School after pursuing what he himself termed as a "progressive education" curriculum, meaning that a selective group of students were able to design their own course of study within broad guidelines supervised by several basic subject teachers (math, science and English). From all indications, and from Bert's own writings, Bert did not fully avail himself of the opportunities afforded by that progressive program of instruction. During summer vacations he worked as a forest ranger intern in the Rocky Mountain National Park near Estes Park, Colorado, which provided resource material for many of his later writings.

After graduating from high school, Bert enrolled in Colorado College located in Colorado Springs. While in college, he was able to pursue his passion for writing as a feature writer for the college paper, *The Tiger*. Bert, at that time between World Wars, often used the college paper to express his pacifist opinions. At one point in his college career, he reportedly locked himself in his fraternity house long enough to write more than twenty-five stories. (There is no indication what this self-enforced vacation from classes did to his grades.)

With the assistance and mentoring of literary agents Max Aley and his wife, Ruth, Bert managed to have a story published in the *Saturday Evening Post*. Not long after that his stories appeared in *Liberty Magazine* and *American Magazine*. Probably his most

Bert Stiles camping out
Courtesy of Tutt Library, Colorado College, Colorado Springs

satisfying experience as a young writer was when the *Saturday Evening Post* published a series titled "The Ranger" that Bert wrote from his personal experiences as a forest ranger intern while in high school.

In January 1943, in spite of his pacifist views, Bert entered the Army Air Corps training program and received his wings and a commission as a second lieutenant in November 1943. Following additional training as a member of a B-17 Bomber crew, he was shipped to England in March 1944, where he joined the 401st Bomber Squadron, a part of the 8th Air Force. It was during his time as a copilot in a B-17 crew that Bert wrote *Serenade to the Big Bird*. Through the personal efforts of Bert's mother, the book was published posthumously in England in 1947 by Lindsay Drummand, Ltd. The book was subsequently published in the United States by W.W. Norton and Company in 1952, and has had several more recent printings.

1LT Stiles (front row, second from left) with his B-17 crew.
Photo by 91st Bomb Group.
Courtesy Tutt Library, Colorado College, Colorado Springs

Although Bert Stiles was only 24 years and 3 months old when he was killed, the collection of his papers at Colorado College fills over half a dozen boxes and includes about 70 short stories, letters, manuscripts, personal memorabilia, photos, and copies of the *Saturday Evening Post* magazines containing his ranger stories.

1LT Bert Stiles is buried in the Ardennes American Cemetery and Memorial near Neupre, Belgium, in Plot B, Row 36, Grave 43.

1LT Stiles' grave site. Courtesy ABMC

1LT Dainotto in enlisted uniform

First Lieutenant
James V. Dainotto[19]
112th Infantry Regiment
28th Infantry Division

1LT James V. Dainotto was killed on 23 December 1944, while a prisoner of the Germans in the German POW Camp called Stalag XIIA located in Limburg, Germany. Lieutenant Dainotto was captured on 18 December, two days after the Germans unleashed their attack, which came to be known as "The Battle of the Bulge," and immediately transported to Stalag XIIA. On 23 December, the British Royal Air Force had been assigned the mission to bomb the railway yards near the town of Dietz, which was located a few miles from the POW camp. Because of strong winds aloft, the British flares, used as aiming points for their bombers, drifted away from Dietz toward the POW camp. Sixty-three American officers in the POW camp were killed when British bombs hit the camp instead of the railway yards.

James V. Dainotto was born in Connecticut but spent most of his early years in Corona, New York. His parents were Vincent and Maria Santangelo Dainotto. James had a brother, Charles, and sister, Carmella, but both died at a young age—Charles of influenza and Carmella suffered deadly injuries while playing with matches in the family's back yard. After the loss of his two siblings, James became very close to a younger cousin, Vincenza (Vinnie), the daughter of his mother's brother. James attended New Town High School and Elmhurst and Stuyvesant High School. A fun-loving youngster who always had a smile on his face, he was liked by everyone and enjoyed playing baseball while in high school.

After graduation from high school, James worked for eight years as a clerk for the Cluett & Peabody Arrow Shirt Company. One evening in the fall of 1940, he attended his cousin's sixteenth birthday party where he met Anna Tanzilli, a friend of a friend of his cousin. James took notice at once and it was not long before the two fell in love. Only eight months later in February 1941, James enlisted in the Army with the hopes that he could serve his time, be discharged, and then marry Anna and start their life together. The

1LT Dainotto and his bride, October 1942

bombing of Pearl Harbor on 7 December 1941, changed those plans forever.

After basic training, James was assigned to Fort Sam Houston, Texas, and was promoted to the rank of corporal on 22 July 1942. He applied for Officer's Candidate School (OCS) and was assigned to Fort Benning, Georgia, from July until he graduated in Class No. 85-A on 19 October 1942. While on leave after OCS, he and Anna were married 25 October 1942, in Our Lady of Sorrows Catholic Church. His cousin Vinnie was maid of honor and Anna's brother, Joseph, was best man. Following the wedding, Anna moved with James from station to station until he was shipped overseas about midnight on 19 September 1943. Earlier that same day James and Anna's baby, Rosemary, was born. James was able to see his new daughter and hold her in his arms for only a few minutes before he left for Europe.

LEST THEY BE FORGOTTEN

James spent time in England training in an anti-tank unit of the 112th Infantry Regiment of the 28th Infantry Division.[20] The 28th Infantry Division was a National Guard Division with most troops coming from or near the state of Pennsylvania. Records show that the 28th arrived on the continent of Europe on 24 July 1944, about six weeks after D-Day. The division fought its way through France, Belgium, and Luxembourg and entered German territory on 11 September. By mid-November the 28th had fought a savage battle against strong German forces in the Hurtgen Forest area. Due to heavy losses suffered during this fighting, the 28th was moved back to defend a large sector along the Our River on the northeastern part of Luxembourg near Wallendorf. While in this sector, the division faced the full force of five German Divisions as the Germans kicked off their surprise attack in the early morning fog on 16 December 1944. The division history recounts that the division was hit hard by the unexpected attack of such a huge force but refused to panic. The division's defense along the Our River during the first five days of the Battle of the Bulge is credited with throwing off the critical German timetable for breaking through the American lines and with causing heavy losses among the German forces. It was during this initial, critical phase of the German attack that First Lieutenant Dainotto was captured on 18 December.

It is not known what type of action First Lieutenant Dainotto was engaged in at the time he was captured. Records reflect that on the night of 17-18 December 1944, the 112th Infantry Regiment, to which he was assigned, received orders to withdraw and defend high ground just west of the Our River. The withdrawal was strongly opposed by German forces that had infiltrated throughout the sector, and the regiment was continually engaged in a rear guard action while covering the withdrawal of the entire right flank of the American First Army units. For this action, from 16 to 23 December 1944, the 112th Infantry Regiment Combat Team received a Presidential Unit Citation. The Presidential Unit Citation ends with the following statement:[21]

> The gallantry under extremely hazardous and physically trying conditions, the stubborn defense of the sectors assigned to them, and the heroic conduct of all personnel of the 112th Regimental

Combat Team, in nine days of continuous fighting, exemplify
the highest traditions of the armed forces of the United States.

James was a POW for less than one week before he was killed.
Mrs. Dainotto received a telegram from the German authorities,
which listed the names of the men killed in Stalag XIIA as a result of
the British bombing.

In May 2005, James Dainotto's daughter, Rosemary, and her
husband, Vinny Cummo, visited Lieutenant Dainotto's grave site
at the Netherlands American Cemetery and Memorial located near
Margraten, the Netherlands. From there, they were able to travel by
train to Limburg, Germany, and the village of Dietz. They were able
to not only visit the Dietz Cemetery, where Lieutenant Dainotto was
first buried by the Germans, but they were granted access to the high
security German Army base where the POW camp, Stalag XIIA, had
been located during the war.

The Cummos were escorted during their visit to the German base
by a German officer who seemed to understand Rosemary's need to
be close to the actual ground upon which her father had walked as a

Cemetery at Dietz, Germany, where 1LT Dainotto was first buried

Rosemary Dainotto Cummo at her father's grave site

POW and where he had been killed by British bombs. After visiting the cemetery and Dietz, Rosemary and her husband returned to the United States, and Rosemary attempted to describe her experience to her mother. Suffering from Alzheimer's, her mother never seemed to grasp the fact that Rosemary had been to James's final resting place, despite the photos Rosemary showed her. Anna Dainotto passed away in September 2005, a little over three months after Rosemary's visit to James's grave site.

1LT James V. Dainotto is buried in Plot J, Row 8, Grave 18, in the Netherlands American Cemetery and Memorial.

Pfc. Patrick in uniform

Private First Class
John McCoy Patrick[22]
11ᵗʰ Infantry Regiment
5ᵗʰ Infantry Division

Pfc. John McCoy (Coy) Patrick was killed by a German sniper near Echternach, Luxembourg, on Christmas Day 1944, during some of the heaviest fighting of the "Battle of the Bulge." Pfc. Patrick was assigned to the First Squad, Second Platoon, Company "L" in the 11ᵗʰ Infantry Regiment of the 5ᵗʰ Infantry Division as the squad BAR (Browning Automatic Rifle) man.[23] Coy's best friend in the Army, Pfc. James Aubrey (Cotton) Almond, gave this account of Coy's death to his own son much later.[24]

> On Christmas Day of 1944 Coy and Cotton were on patrol, just the two of them, near Echternach, Luxembourg. It was a sunny, but frigid, morning as they walked side by side down the snow-covered road. It was the coldest winter in more than 50 years. Suddenly, from a stone farmhouse down the road, a single rifle shot from an enemy sniper struck Patrick, killing him instantly. As Patrick fell, Almond dropped into the snow, brought up his Garand M-1 rifle, and returned fire. Help arrived, and seeing the GI reinforcements, the enemy sniper threw his weapon through the shattered window, emerged from the doorway with his hands held high, and surrendered. Almond was told later that the enemy sniper was shot while trying to escape.

Following intensive training in England and Ireland, the 5ᵗʰ Infantry Division arrived in France on or about 9 July 1944. The Division fought its way through France as part of GEN George S. Patton Jr.'s Third Army. Pfc. Patrick's niece, Mrs. Donna O'Brien, has researched the movements of the 11ᵗʰ Infantry Regiment from a few letters written by Coy, from the book titled *The Fifth Infantry*

Division in the ETO, 1945, written by the Fifth Division Headquarters Historical Section, and from information provided by veterans of the Division. The Division's major engagements from July 1944 until Christmas Day are summarized by Donna as follows:

- Spent most of July moving across France and liberated the town of Angers in early August. The women of Angers served their liberators omelets with fresh fruit and vegetables. (NOTE: There is a monument to the 5th Division in Angers.)

- Moved to vicinity of Fontainebleau, France, in late August and then to Verdun on 30 August, the site of heavy fighting in WWI. Company "L" was assigned the mission to secure a bridge over the Meuse River near Bannoncourt, about 15 miles south of Verdun.

- The month of September was one with a lot of combat and the crossing of the Moselle River. After crossing the river they moved into Dornot where they were engaged in heavy, hand-to-hand fighting as the Germans fought from well-fortified defensive positions and concrete pill boxes. By mid-September fighting centered around Arnaville where heavy fighting finally resulted in the capture of several important hills and pill boxes.

- From 27 September to 13 October, the heavy fighting resulted in the capture of Fort Driant, located south of Metz on the Moselle River. This was followed by a week during which they were tasked to defend positions recently secured along the Moselle River. For about ten days, starting on 20 October, the division was afforded time to rest, take showers, receive fresh uniforms, replace lost or worn out equipment, and stock up on ammunition. They also received hot chow, mail, movies and support from both the USO and the Red Cross. All was not rest though. The men received training on measures required to avoid the kinds of losses they had sustained capturing the enemy pill boxes during the previous thirty days of combat.

- On 30 October the division moved again as a part of the force tasked by General Patton to attack and capture the key city of Metz, France.[25] The attack kicked off on or about 9 November, and Metz was not secured until almost two weeks later on the

21st. Even then several of the German defensive positions around Metz were not taken until the end of November.

- By 1 December the division was again on the move with the objective of attacking the strong German defense line known as the Siegfried Line. It was on 16 December that Hitler launched his last major offensive thrust of the war, code-named "Wacht am Rhein," (Watch on the Rhine), better known today as the Battle of the Bulge.
- On 21 December the division was moved into Luxembourg to defend Luxembourg City itself.
- By Christmas Eve, elements of the division were in Christnach, Luxembourg, and pressing an attack against German forces that continued into Christmas Day itself. It was on that day that Pfc. John M. Patrick was killed.

John McCoy (Coy) Patrick was born on 4 February 1920, in Cagle, Tennessee, the fourth child of James William and Laura Slaughter Patrick. James and Laura married in 1907 and had two older sons, Marcus, born in 1908, and Jesse, born in 1916, as well as one older daughter, Nannie, born in 1911. The youngest child, Clifton, was born in 1923. Coy's father farmed and logged timber, causing the family to move frequently, mostly in Grundy and Warren Counties, Tennessee. Following Laura's death in 1940, James married Amanda

"Coy" Patrick (top right) with his sister, her husband, and their children. Molly Jo, the mother of Donna O'Brien is second from left in front row

Pearson Patrick, who was the widow of Lafayette Patrick, James's cousin. James's father and Lafayette's father were brothers.

Records are not available to document Coy's education, but a group photo exists of his class at Werner's Log Camp School in Grundy County, and the letters he wrote home are clear evidence that he could read and write well. As was common with most young men in rural Tennessee, Coy was an experienced hunter and mentioned hunting in several of his letters. He became interested in collecting foreign currency once he was overseas and sent home some currency in his letters. A total of 440 German marks were found among his personal possessions after his death. The marks were converted to U.S. currency at a rate of ten cents per German mark, and Coy's father received a check for $44.00 in May 1950, four and one-half years after Coy's death.

Coy was among the first young men to be drafted when he was called to duty on 5 October 1941, about sixty days before the Japanese bombed Pearl Harbor. After first reporting to Fort Oglethorpe, Georgia, he was transferred to an Infantry Replacement Training Center at Camp Croft, South Carolina, where he received basic training. Following his stateside training, Coy was sent to Iceland early in 1942 and was there for about fifteen months where he experienced occasional strafing attacks by German planes.

Coy's unit moved to England in August 1943, and spent three months training near Tidworth Garrison. In late October 1943, the unit moved again to Northern Ireland where it underwent rigorous training for combat for about eight months until the unit boarded a transport on 4 July 1944. The unit then moved across the English Channel and dropped anchor off the coast of France on 9 July 1944.

Two important dates in the lives of all Americans figured prominently in the life and death of Pfc. John McCoy Patrick. He boarded a ship for the move to France on 4 July 1944, and he was killed on Christmas Day 1944.

Like many World War II casualties, Private First Class Patrick was first buried in a temporary cemetery near the location where he was killed. He was initially buried near Grand Failly, France. After Coy's father made the decision to have his son's remains permanently interred overseas, they were disinterred on or about 6 August 1948 and taken to Luxembourg where he was permanently buried on 11 February 1949.

Pfc. John M. Patrick is buried in the Luxembourg American Cemetery and Memorial in Plot I, Row 12, Grave 4.

Pfc. Patrick's grave site

Private Joseph T. Lippi[26]
334th Infantry Regiment
84th Infantry Division

Pvt. Joseph T. Lippi was killed on 8 January 1945, while his unit was attacking German positions in the vicinity of Cielle, Belgium. One of Joe Lippi's fellow soldiers, Sgt. Jack O'Leary, recalled the action leading to Joe's death as follows:

Pvt. Lippi in uniform

> About noon of January 8, 1945, we started an attack across a long sloping field with a small wooded area at our back that was protected by 500 yards to another row of trees and perhaps a house or two that could have been on a road. As we started across the field, after getting perhaps 100 yards from the protected area, the Germans opened up with machine gun fire and also started to drop mortar shells on us. Fortunately I was right beside a fairly large shell hole and was able to get some protection in the hole. Lippi was perhaps 25 to 30 yards to my right and at about that time apparently was hit by a fragment from a mortar shell. He was laying [*sic*] in the snow and called for a medic, but the medic who usually was near us was killed that morning back in a draw were [*sic*] Sergeant Smith of the first platoon was hit in the legs. At any rate after hearing him for a while, I hoped that the Jerries would respect what I was doing and I left my rifle in the hole and went to Lippi. I was able to get him on his feet and he half walked and I half carried him back to the protected area. We checked and there was a wound, I believe toward his back on the right side and it was apparent that the shrapnel was still inside.…
>
> We tried to keep Joe warm and kept encouraging him that we would be able to get him out. Someone went to the Company CP and I understand they radioed for a medic and a Jeep to take Joe out. In the meantime, we had a really heavy blizzard which didn't help matters at all.…It was after midnight before they were able to get him out and the next day we heard that he had

died in the aid station, although I am not sure he was still alive when they evacuated him. I think that medics did come and administer some drugs to Joe during the long wait.

Twelve days after Private Lippi was killed, his wife, May, received the official Western Union telegram from the Adjutant General advising her that Joe had been killed in Belgium on 8 January. That was followed a few days later by a confirming letter from the Adjutant General. In addition to validating that Joe had been killed in Belgium on 8 January 1945, the letter included the following sentence: "I know the sorrow this message has brought you and it is my hope that in time the knowledge of his heroic service to his country, even unto death, may be of sustaining comfort to you."

Joseph T. Lippi was born on 15 February 1922, in Brooklyn, New York, to Joseph A. and Henrietta Lippi. The Lippis also had one daughter, Henrietta. Raised in Brooklyn, Joe attended Eastern District High School and graduated in 1941. Because he worked after school to help with the family finances, Joe was not involved in sports or other extracurricular activities in high school. He worked at the neighborhood drug store, Huffman's, both during his high school years and following graduation until he was drafted. Some of Joe's friends were also friends with a young woman, May Lauber, and they introduced May and Joe on a neighborhood street corner when May was only fifteen years old. They saw each other periodically after that and were engaged in November 1942. Joe and May were married in St. Leonard's Church in Brooklyn on 27 June 1943. Eleven months later Joe was inducted into the Army and sent to Fort McClellan, Alabama, for basic training. When Joe Jr. was born on 3 July 1944, Joe was given leave and was able to spend ten days with his wife and baby boy. That was the only time Private Lippi saw his son.

Pvt. Lippi holding his son with wife May

On 1 November 1944, Joe Lippi was one of about 12,000 replacements who boarded the converted luxury liner *Isle de France* for the Atlantic crossing. During the crossing, the ship had to take evasive action and managed to outrun at least one German submarine. After reaching port in Scotland, the replacements endured a seventeen-hour train ride to Portsmouth, England, where they boarded another ship. After crossing the English Channel, the troops landed in the port of Le Havre, France. Following a rather miserable train ride in the infamous French Forty & Eight rail cars (designed to accommodate forty men or eight cows), Joe arrived as a casualty replacement in "E" Company of the 334th Infantry Regiment of the 84th Infantry Division, nicknamed the Rail Splitters. The division saw its first combat, and sustained heavy casualties, barely a week before Joe and the other replacements arrived.

The 84th Infantry Division[27] had initially been assigned along the northern sector of the front lines in the Ninth U.S. Army area but was hastily moved south to the vicinity of Marche, Belgium, on 20 December, four days after the start of the Battle of the Bulge. The division dug in, establishing defensive positions in order to deny enemy access to a crossing site over the strategically important Meuse River. A full German corps attacked these positions the night of 26 December 1944. The division remained in close contact with the Germans for the next several weeks while exchanging mortar and artillery fire and resisting repeated enemy attempts to cross the Meuse River. Both sides repeatedly sent out patrols in an attempt to pinpoint enemy positions and capture troops who could be interrogated in order to learn more about the nature and strength of the enemy. It was during this period of intense combat that Pvt. Joseph T. Lippi was killed by enemy mortar fire on 8 January 1945.

Joseph's widow, May Lippi, married Boatswain Mate First Class Leroy S. Reed, U.S. Navy, on 10 August 1946 in the U.S. Naval Hospital Chapel, Brooklyn, New York. Joe Jr. has always considered Leroy as his "second father."

In December 1948, May Lippi Reed and Joe's father received correspondence from the Army advising that they had the option of having Joe's remains returned to the United States for final burial or they could have his remains buried in one of the permanent American cemeteries to be established in Europe. Since it had been four years since his death, May and Joe's father agreed he should stay near the men with whom he had served and died. Pvt. Joseph T. Lippi was laid to rest in the Henri-Chapelle American Cemetery and Memorial near the village of Henri-Chapelle, Belgium, on 24 August 1949.

Private Lippi's son, Joe Jr., along with Joe Jr.'s wife, Mary, visited Henri-Chapelle Cemetery on 12 September 1994, and placed a floral arrangement on the grave. Only three days later, Mr. Gene Wayne, who was with Private Lippi in combat, visited the grave site along with other members of the 84th Division who were taking a tour on the 50th anniversary of the Battle of the Bulge. After learning that the floral arrangement on Private Lippi's grave had been placed there by Lippi's son, Joe Jr., Mr. Wayne was inspired to try to find Private Lippi's son. A personal message published in a magazine was seen by a family friend and resulted in Joe Jr. and Mr. Wayne meeting in 2001. Then, in 2004, another family friend had a conversation with Mr. Arthur Mahler when it was discovered that Mr. Mahler had gone through basic training with Private Lippi and was with him in Belgium. Joe Jr. was able to meet Arthur and subsequently Jack O'Leary and Walter Wright, all of whom served with Private Lippi during the Battle of the Bulge. Mr. Mahler explained that he had been with Private Lippi when he learned that Joe Jr. had been born. Thus, over fifty years after his father was killed, Joe Jr. was able to meet with veterans from his father's unit and learn more about the conditions which the unit endured during the Battle of the Bulge and the circumstances surrounding his father's death.

Pvt. Joe Lippi is buried at the Henri-Chapelle American Cemetery and Memorial in Plot G, Row 7, Grave 66.

Joseph Lippi Jr., at his father's grave site, September 1994

**Private First Class
John Warren Downs**[28]
**346th Infantry Regiment
87th Infantry Division**

Pfc. Downs in uniform

Pfc. John W. Downs was seriously wounded on 7 January 1945, while occupying a position on the edge of a small town southeast of Tillet, Belgium, during the Battle of the Bulge. Private First Class Downs' unit, Company "G," was in a defilade position near a road junction waiting for orders to attack what was still a very determined enemy. The U.S. forces were slowly regaining positions lost to the Germans when Hitler launched "Operation Watch on the Rhine" on 16 December 1944, that later proved to be his last gasp gamble to split the U.S. and British forces in Belgium and deprive them of the use of the vital port facilities in Antwerp. The German forces were still very active in the area fronting the positions held by the 346th Infantry Regiment on 7 January. During a German artillery attack, one or more shells burst near Private First Class Downs and he was hit by multiple shell fragments. After medics treated his wounds, he was taken to the 107th Evacuation Hospital near Sedan, France, where he died from his wounds on 9 January 1945. John Downs was first buried in the U.S. Army temporary cemetery at Grand Failly, France, with burial services performed by a Protestant chaplain.[29] Following the end of the war, his remains were transferred to the American Cemetery and Memorial located in Hamms, Luxembourg, just outside of Luxembourg City.

John Warren Downs, known as J.W. to family and friends, was born in Pana, Illinois, on 22 October 1922, to Frank Palestine Downs and Isabel Penwell Downs. He was named after his two grandfathers, John Downs and Warren Penwell. Mr. Downs owned a Ford Motor Company dealership in Pana and Mr. Penwell owned a coal mining company in the area. J.W. had two younger sisters, Barbara, who was about three years younger, and Dorothea, who was about five years younger. When J.W. was still a young boy, his parents moved to the nearby town of Shelbyville, Illinois, where his father owned a Chevrolet dealership. J.W. was active in the Boy Scouts, earned the Eagle Scout Badge, was selected to the Shelbyville High School chapter of the National Honor Society, and was awarded the Daughters of the American Revolution (DAR) Good Citizen Medal. Graduating from Shelbyville High on 29 May 1940, he received a diploma signed by his father, who was on the Board of Education.

J.W. enrolled in Antioch College at Yellow Springs, Ohio, and attended that institution until he enlisted in 1943. Following basic training, he was selected to participate in the Army Specialized Training Program (ASTP) at North Carolina State College of Agriculture and Engineering at Raleigh, North Carolina (now North Carolina State University), and graduated in March 1944, in basic engineering. His Army test scores would have qualified him for the ASTP Medical Program, but he opted for engineering because he hoped to join his father's Chevrolet dealership after his military service, thinking that the engineering program would be more beneficial. J. W.'s military records were among thousands destroyed in a massive fire at the National Personnel Records Center in St. Louis, Missouri, in July 1973; therefore it is not possible to tell how or why he was assigned to an infantry regiment instead of an engineer unit. Most likely, it was due to the critical shortage of troops to fill the divisions deploying to Europe at that time, as well as the need for replacements for the losses in North Africa and Italy.

About two months after graduating from the ASTP course, J.W. married Mary Bob Seiler on 19 July 1944, in the Presbyterian Church of Pana, Illinois. J.W. and Mary Bob met at one of the gathering spots for youth in Pana. There had also been several marriages among relatives, so the two young people could also have met at various family

Pfc. Downs and his bride

gatherings. After all, Pana and Shelbyville were two small towns where most residents knew just about everyone. Following the wedding, J.W. was stationed at Fort Jackson, near Columbia, South Carolina. Mary Bob accompanied him to South Carolina and was with him until he shipped out for Europe. A history of the 87th Infantry Division in World War II notes that the troops sailed from New York on 17 October aboard the liner *Queen Elizabeth*, which had been converted to a troop ship. Arriving at Glasgow, Scotland, on 22 October after less than a week at sea, the division then moved by train to the vicinity of Chester, England, received new equipment, new vehicles, and completed training for movement to France. The division landed in France on 28 November 1944, about 175 days after D-Day.[30]

J. W. and Mary Bob's only child, Carol Ann, was born on 31 May 1945, in the same Pana, Illinois, hospital in which J.W. had been born and more than four months after her father's death. J. W. never got to see or hold his baby daughter.

Following J. W.'s death, Mary Bob decided to finish her education at Washington University in St. Louis. During that time, Carol stayed with her maternal grandparents in Pana, maintaining a very close tie to her grandparents. Mary Bob traveled to Pana by train each weekend to spend time with her daughter. After graduation, Mary Bob returned to Pana to work in the family business, the Paddock Lumber Company. Mary Bob, by then called Bobbie, remarried in

1951 to a World War II Navy veteran, John L. Miller, and they had two children of their own.

Pfc. John W. Downs is buried in the Luxembourg American Cemetery and Memorial outside of Luxembourg City in Plot E, Row 9, Grave 7.

Carol Ann Downs at her father's grave site on Memorial Day, 2009

Private First Class
John I. Pinkerman[31]
157th Infantry Regiment
45th Infantry Division

Pfc. Pinkerman in uniform

Pfc. John I. Pinkerman was killed on 12 January 1945. Four other men were also killed at the same time in the vicinity of the small town of Rambervillers, France, about twenty kilometers from Avold, France. The day before Private First Class Pinkerman was killed, he wrote a letter to a cousin in which he expressed his deep desire to get home soon to see his wife and son. A day or two before Private First Class Pinkerman's wife, Geneva, received word that her husband was missing, she learned that her brother was missing in action in the South Pacific. Fortunately, about a month later, her brother called home from an Army hospital in California.

John I. Pinkerman was born on 25 September 1921, to Ira Frank Pinkerman and Bertie Wade Shepard Pinkerman. John had five sisters and one brother: Raphel, born in 1908; Mable, born in 1909; Ruth, born in 1911; Josie, born in 1918; Edra, born in 1924; and Betty, born in 1928. As John was growing up, the family lived on a farm in Cabell County, West Virginia, not far from Huntington. Cousins have told John's son that his father loved to trade "things," whether it be cars, horses or other items of value. He was a Boy Scout in his youth and graduated from Barboursville High School in Barboursville, West Virginia, in 1939.

Frank and Bertie Pinkerman raised their family of six children while living on a farm and growing most of their own food. Frank also worked for a chemical plant about ten miles away from Huntington and advanced to become a foreman in the plant. Frank was a strong-willed man who eventually became a Baptist minister. When Pfc. Pinkerman's son asked his grandfather why he did not have his father's remains returned to the United States for burial after the war, Frank replied that there was a passage in the Bible that states, "Where a tree falleth, there shall it lay."

Following graduation from high school, John worked on his father's farm and also at construction when he could. He and Geneva Frances Alley met in the summer of 1941 in the coal mining community of Clothier, West Virginia, where John's sister, Ruth, lived. Ruth introduced her brother to Geneva, and they were married in Ironton, Ohio, across the Ohio River from Huntington, on 1 October 1941. Their only child, John Alan, was born on 19 May 1943, while John and Geneva were living in Huntington. Grandmother Pinkerman later told John Alan that his father had quite a temper. She said he would be working on a car and if he couldn't get it started he might take a sledge hammer to the fender, hook a team of horses up to the car, and tow the car away.

Sometime later he would return with a different car or perhaps another team of horses. John was an avid hunter, and many years later his sister, Mable, gave John Alan his father's Iver & Johnson 12-gauge shotgun, which he displays proudly in his office.

John received his draft notice on 28 December 1943, and entered the service at Fort Thomas, Kentucky, on 18 January 1944. His mother, wife and young son were able to visit him at Camp Blanding, Florida, where he received basic training before his unit was shipped overseas. Private First Class Pinkerman was

Pfc. Pinkerman with his son, John Alan

sent to Italy and assigned as a replacement in the 157th Regiment of the 45th Infantry Division.[32] Before John's arrival, the 45th Division had already fought on Sicily, in southern Italy near Naples, and in the bloody Anzio beachhead east of Rome. After John arrived, the division took part in the capture of Rome. The division became part of the invasion force for "Operation Dragoon," in which the U.S. Seventh Army invaded southern France along the French Riviera. The division then participated in the breakout offensive that forced the Germans back toward the Rhine River, through the Ardennes-Alsace area, and into the Rhineland area itself. A summary of the 45th Division's World War II combat action indicates that from 2 January 1945, until about 17 February 1945, the division was in defensive positions along the German border and the Moder River. It was during this period that Private First Class Pinkerman was killed, most likely while taking part in a combat patrol to determine the location and strength of enemy positions.

Geneva Pinkerman remarried after the war, and she and her husband had three children. John Alan was raised by his maternal grandparents, Mose and Pauline Alley, two of the finest people John Alan has ever known. They taught him values, helped to develop his character, and introduced him to God. His paternal grandparents, Frank and Bertie Pinkerman, lived about sixty-five miles away near Huntington, West Virginia. They visited frequently and let him spend summers and Christmas vacations with them on their farm. John Alan feels blessed to have had two wonderful sets of grandparents. He told the author, "Had my father returned home, who knows what direction my life would have taken and how different I would be today. God works in mysterious ways, his blessing to bestow."

John Alan Pinkerman, his wife, Donna, their daughter, Kris, and a close friend, Harold Hicks, visited Private First Class Pinkerman's grave site at the Epinal American Cemetery and Memorial near Epinal, France, in September 2005. While there, John Alan was privileged to lay a beautiful floral wreath on his father's grave. (Author's Note: Coincidentally, the author and his wife were visiting the Epinal Cemetery at the same time and met John Alan and his family before they laid the wreath on his father's grave.) It is John Alan's intention to revisit the cemetery with his youngest daughter, Johnna, his son-in-law, David, grandson, Jordan, and granddaughter, Sydney. He stated, "It just didn't seem like I had enough time to spend with my father in 2005 and I would like to go back."

Pfc. John I. Pinkerman is buried at the Epinal American Cemetery and Memorial in Plot B, Row 44, Grave 2.

Pfc. Pinkerman's grave site

Pfc. Scalf in uniform

Private First Class
Andrew J. Scalf[33]
137th Infantry Regiment
35th Infantry Division

Pfc. Andrew J. Scalf was killed in action near Gerderath, Germany, on 27 February 1945. Private First Class Scalf had been a member of the 455th Anti-Aircraft Artillery Battalion until the 3rd Army Commander, General George S. Patton Jr., asked for volunteers to fill the hard-hit front-line infantry battalions. The infantry units had taken heavy casualties in the fighting to push the Germans back into their homeland. Private First Class Scalf volunteered for that hazardous duty, much as he had originally volunteered for the Army in October 1942. He was a true "Tennessee Volunteer." An Army buddy, Roy Clark, later told Private First Class Scalf's daughter, Brenda, that he was with Andrew when he was killed instantly by shrapnel from a German mortar round. Clark was also severely wounded and remained in military hospitals until after the war ended.

Andrew J. Scalf was born on 7 April 1921, to William and Vesta Astin Scalf at a time when his parents lived on a farm in Washington County, Tennessee. His only sister, Mable, died at age twelve when Andrew was about nine. Mable apparently suffered an attack of appendicitis and died when her father's car had a flat tire, which he could not repair in time to get Mable to the hospital. Andrew probably felt that he had to over-achieve in order to fulfill the dreams his parents had for the two children. Andrew loved to play baseball and was an excellent player. His father played semi-pro baseball in California in his younger days and had hopes Andrew could make it to the major leagues. Andrew was said to have had a great sense of humor and could find something to laugh at in almost any situation. While in school, he was called Andy, but he was known as Andrew after he enlisted in the Army. A very handsome young man, Andrew had dark hair and dark brown eyes. His friends joked that all the girls stood in line just so Andy would look their way.

Andrew met and fell in love with Ruth Jones while they were both attending the Liberty School in Washington County, Tennessee, near the Greene County line. Ruth was one of fourteen children. Neither Andrew nor Ruth was able to attend high school because the nearest high school at that time was a boarding school, which their parents could not afford. Andrew and Ruth were married in 1941 and Ruth soon gave birth to a baby daughter, Brenda. Andrew worked for a short time in Detroit, Michigan, at a Revere Ware plant. Many young men from the South migrated to Detroit during those years looking for work in the automobile factories and other factories "up north." He soon returned to Tennessee and was living in Chuckey, Tennessee, when he enlisted.

Andrew volunteered for the Army in October 1942. Following basic training and advanced training with the 455th Anti-Aircraft Artillery Battalion[34] at Fort Stewart, Georgia, Andrew shipped out on the USS *George Simmonds* in September 1943. When the ship developed mechanical problems, it had to detour to Halifax, Nova Scotia, where the men were transferred to the

Andrew and Ruth Scalf

converted luxury liner, the *Queen Elizabeth*, to complete the cross-ing to Glasgow, Scotland. After moving by train to the vicinity of Watton, England, the unit established anti-aircraft defenses around the air bases in that area.

Letters to his wife from England frequently mentioned what a great experience he would be enjoying if it were not for the war and his forced absence from his wife and baby daughter. Andrew's letters told of his desire to have lots more children, but the war precluded the fulfillment of those hopes. His letters expressed how much he loved his little girl and how she was "the best thing that had ever happened." Brenda recently met a former member of her father's unit who told her that he had seen a photo on Andrew's foot locker in which she was wearing a "cute little sailor's dress." He also told how proud Andrew was of his little girl.

The 455th Anti-Aircraft Battalion remained in England until the end of June 1944, when it prepared for movement to France. The first element arrived at Utah Beach, France, on 6 July 1944. The 455th fought through France, passing near Chartres, Reims, Metz, and eventually into Germany. In November 1944, Private First Class Scalf again volunteered and was transferred to the 137th Infantry Regiment, 35th Infantry Division,[35] which was part of the Third Army force tasked to attack the heavily defended city of Metz, France, along the French-German border. Division records indicate that starting on 7 November 1944, the division was involved in al-most constant engagements with the enemy as the enemy retreated toward Germany. Those engagements included not only the battle for Metz, but also the battle for Aachen in Germany.

When Germany launched the surprise attack on 16 December 1944, which became known as the Battle of the Bulge, the 35th Infantry Division was already in Germany attempting to break through the vaunted Sigfried Line. On Christmas Day 1944, after only two days of rest near Metz, the division was suddenly ordered to move that very night toward Bastogne, Belgium, to help relieve the embattled 101st Airborne Division which was surrounded by German forces. The 35th Division captured over 1,000 German prisoners and killed or wounded many more during the move to Bastogne. By late February, the division had moved more than 450 miles north to join the U.S. Ninth Army. It was during this time that Private First Class Scalf was killed.

Brenda now recognizes that she always had a hole in her heart by not having a dad she could talk to as she was growing up. She and her mother never talked about her father, and Brenda knew little about him, not even his birthday. In June 1998, Brenda finally was able to travel to Europe. After arriving at the Netherlands American Cemetery and Memorial located near Margraten, the Netherlands, she walked straight to her father's grave site. She felt a strong connection to the father she had never known. Since that initial visit, she has made numerous visits to the cemetery and has attempted to learn all she can about her father. Brenda said, "I feel that I've come to know him gradually over the last ten years, and I know that if he were alive today we would not only be father and daughter but also the best of friends. I have found out from his friends that I am so much like him in looks and temperament. So, I suppose that he probably felt the same as I do on many things."

Pfc. Andrew J. Scalf is buried in the Netherlands American Cemetery and Memorial in Plot C, Row 15, Grave 30.

Pfc. Scalf's grave site

Private First Class Elmer B. Heath[36] 47th Infantry Regiment 9th Infantry Division

Pfc. Heath in uniform

Pfc. Elmer B. Heath was killed on 9 March 1945, near Bruchhausen, Germany. Elmer had arrived in France on or about 11 December 1944, and was assigned as a replacement in the 2d Battalion, 47th Infantry Regiment (nicknamed "the Raiders"), 9th Infantry Division. The division became known as "The Old Reliable" after its performance in slowing the massive German counterattack that became famous as "The Battle of the Bulge." At the time Elmer joined the division, just before the German attack, it was in defensive positions following an offensive thrust that had taken the villages of Echtz and Schlich in Germany. The division was protecting a wide front near Elsenborn, Belgium, when the Germans attacked in force on 16 December 1944. Elmer was personally involved in some of the worst conditions of the war with fog, sleet, snow, and temperatures dropping well below zero. By the time of Elmer's death, the German offensive had been halted well short of its twin objectives of driving a wedge between the British forces in the north and the American Allies in the south and capturing the critical port city of Antwerp, Belgium.

Elmer and his twin brother, Delmar Ray, were born on 4 August 1918, the first of Scott and Nora

Elmer and his twin brother Delmar

Moser Heath's children. Scott and Nora lived in the foothills of south-west Virginia near Chilhowie, Virginia. The Heaths were a close-knit farm family which managed to survive the Depression years by raising their own food and selling or trading excesses for other essentials. The Heath family quickly expanded with the addition of four brothers (Roy, Marvin, Cecil and Ernest), and three sisters (Anna James, Hazel and Dorothy), a total of nine children. As a young man, Elmer loved baseball and hunting. Elmer did not finish high school, but he worked on the family farm, drove a truck, and worked as a hired hand on a neighbor's farm. He also worked for a time with the Civilian Conservation Corps on various construction projects.

In 1939 Elmer and Virginia Jones were married, and their first child, Nancy, was born in 1941. With World War II now in full force and the Allies advancing in all theaters, Elmer and Virginia struggled to support their family in rural Virginia by whatever jobs Elmer could find. By the time a second daugh-ter, Helen, was born in 1943, Elmer knew that the critical need for re-placements would soon result in his being drafted into the Army even as a married father with two children. Elmer was, in fact, inducted in May 1944, at Fort Meade, Maryland, and was then sent to Camp Wheeler, Georgia, located near Macon, for basic training. Although D-Day was still a month away, Elmer was op-timistic that the war might be won before he would have to face the enemy. His concern for the safety of his twin brother, Delmar Ray,

*Pfc. Heath and his wife
Virginia*

caused Elmer to urge his twin to do all he could to be assigned to a different type of unit that might be less dangerous. Three brothers survived military service and returned home safely after the end of the war. The two youngest brothers were too young to serve.

Elmer's sister, Anna James, stayed with Elmer and Virginia when Virginia was pregnant with Nancy because Virginia was sick during much of her pregnancy. Anna James recalls that Elmer would put his arms around her after she had prepared supper for the three of them and tell her how much he appreciated her helping them while Virginia was sick. Anna James even accompanied Virginia and the two little girls on a train from rural Virginia to Camp Wheeler, Georgia, to visit Elmer while he was in basic training.

Never having been on a train before, Virginia and Anna James were frightened to be traveling by rail with two small children. After reaching Camp Wheeler without incident, Elmer was allowed to stay with them at night. Virginia described that short visit as a "wonderful time." It would be Elmer's last extended contact with his wife and two daughters.

Elmer and thousands of other men were destined to be replacements in the front line combat units, which had fought from the beaches of Normandy to the very borders of Nazi Germany. He probably sailed in October of 1944 aboard the converted luxury liner, the *Queen Mary*, arriving first in Scotland and then, less than sixty days later, moved aboard the USS *Monrovia* from England to France. Prior to Elmer's assignment to the 9th Infantry Division in mid-December 1944, the 9th Division had already been involved in combat operations in Algeria, Tunisia, Sicily, Normandy, the sweep through France, and then the Rhineland border area separating Belgium, Luxembourg, and France from Germany. A summary of the 9th Division actions during WWII shows that the division suffered over 18,600 battle casualties, of which over 2,900 were killed in action,[37] more than 130 percent of the division's authorized strength.

The 9th Infantry Division crossed the famous Luddendorf Bridge at Remagen on or about 7 March 1945, with the 47th Regiment claiming the honor of being the first complete regiment to cross the bridge. The division immediately was assigned the mission to break out of the shallow bridgehead established on the east side of the Rhine River. On the following day, 8 March, Elmer's unit passed through the village of Orsberg and continued to attack toward Bruckhausen, Germany. The Germans had been using the forested area near Bruckhausen to hide the launching sites for their "secret weapon," the V-1 Rocket. It was during this attack against the fierce German defenses that Pfc. Elmer B. Heath lost his life on 9 March 1945.

Elmer's wife, Virginia, did not receive notification of his death until 21 March 1945. Their daughters, Nancy and Helen, were three and one-half years and seventeen months old respectively. Virginia later told the girls that Elmer stated that should anything happen to him he did not want his remains returned to the United States. His rationale was that they could never be sure that it would actually be his remains that were returned. Virginia also told her girls that after spending years recovering from the loss of her husband, she didn't think she could endure the trauma of going through the grief a second time if the body was returned for burial in the United States. Virginia taught the two girls to love and respect the father they could not recall. She maintained close contact with grandparents, aunts and uncles so that Nancy and Helen always had the benefit of a close relationship with Elmer's parents, brothers and sisters.

Private First Class Heath was initially buried in a temporary cemetery, but the location is not known. His remains were moved to the temporary cemetery at Henri-Chapelle, Belgium, in May 1947, and finally buried in the permanent Henri-Chapelle American Cemetery and Memorial near the village of Henri-Chapelle in 1948. Pfc. Elmer B. Heath is buried in Plot D, Row 12, Grave 40.

In May 2006, Nancy, Helen, and their husbands were present at the Henri-Chapelle American Cemetery and Memorial to participate in the Memorial Day wreath-laying services held each year at all American overseas cemeteries. The two sisters describe that emotional experience as a highlight of their lives.

Pfc. Heath's daughters, Nancy and Helen, at his grave site, May 2006

Private
Norman Leroy Burkey[38]
85th Regiment
10th Mountain Division

Pvt. Burkey in uniform

Pvt. Norman Leroy Burkey was killed near the small town of Castel d' Aiano, Italy, on 12 March 1945. Private Burkey and a buddy were in a shallow foxhole when his buddy went to the company rear area to get food for both men. The unit, Company C of the 85th Regiment, 10th Mountain Division, had succeeded in the assault on a mountainous area called Mt. Della Spe which was defended by German troops, but the unit had not yet had time to dig deep foxholes or to remove trees nearest to the company area. While his buddy was gone, a German artillery shell struck a tree behind Private Burkey's foxhole and he was killed. Although not known for sure, it is most likely that either a shell fragment or splinters from the trees struck Private Burkey. At the time Private Burkey was killed, the 10th Mountain Division had been in Italy less than ninety days. The division was involved in some of the heaviest fighting as U.S. and Allied units attempted to push the German troops north toward the Alps and the passes into Austria. By this time, Italy had withdrawn from the fighting and German forces had become the occupiers of Italy instead of Italy's ally. Only about a month after Private Burkey was killed, former U.S. Senator Bob Dole was seriously wounded approximately one mile from the same area.

Norman Leroy Burkey was born on 28 July 1919, on a small farm near Reading, Pennsylvania. He was the oldest child of Raymond and Naomi Hartman Burkey. Norman was only ten years old at the time of the stock market crash of 1929, so he was a true child of the

Depression. Fortunately, he was able to stay in school and graduate from Ontalaunee High School (now a part of the Schuylkill Valley School District) in Leesport, Pennsylvania. Well liked in the community and very spiritual, Norman was active in the Bern Reformed Church where he played violin in the Sunday school orchestra.

Following graduation, Norman was lucky to be employed by the Berkshire Knitting Mills in Reading, Pennsylvania. Sometime later, he worked at the American Chain and Cable Company until he was drafted in 1944.

Norman and his childhood sweetheart, Anna F. Miller, were married in 1940. The wedding took place in a church parsonage in Bern Township, Berks County, Pennsylvania. Married life began on the family farm, but soon they were able to purchase a home in nearby Mt. Pleasant in 1943. Norman and Anna had three children: Norman, born in August 1940, David, born in October 1941, and Anne, born in July 1943.

By 1944 the buildup of troops in both Europe and the Pacific, coupled with the critical need for replacements, led to the demand for local draft boards to reconsider the status of many men who had previously been deferred

Norman and Anna Burkey

because of age, occupation or family status. Even though Norman was married with three children, he was drafted in 1944 at the age of twenty-five. Following completion of his basic training at Fort Blanding, Florida, in 1944, Norman was assigned to the newly formed

10th Mountain Division. He joined the division at Camp Swift, near Austin, Texas. Norman Burkey's son, Norm, commented, "Only in the Army could a farm boy from eastern Pennsylvania, who never saw a pair of skis in his life, be assigned to an alpine unit." The division left for Italy in January 1945 and was quickly involved in heavy fighting in some of the most difficult and inhospitable terrain in Italy. The Germans, who were masters at using terrain to their best advantage, had fortified each hill and had heavy weapons and infantrymen covering all the rivers that the Allied forces had to attack. The Germans defended these natural obstacles fiercely and exacted a terrible toll on the attacking Allied forces.

Private Burkey's widow, Anna, never remarried, but she seldom discussed Norman with the three children. There were a few times when the children recalled their mother letting them look at their father's medals and other mementos, but those times were rare. Anna Burkey and the three children received a great deal of support from both sides of their extended family, but Norm advised that his mom was always the primary care giver. It is his opinion that his mom was every bit as much a hero after the war as his father was during the war.

One summer while Norm was in college, he met a man who told him that he could remember the day the Burkey family received the War Department telegram advising of Private Burkey's death. He said young Norm, only about five years old at the time, ran up and down the street crying for his dad. Although Norm recalls very little about his father, he does remember a time when his father was hauling ashes in a pickup truck. His father was concerned Norm might get ashes in his eyes.

In 2003, Norm Burkey traveled to Italy with members of the 10th Mountain Division Association. While in Italy, they were able to visit many of the battlefields on which the division had fought. Norm was even able to take a side trip to the area where his father was killed and to stand in a hole in the ground believed to be the exact spot where his father was killed in March 1945.

Norm created a scrap book about his father to ensure his own children, grandchildren, and future generations yet to come can have some appreciation for who and what his father was and what he might have become had he not been killed fighting the Nazis.

Pvt. Norman Leroy Burkey was first buried in a temporary cemetery near Florence, Italy. When offered the option after the war to have Private Burkey's remains buried in a permanent American Cemetery, which was to be established south of Florence, or have them returned to the United States, the family decided to have his remains returned to the U.S. for burial.

Pvt. Norman Leroy Burkey is buried in the Bern Church Cemetery on Route 182 near Reading, Pennsylvania.

Norman Burkey, son of Pvt. Burkey, at spot near where his father was killed, 2007

1LT Sears in uniform

**First Lieutenant
Thomas H. Sears[39]
700th Bomber Squadron
445th Bomb Group**

First Lieutenant Sears was killed in action on 23 March 1945, when his B-24 bomber was shot down near Munster, Germany. One of Lieutenant Sears' friends, Mr. F. Max Schutte of Houston, Texas, received the following information from Mr. Horst A. Munter of Dortmund-Wanbel, Germany, in a letter dated 12 June 1998:

It was not easy to find the crash site of 1LT Thomas Sears' "B-24," because most of the old farmers are dead! Even the archive of the city of Munster could not help! However, three weeks ago I was lucky and got a hint of a farmer on whose plot a plane had crashed! He could still remember the exact date! It was 23 March 1945! The farmer, Walter Konerding, took me to the crash site where I could still find some pieces of metal with the help of my detector...As far as the farmer could remember the plane was hit by a bullet from an anti-aircraft gun and broke into two pieces. The fuselage with wings and motors went down in a spin. In the meantime seven men felled [*sic*] out of the plane! But only three were safed [*sic*] by parachutes. The wreck hit the ground and turned over a street [*sic*] and started burning. Sometime later, Russian POWs recovered the both [*sic*] burned crew members and buried all on the "Honour Cemetery" of the former sick bay "Haus Spital" of the Great War. In the years 1946/1947 the dead crew members were transported to different cemeteries:
1. "ARDENNES" – Neuville-en-Condroz – south of Liege (Belgium)
    1LT Thomas Sears
    T/Sgt. Elton Billings – later reburied to U.S.A.

S/Sgt. Richard McLain – later reburied to U.S.A.
2. "Netherlands" – Margraten –east of Maastricht (Netherlands)
2LT Solon Briskin – still missing!
S/Sgt. Calvin Wilson
Sgt. Henry Bateman"

(Author's Notes:

1. Mr. Horst Munter died in 2008 from diabetes. In spite of his efforts on behalf of the families of missing Americans, and the efforts of others, no trace of Second Lieutenant Briskin has been found.

2. The remains of Second Lieutenant Briskin were not identified after the bodies of the crew were recovered from the "Honors Cemetery." Neither was his military identification tag found. First Lieutenant Sears' I.D. tag was not found either, but identification was made possible because of his Purdue University signet ring.

3. It is not known why First Lieutenant Sears' remains were subsequently interred in the Ardennes American Cemetery in Belgium while the remains of Staff Sergeant Wilson and Sergeant Bateman were interred in the Margraten American Cemetery in the Netherlands. First Lieutenant Briskin's name is on the Wall of the Missing at Margratin.)

Tom Sears, born at Cincinnati, Ohio, on 16 June 1924, was one of four sons born to Charles and Vivian Fosdick Sears—John, James, Thomas, and Robert.

Left to right: John, Thomas, Robert and James Sears receiving their Eagle Scout Badges from the chief of the local Boy Scout Council

All four brothers were active in the Boy Scouts. Thomas (Tom) graduated from Webster Groves High School in Webster Groves, Missouri, on 24 June 1942. While in high school, Tom was a member of the Senior Student Council, the Chemistry Club, was president of the Hi-Y Club, and was a member of the track team. He went to Purdue University to major in science and engineering but entered the service on 27 February 1943.

After training in the United States, Tom was assigned as a pilot to the 700th Bomber Squadron of the 445th Bomb Group stationed near Tibenham, Norfolk, England. While stationed there, Tom met an eighteen-year-old British girl, Gladys Ivy Pease, who was in the British military assigned to food service activities, stationed in Wales. Love flowered between the two, and, although stationed in different locations, they continued their romance through the exchange of letters and infrequent meetings. Gladys soon found that she would have Tom's child, and Tom told her that if anything should happen to him she and their child should go to the United States to live with his parents.

Lieutenant Sears was initially reported as missing in action in March 1945. About three weeks after he was reported missing, Gladys gave birth to a baby girl, Diana, on 11 April 1945. The young girl's family could not accept the situation; their unmarried daughter had given birth to a child whose father was probably dead. The official British birth certificate lists the mother's maiden name and leaves blank the name of the father. Gladys was discharged from the military, but her family refused to accept her back in their house. Unable to provide for herself and her baby, she had to find a workable solution. She made friends with a family that had lost a baby girl, and that family agreed to look after the baby (Diana) until the new mother could get herself sorted out. Gladys managed to find work nearby caring for young children and visited regularly to feed and help care for Diana. Later, she left the area to make a new life for herself, secure in the knowledge that her and Tom's baby daughter was safe and secure with her new "family."

It was not until many years later that Diana, now a grown woman, managed to uncover the facts of her parentage and was finally able to visit the remaining members of her biological father's family in the United States. She learned that her father's parents had apparently not openly shared with other members of the family the fact that Thomas had fathered a child before he was killed. However, Diana's cousin, Uncle Bob's son, told her that when their grandmother was nearing the end of her life, she suddenly blurted out, "I have a grandchild someplace in Europe – GB!" Uncle Bob thought his mother must be talking nonsense; it had been more than thirty years since Tom was killed.

Diana Sears Vuillemin, the daughter of Tom Sears, currently lives in Lausanne, Switzerland. She has been trying to learn all she can about the father she never knew and who was killed before she was born. In addition to visiting her father's living relatives in the United States and meeting many members of the extended family, Diana managed to contact the three members of her father's flight crew who were fortunate enough to have survived the crash that killed her father.

One crew member, Frank Morgan, wrote Diana a two-page letter in 1996, which included the following comments:

> He was a personable, tall, lanky kind of person....He was a pilot on a B-24 Liberator Bomber, and I was his radio operator. There were ten of us on the crew....Tom looked too young to be commander of such a large aircraft. We flew 28 1/2 missions over Germany. Tom had an additional one, for he flew his first as a copilot on another crew before taking us along.
>
> On March 23, 1945, we were on a very short mission to Munster, Germany, in the Ruhr Valley. We were to bomb the rail yard at 26,000 feet and return home shortly after noon. Just as we released the bomb load and I had closed the doors, an antiaircraft shell exploded near the plane. I saw the red center. Brisken, [sic] the copilot, was flying formation. When he yelled that the left rear rudder of the twin tail was hit, Tom called to the crew to prepare to bail out. The plane went out of control. He ordered us to bail out. By then the aircraft was rolling over. For a moment I was unable to move because of the centrifugal force. Suddenly I found myself falling into space and pulled the ripcord of my parachute. I never saw the plane again. There were two parachutes below me, and before nightfall I met Meyer and Kelly in a prison cell. Obviously, we were the only survivors. It was a grievous time for us. We had almost finished our tour of

1LT Sears, top left, and his bomber crew, March 1945

duty; the war was almost over; we had come so far together; it was a pity it had to end this way.

One final word – perhaps the best. Tom Sears was my friend, my senior officer, and one who cared for his fellow crew members. He was an excellent pilot, and I had complete confidence in him. He brought us safely home many, many times. I have always believed that Tom fought to regain control of the plane and may have made it possible for me to overcome the forces and to exit.... He never included us in his personal life; he never talked about his family; nor your impending birth. Surely, he must have been struggling under enormous pressure to survive and return home. But he kept it all to himself. Maybe all of us did.

Diana was able to have her maiden name changed to Sears in Great Britain, but until recently was not successful in obtaining American citizenship. She tried for well over ten years to accumulate the necessary documentation but was repeatedly rejected for one reason or another. Diana even managed to obtain validated DNA tests which determined with a 99.9% probability her biological relationship to two of Tom Sears' brothers, John and Robert. Finally, in August 2008, her efforts were rewarded, and Diana was sworn in as an American citizen. She is very proud of her new citizenship as well as being proud of her hard work—over thirty-three years of research and dogged persistence required to reach her goal. Tom Sears would be proud!

1LT Thomas H. Sears is buried in Plot A, Row 43, Grave 26, in the Ardennes American Cemetery and Memorial located near Neupre, Belgium.

Diana has visited her father's grave site in Belgium and has a photo of his marker with a wreath she had placed there. Diana wrote the following poem in honor of the father she never knew:

Thomas

One spring day in '45 a "Freedom Bird" flew high to the skies.
I slumbered, still, in my nest so warm, awaiting the long journey to be born.
My cry of life joined yours of pain, our breaths as one,
in this great shame called ....war.
The light of day called out my name as midnight felled your flame.
Since, peace has reigned 50 years and one, but in my heart,
loss and tears have been my everlasting spears.
To you, for always and forever after,
This a tribute, to my hero,
My dearest father.
Diana Sears 1997

1LT Sears' grave site.
ABMC photo

Pvt. Gilbert Bush relaxing

Private Gilbert M. Bush[40]
313ᵗʰ Infantry Regiment
79ᵗʰ Infantry Division

Pvt. Gilbert M. Bush died 8 May 1945, as a result of what the official Army investigation report termed "an accidental death." He was on duty near the town of Unna, Germany. Private Bush's story is like other stories in this book in some ways but very much different in at least two very significant aspects: First, his story was brought to the attention of the author by an e-mail from his daughter, Ms. Angela Christian, who lives in Great Britain. Second, his death was not due to combat with the enemy or even as the result of a vehicle accident.

According to a letter received by Angela in 2006 from a former member of her father's unit, Gilbert had served with an antitank company of the 313ᵗʰ Infantry Regiment as the unit made an assault crossing of the Rhine River in late March of 1945. At that time in the war, the Allies were steadily pushing the German Army to the east and southeast while anticipating the linkup with Russian forces which were rapidly advancing from the east and nearing Berlin.

As the war moved steadily toward a successful conclusion, the tactical situation became very confused. The Americans continued to engage the hard-pressed Germans, but at the same time, had to be alert for possible interference from the German civilian populace. The Americans also had to house, feed and protect the hundreds of thousands of French, Poles, Czechs, Yugoslavs and Jews who were being liberated from slave labor camps, concentration camps and death camps. Amid all of this confusion, Private Bush's unit was detailed to provide security for a camp where many of the "displaced persons" were being held. The American soldiers had sympathy for the pitiful circumstances under which the displaced persons had to live, and the GIs would share their own food rations and cigarettes or trade for souvenirs.

When it was officially announced that Germany had surrendered and the War in Europe was over, the displaced persons in the camp wanted to thank their liberators. Unbeknown to the Americans, the displaced persons in the camp had somehow managed to obtain alcohol-based fuel used for the German V-1 Rockets (the infamous Buzz Bombs). They mixed the "alcohol" with other locally available juices and provided the "booze" to their American friends. Russian troops were also nearby at the time, so the Americans, Russians and some of the displaced persons apparently toasted Germany's defeat using the deadly brew. The following morning, Private Bush and one of his good buddies were found near a sink in their barracks where they apparently had been trying to disgorge the poison that was causing their extreme discomfort. Both men were taken to a nearby Army hospital. Private Bush and his close friend, as well as a number of displaced persons and several Russians, died. After avoiding death or injury in combat, Private Bush died of acute alcohol poisoning!

Although Private Bush trained with the 29th Infantry Division in the United States and had shipped out of the United States with the 175th Regiment of the 29th Division in October 1942, he was transferred to the 79th Infantry Division[41] at some point after June 1943. It is known that he received the highly regarded Combat Infantrymans Badge in December 1944, while a member of Company H, 313th Infantry Regiment of the 79th Infantry Division. Private Bush was returned to England about January of 1945 for unknown medical reasons. Upon returning to the 79th Division, he was assigned to an antitank company in the 313th Regiment of the division.

The 79th Division may not be as well known as some other divisions such as the 1st Division, the 29th Division, or the 3rd Armored Division, but its combat record was outstanding. The 79th Division saw its initial combat action in late June 1944, during the battle to take the vital port city of Cherbourg in Normandy, France. The division captured over 6,000 German troops during that engagement, and then fought across France and Belgium on its way to Germany. During the months of September and October 1944, the division battled against strong German forces in the Vosges Mountain area. By 17 December 1944, the division was attacking the infamous Siegfried Line.

If casualties are any indication of the fierce nature of combat, then the 79th Division must be near the top. The division sustained 2,476 killed in action, 467 dead from wounds received, 10,971 wounded in action, 1,699 captured or Missing in Action, and 14,875 casualties from disease or other non-battle injuries. That was a total of over 30,400 casualties for a division with a normal strength of about 15,000.

Gilbert M. Bush was born in Princeton, New Jersey, on 15 January 1916, and was the youngest of five children born to Gilbert and Annie Yates Bush. His father died when Gilbert was only fourteen years old, and Gilbert did his best to help the family survive through the hard times of the Great Depression. Like many young men during the Depression, Gilbert spent time working on "New Deal" construction projects, reportedly working to build new roads in New Jersey. At some point before being inducted into the Army, Gilbert married Mary Dunk of Pennsylvania and fathered three children. Available Army records at the time he was inducted state that he and his wife were separated. No information is available to indicate what became of his estranged wife and their three children.

Gilbert enlisted in the Army on 18 May 1942, at Fort Dix, New Jersey. Following basic training and advanced training in the United States, he was assigned to Company M, 3rd Battalion, 175th Regiment, 29th Infantry Division. He shipped out for England with the division in early October 1942, only five months after his enlistment.

During the eighteen months of intensive training in England as preparation for the anticipated invasion of France, Gilbert met a young British woman in London, Annie May McGuinness. Annie May later told her daughter, Angela, that Gilbert loved music, dancing, and gambling, and was incredibly romantic with an eye for the ladies. He had boyish good looks, was a charming man, and lived life to the fullest. Gilbert apparently swept Annie May off her feet. At some point before Gilbert and his unit moved across the English Channel to France, Annie May became pregnant with their daughter, Angela. Angela does not know if her father knew about the pregnancy before he went to France. Angela was born in October 1945, about five and a half months after her father died.

Angela Christian was raised by her mother and stepfather. She was twelve years old before learning who her real father was. Angela now asks herself what might have been achieved in her life if her "Dad" had lived to advise her and give her the confidence she now lacks. Much about her father's life in the United States is still unknown, but she feels that Gilbert "is probably a little bit proud of me, after all, I (little old me), against all odds, have found him, and I am making sure he will be remembered and justly honored." As Angela noted, it was ironic that Private Bush participated in some of the most severe fighting as the Allies pushed the Germans back from the beaches of France into the German homeland itself, only to die of alcohol poisoning after the German surrender.

Angela was able to locate her father's burial site in the Netherlands American Cemetery and Memorial at Margraten. She now visits his grave site as often as possible. Pvt. Gilbert M. Bush is buried in Plot M, Row 8, Grave 10.

Angela Christian at her father's grave site

NOTES

[1] Family information and photos provided by Mr. Ron McEntyre, Knoxville, TN, son of Pfc. McEntyre.

[2] Information related to the 4th Infantry Division extracted from the Normandy Allies web site for the 4th Inf. Div.

[3] Family information and photos provided by Mr. Larry G. Graber, Sugar Creek, OH, son of Pvt. Graber.

[4] Information related to the 9th Infantry Regiment extracted from *Ninth Regiment History 1798-2000* at www.Manchu.org and from information about the 2d Infantry Division at http://wikipedia.org.

[5] Family information and photos provided by Mrs. Virginia Hallman, Reading, PA, widow of S/Sgt. Hallman.

[6] Information related to the 29th Infantry Division actions in Normandy and Brittany extracted from the following sources: Chester County, PA, "Hall of Heroes: Sherwood Henry Hallman;" www.sprol.com/+/29thinfantry. html; www.lonesentry.com; "29th Let's Go! The Story of the 29th Infantry Division"; www.dix.army.mil/pao.

[7] Staff Sergeant Hallman's Medal of Honor Citation at www.army.mil. cmh.

[8] Family information and photos provided by Ms. Gail Eisenhauer, Hamden, CT, daughter of 2LT Eisenhauer.

[9] Information related to the 9th Infantry Division obtained from www. lonesentry.com which contains a number of historical booklets about various WWII divisions prepared by the I&E division, ETOUSA.

[10] Family information and photos provided by Ms. Merrill Baker, Staten Island, NY, niece of Pfc. Baker.

[11] Information related to the 79th Infantry Division extracted from: "The 79th Infantry Division (United States)" at http://en.wikipedia.org; the 79th Infantry Division in World War II" at http://home.earthlink. net~jwittimeyer/314/reunion/79idhtml; and the National Archives of the U.S. at College Park, MD.

[12] Quoted from "The Cross of Lorraine Division: the Story of the 79th," as provided by Ms. Merrill Baker.

[13] Family information and photos provided by Ms. Jo Anne Rowman Morrissey, Brooksville, FL, daughter of 2LT Rowman.

[14] Information related to the 106th Reconnaissance Squadron extracted from "officers 106th Squadron, 106th Cavalry, Group Roster" at http:// mars. Wnec.edu/~dwilliam/history/106off.htm.

[15] Family information and photos provided by Mr. C. Joe Farris, Montpelier, VT, son of Pvt. Farris.

[16] Family information and photos provided by Mr. Barry Barr-Finch, Seatac, WA, son of 2LT Finch.

[17] Information provided by Mr. Barry Barr-Finch.

[18] Information related to 1LT Stiles was obtained from three primary sources: the Tutt Library at Colorado College, Colorado Springs, CO; www.acmedepot.com "A Tribute to Bert Stiles: An Unfinished Story"; http://wikipedia.org.

[19] Family information and photos provided by Rosemary Dainotto Cummo, Oak Ridge, NC, daughter of 1LT Dainotto.

[20] Information related to the 28th Infantry Division and the 112th Infantry Regiment extracted from "Fact Sheet of the 28th Infantry Division" at www.battleofthebulge.org, and from declassified "Organizational History" records of the Anti-Tank Company, 112th Infantry Regiment.

[21] Extracted from "HQ Company: a WW2 Unit History" by Lt. Robert "Bud" Flynn of the 112th Infantry Regiment, 28th Infantry Division" available at http://students.usm.maine.edu.

[22] Family information and photos provided by Ms. Donna O'Brien, Chicago, IL, niece of Pfc. Patrick.

[23] The BAR was an intermediate weapon, lighter than a machine gun, but heavier than the standard M-1 rifle. It was capable of slow fire at a rate of 300 to 450 rounds per minute or fast fire at a rate of 500 to 650 rounds per minute. The BAR was often called the Infantry Squad's best friend.

[24] Provided by Mr. Michael A. Almond, Charlotte, NC, son of Pfc. James A. (Cotton) Almond.

[25] Metz, France, is located at the intersection of two major axes: west toward Paris and east toward Prague, Czech Republic; north toward Luxembourg and south toward Nance, Dijon, and Lyon, France.

[26] Family information and photos provided by Joe Lippi Jr., Snoqualmie, Washington, son of Pvt. Lippi.

[27] Information about combat actions of the 84th Infantry Division provided by Joe Lippi Jr.

[28] Family information and photos provided by Carol Downs Brooks, Rochester, NY, daughter of Pfc. Downs.

[29] Information related to Pfc. Downs' death and temporary burial is extracted from a letter written to Pfc. Downs' father by the 346th Infantry Regiment chaplain.

[30] Information related to the 87th Infantry Division extracted from www.history.army.mil/html; http://en.wikipedia.org; and from www.lonesentry.com which contains a number of historical booklets about various WWII divisions prepared by the I&E Division, ETOUSA.

[31] Family information and photos provided by John A. Pinkerman, Lesage, WV, son of Pfc. Pinkerman.

[32] Information related to the 45th Infantry Division extracted from article titled "45th Infantry Division (United States)" found at http://en.wikipedia.org and from www.lonesentry.com which contains a number of the historical booklets about various WWII divisions prepared by the I&E Division, ETOUSA.

[33] Family information and photos provided by Brenda Scalf Burchfield, Knoxville, TN, daughter of Pfc. Scalf.

[34] Information related to the 455th Antiaircraft Bn. Provided by Brenda Scalf Burchfield.

[35] Information related to the 35th Infantry Division extracted from "Combat Chronicles – 35th Infantry Division" at www.army.mil.cmh/lineage; and from www.lonesentry.com which contains a number of the historical booklets about various WWII divisions prepared by the I&E Division, ETOUSA.

[36] Family information and photos provided by Helen Heath Vernon, Marion, VA, daughter of Pfc. Heath.

[37] Casualty data extracted from www.army.mil/cmh file titled "9th Infantry Division: Hitler's Nemesis."

[38] Family information and photos provided by Norm Burkey, Forest Hill, Maryland, son of Pvt. Burkey.

[39] Family information and photos provided by Diana Sears Vuillemin, Lausanne, Switzerland, daughter of 1LT Sears.

[40] Family information and photos provided by Angela Christian, Great Britain, daughter of Pvt. Bush.

[41] Information related to the 79th Infantry Division extracted from www.gomilspec.com/libertyroad/79th and from article titled "79th Infantry Division in World War II" at http://home.earthlink.net.

Chapter Six

THE AMERICAN WORLD WAR II ORPHANS NETWORK (AWON)

*"The power of noble deeds is to be preserved
and passed on to the future."*
Brigadier General Joshua Chamberlain,
Commander of Federal Forces
at the surrender of General Lee's forces
at Appomattox Court House,
Governor of Maine, and President of Bowdoin College.

(Author's Note: This chapter describes the purpose of and the creation of the organization. The information in this chapter was contributed by Mrs. Judith Hoffman, a past president of the AWON Board of Directors.)

The American World War II Orphans Network (AWON) was founded in 1991 by Ann Bennett Mix in order to bring war orphans together. Most of the orphans of WWII grew up in isolation, not knowing other such orphans existed. The estimated number of children who lost fathers in WWII is 183,000. Through Ann's efforts and the work of many AWON volunteers, AWON has become a national organization which holds biannual conferences, publishes a quarterly newsletter, coordinates wreath layings at memorial services worldwide, and provides support and guidance for members' research about their fathers.

The mission of the American World War II Orphans Network is: to locate and bring together sons and daughters of those who died or are missing as a result of American involvement in World War II; to honor the service and sacrifice of their fathers; and to provide information and support to those people who were orphaned by the war.

When many American WWII orphans were growing up they knew little about their fathers and, when questioned, could only answer, "My father died in the war." It was a mantra, said with little emotion or inflection. In Ms. Hoffman's personal experience, people just replied with an "oh," and turned away with some degree of discomfort. In many cases, the widows of WWII did not discuss the fallen fathers with their own orphaned children. At that time no one knew about the stages of grieving nor were there support groups for the widows and orphans as there are today. During that period there was no thought given to children who needed help working through the grief process. Neither did the widows receive counseling to assist with their own grief, nor did they have the time, even if such support had been available. They were too busy trying to provide for themselves and the child or children who no longer had a father. The widows were expected to "just get on with their lives." And most did. They supported themselves and raised the children as well as possible. Some widows experienced problems later, which may possibly have been traced back to the mental trauma of the loss of their husband and the strain of "just getting on with their lives."

When Ann Bennett Mix began her own journey to learn about her father, a Bellingham, Washington, newspaper printed an article about her search for other orphans in order to write a book about their shared experiences. As a result of that 1990 article, Ann found five other WWII orphans and, in 1991, she registered the name "American World War II Orphans' Network" as a 501 c(3) non-profit business corporation. Articles in several other publications followed and membership in the fledgling organization continued to grow, although slowly.

In 1991, following an article in *Parade* magazine about a tree planting in Arlington National Cemetery for children of war dead, which was being sponsored by the group "No Greater Love," Ann contacted Carmella La Spada, founder of the group. Later, Ann went to Washington, D.C., to attend the tree-planting event, taking with her fliers to distribute, which described AWON and its mission. Ms. La Spada later sent Ann a list of WWII orphans who had attended the tree-planting event, and the number of identified WWII orphans jumped to 200.

Senator Bob Dole spoke at the tree dedication and, afterwards, Ann introduced herself to him. He had served in the 10th Mountain Division as had Ann's father, Private Sidney Bennett. Senator Dole asked how he could help the orphans and graciously agreed to become the group's national advisor.

Ann Mix then coauthored the book, *Lost in Victory, Reflections of War Orphans of World War II*, with AWON member Susan Hadler. Following the book's publication, Ms. Hadler wrote an article published in *Reader's Digest*. As a result of that article many more war orphans made contact with AWON and found they had not been alone for all those years.

About that time, Mr. Lorin McCleary, a WWII orphan who lived in the state of Washington, proposed that a group of AWON members meet in Washington, D.C., to hold a planning session. Twelve of the attendees at the session, now known as "First Founders," each contributed $500 to underwrite the cost of the AWON network. Those First Founders were Anne Maloney Black, Clatie Cunningham, Nick Etchevery, Clint Frederick, Susan Johnson Hadler, John and Walter Linne, Lorin McCleary, Eric Rosen, Mary Swaggerty Slowey, Sam Tannenbaum, and Jeffrey Ward. The group also formed a task force, headed by Lorin McCleary, to draft bylaws and to plan for a conference at which a board of directors and officers could be elected.

In November 1995, the very first national conference of AWON members was held in Seattle, Washington. At this first conference, attendees elected a governing board and officers for the organization. This first board consisted of Ann Mix, Founder; Walt Linne, President; Sandra Walker, Vice President; Lorin McCleary, Secretary; Anne Maloney Black, Public Relations; Clint Frederick, Treasurer; Diane Glasgow, Accountant; and Directors at Large Pat Lahey, Gloria Layne, Joan Marlow, Kay Sandhoff, Suzanne Turpin, Jeff Ward, and Patty Wheeler.

Among the notable attendees at the first national conference were the late Gen. Wayne Downing and his wife. A World War II orphan himself, General Downing knew his father was killed while on a mission to rescue POWs. His mother raised him and two younger sisters. A West Point graduate, Downing was revered throughout the Special Operations Forces as a soldier's soldier. Following the 9/11 (2001) bombing of the World Trade Center, President Bush recalled General Downing from retirement to serve as National Director and

Deputy National Security Advisor for Combating Terrorism. General Downing died in 2007 from complications of meningitis.

Mr. Howard Kleinberg, a nationally syndicated columnist, happened to be staying in the same hotel where the first conference was held. Upon learning about the AWON conference, Mr. Kleinberg changed his own plans for the weekend and attended the AWON events. As a result of his subsequent column about the new organization, twenty-four more members joined AWON.

Three years later, the second AWON conference was held in St. Louis, Missouri. St. Louis was, and still is, the home of the National Personnel Records Center, Military Personnel Records (NPRC-MPC). The NPRC-MPC is the official repository for millions of military personnel records, including medical records of discharged and deceased military veterans of all services during the twentieth century. Ann Mix contacted the Archivist of the United States and persuaded him to allow AWON members to tour the facility. She went a step further and asked if the records and medals of the members' fathers could be made available during the tour. The late COL Jack O. Forgy, U.S. Army Retired, agreed to be the contact for that part of the event. It was a very emotional moment for each AWON member when they were presented their father's records. Colonel Forgy continued to assist AWON members in their efforts to learn where and how their fathers had served and died. Colonel Forgy is now deceased, but the time he spent poring over government forms and searching for records of those who died in WWII was a labor of love for him. He is greatly missed by all those whose lives he touched. (Author's Note: A major fire at the NPRC-MPC in 1973 destroyed thousands of irreplaceable personnel files, but efforts were made to recover as many files or portions of files as modern technology permitted.)

The AWON organization continues to expand its membership and offers significant services to both AWON members and to the general public. An outreach to all families of those missing in WWII, headed by President Emerita Patricia Gaffney Kindig, has had a significantly positive impact on the way the government interacts with families of the missing.

An AWON web site was created by Mr. Rik Pierson, a very talented graphic artist and web designer. AWON members can publish tributes to their fathers on the web site along with photos. The web site (www.awon.org) also contains valuable information about AWON, how to become a member, advice on obtaining military records, advice for dealing with the loss of a loved one, and a listing of the books available for purchase from the AWON Bookstore. Mr. Pierson also created and maintained a list server containing information that enables AWON members to contact each other by e-mail, announces meetings and regional get-togethers of members, highlights conferences of interest to members, and provides access to other data, which helps cement bonds of friendship among AWON members.

Among her many efforts on behalf of AWON, Ann Mix edited and published an AWON newsletter, *The Star*, which was taken over and ably edited for many years by Doni Morrison Troglio. It is currently edited by AWON granddaughter Kathy Le Comte Lupton. Each issue of *The Star* contains stories about AWON members, stories about members' fathers, reports of regional meetings, reports by the AWON Board, and other items of general interest to the membership. A version of *The Star* is accessible by the general public at the AWON web site.

One of the most significant events in the history of AWON was the dedication of the National World War II Memorial on the National Mall in Washington, D.C., in May 2004. The dedication of the new memorial coincided with AWON's 2004 National Conference which was appropriately titled "In Their Memory." Ann Mix traveled to Washington, D.C., to attend the National Planning Commission meetings for the National World War II Memorial and represented AWON. After seeing the proposed design, which included a "sacred space" with a stone coffin to represent the sacrifice made by Americans, Ann suggested that instead of the stone coffin, gold stars should be considered to represent all the lives which were lost. Friedrich St. Florian, the architect who created the design, told Ann he liked her idea about the stars and he would do something with it. He then drew a new design for the sacred space which became a wall of 4,000 stars. Each star represents about 100 of the 407,000 war dead. The gold stars remind everyone of the flags that hung in all too many American windows during the war to signify a family's loss.

Due to her efforts to ensure that the World War II Memorial included an appropriate tribute to those who gave their lives in the war, President George W. Bush invited Ann Mix to the White House to witness the signing of the bill authorizing the construction of the memorial. She and Patricia Gaffney Kindig, the AWON board president, attended the ceremony.

When the new memorial was formally dedicated by President George W. Bush on Memorial Day 2004, the AWON members were seated with the World War II veterans themselves. Ann Mix was seated on the dais with President Bush, former President Clinton, Senator Bob Dole, Tom Hanks, and other dignitaries. The evening of the dedication, AWON was honored by allowing it to hold the very first memorial service at the new monument. During the AWON Memorial Service, the names of the family members who died during the war were read by their grandchildren.[1]

(Author's Note: The following is Ms. Hoffman's perspective of the WWII Orphan experience.)

While still a young child playing in my mom's closet, I found a photo of a man who looked a lot like me, but I didn't know who he was. My mother walked in, took the photo away from me and simply said, "That's your father." I didn't see that photo again until I was about forty years old when Mom gave me that same photograph and a scrapbook of my father's life, which had been kept by my grandmother. We, in AWON, call this attitude "The Wall of Silence." As children, we did not understand, but we still had to maintain "The Wall of Silence" to our own eventual detriment.

When I received a copy of my father's military personnel records in the mail from the NPRC-MPC, it had been more than fifty years since my father had been killed in Italy two months before I was born. My husband came home that evening to find me sitting in the kitchen weeping for a man I had never met. I have been told that I was experiencing delayed grief for one I really hadn't known until that day. Those records were precious beyond price. They told me how tall he was, that he often had a sore throat, as I did. I saw his signature for the first time, but most importantly, it told me when, where and how he died. He died in a small place in Italy called Piccilli as a result of an accident in a Jeep he was testing. A skilled mechanic, the

Army had put him in charge of a motor pool; he was testing the jeep after it had been repaired before letting it be reissued.

As a direct result of my membership in AWON I was able to discover a father I never knew nor would have known. My father's sister, Auntie Em, who was also my godmother, whom I had last seen when I was only ten years old, "found" me on Veterans' Day in 2005. As had happened in many cases, my mother had lost touch with my father's family, and I had not attempted to locate them. Auntie Em, by then a very savvy octogenarian, had read an Ann Landers column about adding names of any of the greatest generation to the WWII National Memorial website. She wanted to add the name of her brother, my father. When she tried to do that, she found that his name was already listed with my name, his daughter, as the contributor. She then "Googled" my name and found the AWON Web Site, which contained the tribute that I had written to my father. Somehow, I still don't know quite how, she found my unlisted phone number and called. I can never explain how much that call meant to me. In a subsequent visit, Auntie Em gave me all of my father's letters, which he had written to his family from the war zone, as well as a family genealogy document. My mother had burned all of my father's letters, which he had written to her from the war zone. Therefore, the family letters were a revelation to me about his personality and thoughts, which always will be the greatest treasure and gift of my lifetime.

Auntie Em has shared many stories about my dad, the good as well as the not so wonderful, as one would expect from a kid sister, but all have been appreciated. I now have an idea of what his personality was like and find that it was not so different from my own. Auntie Em's stories have helped to explain many things about my own nature that had puzzled me for years, especially why I was so very different from my own mother in many ways. Although I never saw my dad and didn't have the benefit of his guiding hand as I grew up, I find that I am like him in many aspects.

One of my closest friends in AWON was able to locate her father's brother shortly before he died. That contact, and the information he was able to provide about her father, meant the world to her.

There are hundreds of truly amazing stories in AWON. I call them AWON miracles: the recovery of family memorabilia after more than fifty or sixty years; finding the very spot where a father fought and died and feeling his presence there; flying in his airplane or visiting his ship; finding life partners in AWON and feeling that in some way our fathers had a hand in it. The most amazing miracle of all is meeting like souls who really do "get it."

It has been a great honor to serve as President of the AWON Board of Directors and to be directly involved in the work of AWON to help ensure that our legacy as war orphans, as well as the stories of our fathers, will be preserved for future generations.

NOTES

[1] Ms. Hoffman referred to the following publications as background for the information contained in this chapter:

   a. *American WWII Orphans Network, In Their Memory.* Turner Publishing Co., Paducah, KY, 2004.

   b. *Lost in the Victory, Reflections of American War Orphans of World War II*, by Susan Hadler and Ann Bennett Mix, University of North Texas Press, Denton, Texas, 1998.

   c. Personal recollections of Ms. Ann Bennett Mix, founder of the American WWII Orphans Network.

Chapter Seven

JACKSON COUNTY MEN

*"Wars can be prevented just as surely as they are provoked,
and therefore we who fail to prevent them must share
in guilt for the dead."*
General Omar N. Bradley

Jackson County is a small county nestled among the rolling hills of southeastern Ohio, commonly called the Tri-State Area. It is roughly thirty miles from West Virginia and thirty miles from Kentucky with the Ohio River serving as the boundary. In 1941 the total population in the county was about 27,000 with the major population centers being in Jackson (the county seat) and Wellston, about nine miles from Jackson. Each town had a population of more than 6,000. The two villages of Oak Hill and Coalton each had less than 1,000 people, and the remainder were scattered throughout the county on small farms and orchards. The county did not have a higher education institution, but Rio Grande College, a small, private, two-year college was located about fifteen miles away in Gallia County, and many Jackson students attended Rio Grande. Others attended Ohio University in Athens, Ohio, or The Ohio State University in Columbus, Ohio.

The major industries in the county included the Globe Iron Company (Globe), the Jackson Iron and Steel Company (JISCO), and the Detroit Toledo and Ironton Railroad (DT&I) car shops in Jackson; the Frick Gallagher Manufacturing Company and the Hercules Trousers Company in Wellston; several brickyards in or near Oak Hill; and some small coal mines near Coalton. Both Globe and JISCO produced a specialty iron, known as Silvery Pig Iron, that was vital to the big steel mills in the east and south, which manufactured finished steel products.

The small village of Coalton, located about five miles from Jackson, is probably best known as the birth place of Ohio Governor

James A. Rhodes. Governor Rhodes served four terms as governor, but his terms were separated into two eight-year periods because of Ohio law which precluded a governor from serving more than two consecutive four-year terms. Coalton is also known as the place where the value of the cash register was first recognized. John H. Patterson owned a small general store in Coalton in connection with his coal mines. In order to stem losses in the store, he purchased three of the very first rudimentary cash registers. Mr. Patterson was so impressed by the cash registers that he bought the patents and the manufacturing rights and established what became the National Cash Register Company in Dayton, Ohio.

Jackson County was also home to numerous family-owned apple orchards as well as dozens of small farms that raised corn, potatoes, tomatoes, beans and other farm products. Held in late September each year, the Jackson County Apple Festival attracted thousands of visitors and featured booths in which orchard owners and various community groups sold apples and products made from apples.

Jackson, Wellston and Oak Hill high schools had a natural and intense athletic rivalry with the annual Thanksgiving Day football game between Jackson and Wellston culminating each team's season. The game was always played mid-morning, so the traditional turkey meal was delayed until mid-afternoon or even early evening for the families of the players, band members, cheerleaders and fans who attended the game.

Jackson County contributed more than its share of men and women to the war effort, either by direct military service or through work in the industries supplying the essential equipment needed by our own forces and those of our allies. Many Jackson County residents moved to the larger cities where planes, trucks, artillery, munitions, clothing and food were manufactured, packaged and shipped overseas. Accurate casualty data is hard to find, but an article in one of the county newspapers at the end of the war listed the following:[1]

Missing or prisoners of war 35
Killed in action 76
Died or killed in training 21

TOTAL 132

This author attempted to contact as many family members as possible of those Killed in Action, but was only able to establish contact with those whose vignettes are included in this chapter.

Private Paul L. Staton[2]
Headquarters Squadron
18th Bomb Wing

Pvt. Paul L. Staton was probably the first World War II casualty from Jackson County, Ohio. Private Staton was assigned to the Headquarters Squadron of the 18th Bomb Wing stationed at Hickam Field near Honolulu, Hawaii, when the Japanese attacked on Sunday, 7 December 1941. In addition to the Headquarters Squadron, the Wing also included the 18th Pursuit Group, the 4th Recon Squadron, and the 5th Recon Squadron. The Staton family was listening to the radio on 7 December when news

Pvt. Staton in uniform

of the surprise Japanese attack was broadcast and mentioned that Hickam Field had been hit by the attackers. The official message received by his family eight days later was terse with no details of how Private Staton was killed. The message did include information that his remains would be interred until "after the emergency was over" at which time the family could request that his remains be returned to the United States for burial. (Interesting to note, the referenced "the emergency" became World War II.)

Paul was the youngest son of Millard and Vina Staton, along with one older brother, Herman, and three sisters, Thelma, Helen, and Dorothy. Herman served as a Military Policeman during WWII, and Dorothy later served as an Army nurse. The family lived at Jefferson Furnace, a small community near Oak Hill, Ohio, in southeastern

Ohio, not far from the Ohio River. Paul's father was a veteran of the Spanish American War. He had celebrated his eighteenth birthday on the same day that the USS *Maine* was sunk in Havana Harbor, and enlisted shortly afterward. Millard also spent several years in the Philippines after the war.

Paul Livingston Staton was born in Kelsa, Virginia, on 22 November 1916, where his father worked at a lumber mill. His mother was a typical rural housewife, taking care of the family needs and all of the normal household chores. In 1920,

Herman and Paul Staton

the family moved to Robinson Creek in Pike County, Kentucky, where they again lived in a rural area and Millard worked in his father's "mercantile store," another name for what many of us would know as a "general store." The store served the basic needs of the families of coal miners living in that area. Paul and his siblings enjoyed the typical life of rural children during the ten years that the Staton family lived in Kentucky. They attended school and church, helped with the chores on a small farm, and played outside. Many friends and relatives still live in that area.

In 1930 the family moved to Oak Hill, Ohio, where the children attended public schools. All of the Staton children graduated from Oak Hill High School, with Paul graduating in 1936. While in school, Paul played varsity football, and continued to help with chores on the small family farm. He would frequently borrow his father's car to go to the movies in Oak Hill. Paul had many friends with whom he could hang out when not in school or helping on the farm.

Following graduation from high school, Paul joined the Civilian Conservation Corps (the CCC), which had been established as one of President Roosevelt's programs to combat the "Great Depression."

Not only did the CCC provide jobs and skills training for young men, but the projects provided public parks, cleared land for lakes and dams, and constructed other public facilities. Paul was assigned to work in Idaho clearing trees to make way for roads to be built in that area.

Returning to Oak Hill after his CCC experience, Paul was unable to find suitable work, so he decided to enlist. He made the short trip to Huntington, West Virginia, where he enlisted on 8 November 1939. Following his basic military training he was assigned to the Army Air Corps' 18th Bombardment Wing. In January of 1940, barely two months after his enlistment, his unit was ordered to Hickam Field, Hawaii, by way of the Panama Canal, reaching Hawaii in February 1940. Paul had an intense desire to become a pilot, so he paid $6.00 per hour for private flying lessons at the John Rogers Airport in Hawaii where he accumulated enough flying time to complete requirements for his basic pilot's certification.

Hickam Field was officially activated on 15 September 1938, and was the only field in Hawaii capable of handling the new, larger B-17 bombers. The first large contingent of twenty-one B-17D aircraft arrived at Hickam on 14 May 1941. By the time of the Japanese attack, the Army Air Corps in Hawaii had a contingent of over 750 officers and more than 6,700 enlisted men, as well as over 230 aircraft assigned to Hickam, Wheeler and Bellows Fields. Hickam Field, the main Army Air Corps base in Hawaii, was located about halfway between Honolulu and Pearl Harbor. This location and the fifty-one aircraft stationed there made Hickam Field a priority target for destruction by the Japanese. An additional twelve B-17 aircraft arrived from the United States on 7 December during the Japanese attack, but had to land immediately because they were almost out of fuel. Most of the twelve new planes were destroyed on the ground by the Japanese attackers without being able to contribute to the defense of Hickam Field.

Hickam Field suffered major property damage, lost most of its aircraft, had 139 men killed, and over 300 wounded during the Japanese attack. Most of the casualties at Hickam were eating breakfast in the dining hall when the Japanese bombed the base. The three airfields (Hickam, Wheeler and Bellows) were targeted by the

Japanese for two primary reasons: to destroy as many of our aircraft as possible; and to preclude U.S. planes from tracking the Japanese planes back to their aircraft carriers and attacking the Japanese fleet while their carriers were recovering planes from the strike force.

Shortly before notification of Paul's death, the family received a package from him in which he sent pictures of Hawaii, a photo of his unit, and the menu planned for his unit's Christmas dinner. After notification of his death, Paul's father said, "This is just the beginning." Mr. Staton probably did not realize the full extent to which his statement would apply. The United States lost over 291,500 killed in action and over 118,800 non-battle deaths before Japan surrendered in August of 1945. Paul's death caused great sorrow among his family and friends. To this day, he is still remembered by those who remain and by their families, to whom many fond memories of the friendly, hard-working young man have been passed down.

Following the end of hostilities, Paul's family elected to have his remains buried with those of other service men and women killed on 7 December 1941. Pvt. Paul Livingston Staton is buried at the National Memorial Cemetery of the Pacific, in Honolulu, Hawaii, more commonly known as "the Punchbowl." This cemetery, administered by the Veterans Administration, is one of only two permanent cemeteries for World War II casualties in the Pacific. The other cemetery, administered by the American Battle Monuments Commission, is located in Manila in the Philippines. The Punchbowl Cemetery is located in what was once an active volcano called Puowaina, which translates to "Consecrated Hill." The first World War II remains were interred on 4 January 1949 with the burial of 776 casualties of the Japanese attack on 7 December 1941. Famed World War II Correspondent Ernie Pyle is also buried there.

Private Staton is buried in Plot C, Row 0, Grave 201.

Pvt. Staton's grave marker in the "Punchbowl" cemetery, Hawaii. Photo by LTC H. J. Callahan, USAF (Retired)

First Lieutenant
Edwin Hurlbut Bicksler[3]
314th Fighter Squadron
324th Fighter Group

1LT Edwin Hurlbut Bicksler
was reported missing in action
on Palm Sunday, 18 April 1943.
Known to his family as Hurlbut,
his friends back home in Oak Hill,
Ohio, and in the service called him
"Bix." His remains were never recovered. The son of a Presbyterian
minister, it is somewhat of a para-
dox that "Bix" was shot down and
probably killed on Palm Sunday.
1LT Bicksler's military career
seems like a work of fiction that
might well form the basis for a
Steven Spielberg movie.

1LT Bicksler in RAF uniform.
Photo from booklet prepared
by his father following his
death

In August 1941, during the height of the Battle of Britain,
Bicksler, along with nine other young Americans, sailed for England
to join the Royal Air Force (RAF) in the desperate battle against
Hitler's Blitz. During the cross-Atlantic trip, the ten Americans were
split between two ships. Four of the original ten lost their lives when
one of the ships was sunk by Nazi submarines. Hitler's plan was to
destroy the RAF before attempting to invade and conquer Britain.
Eventually, enough Americans, Czechs and Poles joined the RAF to
form three fighter aircraft squadrons, which became known as "the
Eagle Squadrons," and Bicksler was a pilot in one of those squadrons. Some of America's greatest World War II Aces first flew with
the RAF in one of the three Eagle Squadrons.

From September 1941 until April 1942, the young Bicksler
flew fighter patrol missions over England and the English Channel
while learning how to best utilize his airplane's weapons and avoid
German fighters. During that same period, five of the remaining six

men who had joined the RAF with Bix were killed in action, including Bicksler's buddy and roommate, Ray Powell of Alabama. By the time Bicksler left England for Africa in April 1942, he was the only survivor of the original ten Americans.

While flying for the RAF in North Africa, Bicksler engaged the enemy in both Egypt and Libya. On 5 September 1942, Pilot Officer Bicksler was shot down by German Messerschmidt 109s. This action took place during what is called The Battle of El Alamein.

The following article from the *New York Journal* newspaper recounts Bicksler's story. A longer version of the Bicksler story appeared in the *London Times*, and the National Broadcasting Company (NBC) reported it in some detail during a 30 September broadcast.

Cairo, Sept. 30 (UP) –Pilot Officer Edwin H. Bicksler, of Oak Hill, Ohio, a volunteer with the RAF, is proud of his membership in the Late Arrivals Club—for fliers who make base after they are overdue—but his main desire is to climb back into a fighter plane and "get even."

> With his right leg in a plaster cast, Bicksler today described the dog fight he lost over enemy territory Sept. 5, and how he escaped being taken prisoner. He said, 'Cannon shells hammered through my plane and one exploded at my feet, smashing the controls and wounding me. I couldn't get out of the cockpit easily, and when I bailed out I dislocated my shoulder.' Bicksler said he hid himself until night behind enemy lines and then started crawling and hobbling toward his own lines. Suddenly an armored car loomed up in the night, heading in his direction. 'I thought it was goodbye to the war,' Bicksler said, 'but it turned out to be British.'
>
> As a result of his being shot down and making it back to British lines after the rest of his squadron, Pilot Officer Bicksler was officially inducted into the 'Late Arrivals Club.' His induction certificate states: 'In as much as he, in a Spitfire on September fifth 1942 when obliged to abandon his aircraft, on the ground or in the air, as a result of unfriendly action by the enemy, succeeded in returning to his squadron, on foot or by other means, long after his Estimated Time of Arrival, it is never too late to come back. This member is permitted to wear the Emblem of the Winged Boot on the left breast of his flying suit.'

1LT Bicksler in RAF uniform. Photo from booklet prepared by his father following his death

In January 1943, Bicksler was transferred to the U.S. Army Air Corps with the rank of first lieutenant and assigned to the 314th Fighter Squadron of the 324th Fighter Group flying the P40-F aircraft. His duty with the Americans was no less exciting than his time spent with the RAF. Lieutenant Bicksler's own flight log tells only part of the story, but sheds some light on the actions in which he took part. The following is an excerpt from his personal flight log after he had joined the 314th Fighter Squadron:

Tunisia, 1943, with the United States Army Air Force flying P40-F.

Mar 14—Gambut to Sirte. Landed on Sirte wheels up, out of gas. Available landing ground mined and US. (Author's Note: "US" may be his shorthand for unstable.)

Mar 29—Dive bombing mission. Bombed road north of Gaber. Hit truck and set it on fire. A lot of Flack [*sic*].

April 2—Fighter Sweep. Heavy Ack Ack encountered.

April 8—Bombed and straffed [*sic*] south of Sfay. Slight flack [*sic*]. Youngblood shot down.

April 13—Shipping patrol.

April 16—Shipping patrol. Ferry from Sekhia to El Djem.

The *Life* magazine issue of 5 July 1943 included an article on the 314th Fighter Squadron, which succinctly tells the story of the mission during which 1LT Bicksler was shot down and declared Missing in Action.

"The Palm Sunday Massacre"
(Author's Note: No corrections have been made to the article as it appeared.)

If only one mission is to be considered "314th Fighter Squadron's Greatest Moment" it would have to be the Palm Sunday Massacre, April 18, 1943, and even this mission was a joint effort. Intelligence had cracked the German code and were eavesdropping on their communications. It was discovered the Germans were planning a mass air transport evacuation from Tunis to Sicily. In preparation for this mission the 57th Squadron and the 314th were placed on alert as well as a squadron of RAF Spitfires based near Sousse. The 66th Fighter Squadron was the lead and low flying squadron. The 314th was the medium flying squadron, the 65th high flying squadron, the 64th flying top cover and the Spitfires flying above the 64th. The mission was briefed for the 64th and the Spitfires to concentrate on attacking the German fighter escort and the other three squadrons would attack the transports. The 314th pilots assigned to this mission follow:

"A Flight"	"B Flight"	"C Flight"
Phillips – flight leader	Powers – flight leader	Werner – flight leader
Stout – wing man	Huser – wing man	Yehle – wing man
Bicksler – element leader	Duffy – element leader	Everest – element leader
Warnke – wing man	McKnown – wing man	Whiting – wing man

The mission was scrambled at 1650 (4:40 PM) [*sic*] and the RAF Spitfire squadron rendezvoused with the P-40's over Sousse and took their position at the top of the formation. Dense flak was experienced after crossing the bomb line and continued until the formation was over the Bay of Tunis. At approximately 1745 (5:45 PM) the mission was on station and patrolling the area from Cape Bon to Tunis. An estimated formation of 100 Ju-52's was sighted with an estimated escort of 50 German fighters. Accounts vary as to the composition of the fighter force. One account says the force was composed of Me-109's, Me-110's and Macci 202's. However, Me-110's had never been seen in the theater and, while Macci-202's were in the theater, all the fighters shot down were Me-109's. The battle started and one might say attacking the slow forming Ju-52's was a "turkey shoot." Even though the 64th and the Spitfires kept many of the enemy fighters engaged several did break through to the battle taking place with the Ju-52's. There was bedlam and the Ju-52 formation turned east toward land and many crash landed on the Cape

Bon beaches. The P-40's and Spitfires returned to their bases at approximately 1900 (7:00PM). Total claimed victories were 58 JU52's and 16 Me-109's destroyed. This includes 314th claims of 23 Ju-52's and 2 Me-109's. The missing pilots and claims by flights follow:

"A Flight"	"B Flight"	"C Flight"
Capt Phillips – missing	Lt. Powers – 4 Ju-52's	Lt. Werner – missing
Lt. Stout – 3 Ju-52's	Lt. Huser – 1 Ju-52	Lt. Yehle – 1 Ju-52
Lt. Bicksler – missing	Lt. Duffey – 5 Ju-52's	Lt. Everest – 2 Ju–52's
Lt. Whiting – 3 Ju-52's	Col. McKnown – 2 Ju-52's	Lt. Warnke – 2 Ju-52's

Lt Huser claims 2 Ju-52's damaged and Lt. Everest claims 1 Ju-52 damaged.

Missing pilots claims not included. Col. McKnown was the Commander, 324th Fighter Group. Lt. Bicksler was a replacement pilot transferred from the RAF. Needless to say there was a big squadron celebration that night. Since the squadron had been in combat for just over a month that was considered pretty good scoring but the losses still had a sobering effect. The Germans had not forgotten us. They came back the next night and bombed and strafed us with Ju-88's. There was loss of property but no casualties in the 314th.

Edwin Hurlbut Bicksler was born on 26 February 1920, at the Greetingsville Manse, Clinton County, Indiana. His father, a Presbyterian minister, was Harry E. Bicksler and his mother was Margie. He had an older sister, Almeda, a younger sister, Margie, and a younger brother, Ned. In 1932 the family moved to the village of Oak Hill, Ohio, a small village settled by Welsh immigrants in Jackson County, located in southeastern Ohio, not far from the Ohio River. Edwin graduated from Oak Hill High School in 1937. A friend who still lives in Oak Hill, James Lloyd, provided the following insight into the young Edwin:

> When he was not into sports, he worked at the Parish of the Templed Hills property, which was a project his father started to combine five county churches into a shelter house in a nice

grove of trees on (Route) 279 east, about 2 miles outside of Oak Hill. They also built a Manse where the Bickslers lived. Bix worked there with the rest of us teenagers, when we could spare the time from the farm, improving the grove and building the shelter house. His father was a promoter who never ran out of ideas for us to do.

Bix was a typical preacher's son. Daredevil and ready to pull a trick on the rest of us when the chance arose. In the grove are many tall trees and there were rope swings hanging from many of them for the young to swing from. Bix was kind of a "muscle man" for he could pull himself by hand up the rope to the top with his legs in the sitting position. None of us could do this and he took every great joy in doing it in front of us to rub it in. (He) worked his way through Rio Grande School for the 2 years he attended. He was a very friendly lad, and I enjoyed his company tho he was 2 yrs older.

As noted by Mr. Lloyd, Bicksler enrolled at Rio Grande College, a two-year college located in the small village of the same name about midway between Jackson and Gallipolis, Ohio. During his two years at Rio Grande, Bix majored in elementary education and was active in extracurricular activities such as the College Christian Association, the Drama Club, and intramural sports. He played varsity football his second year. Following his two years at Rio Grande College, he entered The Ohio State University at Columbus, Ohio, in the fall of 1939. It was while he was at Ohio State that his interest in flying manifested itself and he became an Aviation Cadet.

After only one year at Ohio State, Bix was accepted in the Army Aviation Cadet Program and was assigned to Hicks Field, Texas, and then to Randolph Field, Texas. While at Randolph Field, Bix satisfactorily completed the academic regimen but failed to qualify for his wings because he had been forced to spend three weeks in the hospital suffering from pneumonia. His time spent in the hospital kept him from gaining the total number of flying hours required to be commissioned a second lieutenant and receive his Silver Pilot's Wings. It was during this time that he learned of the young Americans and Canadians who were leaving North America to fly with the Royal Air Force. He jumped at the chance and was soon on his way to fly with the RAF as a member of the Eagle Squadrons.

Following confirmation by the War Department of the presumed death of 1LT Bicksler, his father put together a fifteen-page booklet titled, *Life Record of First Lieutenant Edwin Hurlbut Bicksler.* Thanks to Mr. Lloyd, the author of this book was provided a copy of that booklet. On the frontispiece of the booklet, Reverend Bicksler included the following poem written by John Magee, another American fighter pilot who died while fighting with the RAF during the Battle of Britain:

> Up, up the long delirious burning blue
> I've topped the wind-swept heights with easy grace
> Where never lark, or even eagle, flew,
> And while with silent, lifting mind I've trod
> The high untrespassed sanctity of space,
> Put out my hand, and touched the face of God.
> By John Magee

1LT Edwin Hurlbut Bicksler is listed on the Tablets of the Missing at the North African American Cemetery and Memorial near Carthage, Tunisia.

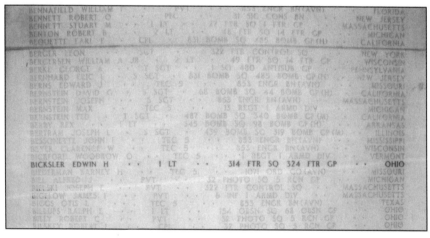

1LT Bicksler's name on the Wall of the Missing, North African American Cemetery and Memorial. Photo by ABMC

First Lieutenant George R. Crick[4]
27th Field Artillery Battalion
1st Armored Division
(Photo not available)

*"I remember the battle for Anzio as the most brutal in which I
fought during World War II. I also remember it as the most futile:
for fifty years its futility has haunted me."*
(Quoted from an article by William Woodruff
in the summer 1995 issue of *Joint Force Quarterly.*)

1LT George R. Crick was killed by an enemy sniper on 3 February
1944, near Anzio, Italy. The allied landings at Anzio on 22 January
1944, were an attempt to break the deadlock which stymied the Allied
advances along the German's Gustov Line near the village of Cassino,
Italy. The Allied plan, named "Shingle," called for a three-division
American force to land in the vicinity of the Anzio-Nettuno area
about eighty miles north of the Gustav Line and only thirty-five miles
south of Rome. The American Fifth Army Commander, LTG Mark
W. Clark, was intent on capturing Rome before the planned invasion
of France in the summer of 1944 captured the attention of the media.
Two divisions were landed at Anzio initially, but the planned landing of the 1st Armored Division, whose tanks were essential to support advancing infantrymen, was delayed because of a lack of landing craft. The Allied forces on the beaches were left without badly
needed armored support. Within two days of the Allied landings, the
German commander in Italy, Generalfeldmarschall (short title Field
Marshall) Albert Kesselring, quickly moved more than 40,000 troops
to the Anzio area in an attempt to throw the Allies back into the water.

Casualties among the Allied troops were high due to enemy attacks from the air, long-distance artillery, very accurate mortar fire,
and localized infantry attacks. Allied artillery units, such as the one
to which First Lieutenant Crick was assigned, would normally have
been positioned well back of the front lines, but the situation within
the Anzio beachhead was not normal. Two divisions and their supporting troops were all crowded into the very restricted beachhead
area. There was no "rear area" in the traditional sense. No place was

safe from the German artillery. Even wounded men on the beach waiting to be evacuated to Navy ships were hit by shell fragments, and Army nurses were killed while attending to the wounded. The German forces were often within shouting distance of the Allied lines, even when they were not attempting to launch attacks against the American positions.

There is no record available to describe First Lieutenant Crick's precise location or duties at the time he was hit by enemy sniper fire. Neither is it known if he was killed immediately or if he died at an aid station or other medical facility.

Not much is known of George's early years. His parents were divorced when he was about fifteen years old. Following his parents' divorce, George lived with the Wick family in Jackson, Ohio, the county seat of Jackson County. He earned his room and board with the Wick family by doing odd jobs, such as loading their furnace with coal and tending to some of Mr. Wayne Wick's vending machines. George was active in many extracurricular activities while attending Jackson High School. The senior year entry for George in the high school yearbook, called the *Osky Wow*, described him as "a man with personality plus." In addition to playing three years of varsity football, he was also on the track team his senior year. George served as home room president during his senior year and was active in the Latin Club, the Biology Club, the Library Science Club, and the Drama Club, holding offices in the latter three clubs.

After graduating from high school in 1933, the Wick family allowed George to live in one of the guest rooms at the Gibson House Hotel, which they owned and operated on Main Street in downtown Jackson. George continued to work for Mr. Wick and is remembered as a sweet kid, outstanding in everything

1LT Crick in Jackson High School football uniform. Photo from the high school yearbook, the Osky Wow

he did. In 1936, George enrolled at The Ohio State University in Columbus, Ohio, probably with financial help from the Wicks, majoring in Optometry. While at OSU he also enrolled in the Reserve Officers Training Corps (ROTC). After graduating from OSU, George was commissioned as a First Lieutenant in the artillery, immediately entered the Army, and was assigned to Fort Knox, Kentucky.

Although specifics are lacking, George eventually went overseas to Ireland with the 1st Armored Division. While in Ireland the division continued to conduct intense training for combat. The division then boarded ships and moved to North Africa where it took part in the Allied invasion. Not long after the invasion, LTG George Patton Jr. assumed command of the American corps there. In one of his letters to Mr. Wick, George provided his opinion of the new corps commander as follows:

> We have a new Corps Commander, Lt. Gen. Geo. Patton who seems very determined – to get himself some publicity – at our expense. Well, we who have about 5 months experience on him so far as being in the combat zone is concerned – can't be too enthusiastic about him.

Lieutenant Crick probably took part in the invasion of Sicily and the defeat of the German and Italian forces there before the Allies assaulted the Italian mainland. At one point, George sent a number of war trophies back to Mr. Wick in Jackson to include a red German banner with a swastika in the center.

1LT George R. Crick is buried in the Sicily-Rome American Cemetery and Memorial near Nettuno, Italy, in Plot H, Row 6, Grave 17.

1LT Crick's grave site.
Photo by ABMC

Sergeant Marion D. Ross[5]
748th Bomber Squadron
457th Bomb Group, Heavy

Sgt. Marion D. Ross was killed while serving as a waist gunner on a 457th Bomb Group B-17 participating in a raid on 25 February 1944, only the fourth 457th Group mission since going operational. The target for the day was a site near Augsburg, Germany, where the ME-210 jet aircraft was being manufactured. The group dispatched twenty-five of its planes for this mission. Sergeant Ross was a member of

Sgt. Ross in uniform

the crew of Aircraft No. 517, aircraft serial number 42-31517, piloted by Lt. James R. Chinn. In addition to Lieutenant Chinn and Sergeant Ross, the crew on that flight consisted of another eight men.

According to the mission narrative of the 457th Bomb Group as found at the unit's web site, http://457thbombgroup.org:

> Plane s/n 42-31517 was piloted on this mission to Augsburg by Lt. James R. Chinn. His plane was hit by flak over France and he had to leave the formation. He salvoed his bombs but was still not able to rejoin the formation and was attacked and shot down by fighter aircraft over Mont St. Martin, France. Seven of his crew were killed, one evaded and two were captured and became POWs.

(Author's Note: As so often happens when researching WWII records, there is a conflict in the records. This account says that one crew member evaded and two were captured. However, the same report from which this account is taken lists the names of two crew members who evaded and one who was captured. Regardless of this disparity, seven crew members, including Sgt. Marion Ross, were killed.)

During this mission, two of the twenty-five 457th Bomb Group aircraft were lost and an additional six suffered damage. A total of twenty crewmen were either killed or missing in action and another seven were wounded.

It should be noted that accounts of World War II bomber missions over enemy territory reflect the absolute importance of all bombers remaining in formation for maximum protection from enemy fighters. Formation flying could not protect against enemy ground fire (flak), but did offer a degree of protection against enemy fighters due to the sheer volume of fire the bombers' gunners could deliver against enemy aircraft. Once a bomber was hit and had to leave the formation, it lost this element of group protection and became a prime target for the enemy. Enemy fighters would then swarm around the damaged plane which was by that time flying alone and at a greatly reduced speed. The usual result was the loss of the straggler aircraft and most,

Sgt. Ross (third from left in back row) with flight crew.
Photo from www.457thbombgroup.org

if not all, of its crew. Disabled aircraft which managed to limp back to their home bases in England were most fortunate indeed.

Marion D. Ross was born in 1923 at Jackson, Ohio, the son of Bill and Sara May Ross. He had one sister, Vida, who was two years younger than Marion, and one brother, Bill, who was about twelve years younger. Marion's father worked at the Globe Iron Company, one of the two steel mills in Jackson. Many Jackson County men worked for either the steel mills or in the local coal mines which supported the steel mills. Marion dropped out of school after his sophomore year and went to work at Globe Iron Company. Marion loved to fish and hunt, but his passion was his Indian motorcycle. During his free time, Marion would ride his Indian all over the country roads of Jackson County and neighboring counties. Friends tell a story of Marion riding his Indian while standing on the seat instead of sitting on it. He was stopped once by the Ohio Highway Patrol and charged with reckless operation of a motor vehicle. Supposedly, that encounter with the law did not stop Marion from riding standing up.

A former Jackson resident wrote the author the following note:

> I am a former resident of Jackson and remember Marion Ross from the time when he worked part-time at my father's Sohio service station at the corner of Portsmouth and Pearl Streets. I was younger than Marion, but was in the same graduating class as his younger sister, Vida. I don't remember too much about Marion, but I do remember reading about his death during WWII. He seemed to be a very pleasant person and had many friends who would stop by the station to see him.

Marion Ross with his Indian motorcycle

After Marion was reported to be missing in action, his father took the Indian motorcycle completely apart and hung the pieces in a garage. His father told everyone that when Marion returned he would want to put the Indian back together. In a telephone conversation with Marion's younger brother, Bill (now deceased), this author was told that the disassembled Indian had hung in the garage (or barn) until just recently when he finally sold it to a man who had repeatedly offered to buy it. One can only guess what a 1930s vintage Indian motorcycle in almost new condition might bring on the market today.

Sergeant Ross's body was never recovered. His name is listed on the Tablets of the Missing at the Luxembourg American Cemetery and Memorial near Luxembourg City, Luxembourg.

Sgt. Ross's name on the Tablets of the Missing at the Luxembourg American Cemetery and Memorial. Photo by ABMC

Corporal Roland T. Crace Jr.[6]
831st Bomber Squadron
485th Bomb Group, Heavy

Cpl. Crace in uniform.
Photo clipped by family
from The Oak Hill Press,
a newspaper no longer
in business

Cpl. Roland T. Crace Jr., was reported Missing in Action as of 20 April 1944, when the U.S. Merchant Marine ship SS *Paul Hamilton* was sunk in the Mediterranean Sea on its way to Italy from the United States. Among the estimated 580 men killed were 154 officers and men assigned to the 485th Bomb Group, Heavy, with most of those members of the 831st Bomber Squadron. A history of the 485th Bomb Group, Heavy, posted on the Internet by the 485th Bomb Group Association at www.485thbg.org/485th_history.htm includes the following paragraph:

> While about 56 of the Headquarters detachment left Hampton Roads in late March, most of the men boarded troop ships on April 2d and began their overseas voyage. On the night of April 20th, 1944 the convoy was attached [*sic*] by JU-88 torpedo bombers in the Mediterranean Sea, off the coast of Algeria. Three ships were sunk, including the liberty ship SS *Paul Hamilton*. The ship carried 154 officers and men from the 485th Bomb Group, most of them from the 831st Squadron. The *Hamilton* exploded and sank within 30 seconds and all personnel aboard were lost. It would later become recognized as one of the greatest liberty ship disasters of WWII. The other 485th Group ground personnel, on various other ships in the convoy, made it safely to Italy and made their way to their new home in Venosa, Italy.

(Author's Note: In addition to the 580 men on board, the SS *Hamilton* also carried a cargo of high explosives and bombs. Crewmen from other ships in the convoy reported that after the torpedo from a JU-88 hit the SS *Hamilton* there was a tremendous explosion with plumes of black smoke sent high in the air and pieces

Night photo of the SS Hamilton *exploding after being hit by German torpedo. Photo from www.ibiblio.org/hyperwar/USN/ships*

of debris could be seen hitting the water where the ship had been. Once the smoke cleared, there was nothing left of the *SS Hamilton* or the 580 men on board. It must be assumed that the single torpedo scored a lucky hit on one of the cargo compartments holding high explosives or bombs.)

According to information now available, the sinking of the SS *Paul Hamilton* was the most costly Liberty Ship disaster as to loss of life in all of World War II. The crossing was to have been the ship's fifth when she was attacked and sunk about sundown on 20 April 1944. At least two other ships in the same convoy were sunk and another two were damaged but not sunk. Over 400 merchant ships were sunk in the Mediterranean Sea during the war, but none sustained the loss of life as did the SS *Paul Hamilton.*

Roland T. Crace Jr. was born at Eifort, Ohio, in Scioto County, on 10 June 1923, the second child of Roland T. Crace Sr. and Ethel Rowlins Crace. He had one older sister, Eva, two younger sisters, Opal and Dolly, and two younger brothers, Joe and Don. Roland's mother and father met in church and later were married in 1919. His father only completed the third grade, but after moving to Oak Hill, Ohio, in Jackson County, he opened a scrap metal business. Roland attended public schools and graduated from Oak Hill High School in 1941. He loved to hunt, fish and play football. He attended Ohio University at Athens, Ohio, for one year and then worked at the Goodyear Aircraft Plant near Akron, Ohio, before enlisting in November 1942. When he enlisted, Roland told his younger sister, Opal, to wait until he returned home and then they could both attend college together. When Roland did not return, Opal did not go to college.

He was initially assigned to Lowery Air Force Base near Denver, Colorado, for basic training as a ground crewman for the B-24 Liberator Bomber. Following his basic training, Corporal Crace served as an armorer instructor until receiving orders for deployment to Italy with the 831st Bomber Squadron. Corporal Crace never saw a single day of combat before losing his life at sea.

The name of Cpl. Roland T. Crace Jr. is located on the Tablets of the Missing at the North Africa American Cemetery and Memorial near Carthage, Tunisia, North Africa. Roland's sisters and brothers had five floral arrangements, one from each sibling, placed near the Tablets of the Missing in his memory.

Cpl. Crace's name on the Tablets of the Missing at the North American Cemetery and Memorial. Family photo

Private Alvin Theodore Swisher[7]
393rd Infantry Regiment
99th Infantry Division

Pvt. Swisher in uniform at age 19, 1944

Pvt. Alvin Theodore Swisher was killed in action on 17 December 1944, while fighting with the 2d Squad, 3rd Platoon, Company "F", 393rd Infantry Regiment of the 99th Infantry Division in Belgium. Private Swisher was only nineteen years old when he was killed.

The 99th Infantry Division was a "green" division that arrived in the Ardennes Region of Belgium in November 1944, and was assigned a nineteen-mile front to defend. This extreme frontage required the division to establish a series of strong points which were separated by large gaps where there were no defensive positions or troops. "F" Company had moved forward to the front along the Belgium-German border in mid-November. Combat action had been rather quiet until the unit was ordered to attack a German position on 13 December, only three days before the Germans unleashed their surprise attack in the Ardennes area. The division was told there would be a USO show in their area with movie star Marlene Dietrich on 16 December. However, on that day, the unit was ordered to move to a new position, in the vicinity of the twin hamlets of Rocherath and Krinkelt, Belgium, to hold a vital road area against a threat by the Germans. This "threat" became known as "the Battle of the Bulge." On 17 December, Alvin was serving as assistant to his squad's point man. The two of them moved ahead of the rest of the unit to determine if it was safe for the men to follow. As Alvin and the point man, J. R. McIlroy, were moving down a hill, they were ambushed by a large body of German SS troops. An enemy round hit McIlroy's Browning Automatic Rifle, shattering it. McIlroy at once hit the ground and Alvin lay across him in order to fire his own weapon at the enemy force. After only a minute or so, Alvin was hit between the eyes and died instantly. The rest of the unit took the Germans under fire, causing them to scatter, thus giving McIlroy time to escape up the hill toward the American lines.

Young Alvin Swisher on tricycle

Alvin Theodore Swisher was born on 1 December 1925, in Piketon, Ohio, in Pike County. His father was Alvin Swisher and his mother was Helen Chloe Brewer Swisher. Although Alvin had his father's name, he was not identified as "junior." He started school in Piketon, but the family later moved to Vinton County, in southeastern Ohio, a neighboring county to Jackson County.

Alvin attended Wilkesville High School in Vinton County and graduated on 24 May 1943. There were only eleven students, five girls and six boys, in his graduating class. His senior year report card shows that Alvin received three "A" minuses and one "B" minus in his core subjects and an "A" in health and physical education. Following graduation, Alvin worked on a nearby farm until July 1943 when he moved to Columbus, Ohio, to work for a freight company.

After about six months in Columbus, Alvin received his draft notice and was inducted into the Army on 28 February 1944. He was initially stationed at Fort Thomas, Kentucky, then transferred to Fort McClellan, Alabama. After time spent in Tennessee, probably on combat maneuvers, he was shipped overseas in October 1944 and joined the 393rd Regiment, 99th Infantry Division. His family first received information from the Army that Alvin was missing in action. It was not until 24 July 1945, five months after his death, that his mother received an official telegram from the Secretary of War advising that Theodore's status had been changed from Missing in Action to Killed in Action. The telegram included the following sentence, "The Secretary of War asks that he express his deep sympathy in your loss and his regret of unavoidable circumstances made necessary this unusual lapse of time in reporting your son's death to you." It is most likely the "unavoidable circumstances" were caused by the initial German success in the surprise attack on 16 December. The German forces probably occupied the area in which Private Swisher was killed, precluding an immediate search for his body. Although some U.S. dead were buried by local civilians, the remains of many casualties of the Battle of the Bulge were not recovered until after the Germans had been pushed back and the spring thaws enabled the Quartermaster Graves Registration units to make extensive searches for the remains of those who had been initially reported as Missing in Action.

Theodore's half brother, James L. Sorrell, states that although he was only four years old, he can remember watching Alvin shave the morning he left home. James also states that it was he who carried the telegrams into the house to their mother advising that Alvin was missing in action and later, killed in action.

Pvt. Alvin Theodore Swisher is buried in the Henri-Chapelle American Cemetery and Memorial near Henri-Chapelle, Belgium, in Plot E, Row 16, Grave 15. The following photo of his grave site was taken in 1989 by his former point man, J. R. McIlroy, when several surviving members of the 99th Infantry Division returned to Belgium to tour the battlefields where so many of their buddies were killed during the Battle of the Bulge and to visit their grave sites.

Pvt. Swisher's grave marker in Henri-Chapelle American Cemetery and Memorial, Belgium. Photo by James R. McIlroy

T/Sgt. Hill in uniform

Technical Sergeant Keith W. Hill[8]
751st Bomber Squadron
457th Bomb Group, Heavy

T/Sgt. Keith Wellington Hill was killed while serving as the radio operator on one of 36 B-17 bombers which participated in Mission No.173 conducted by the 457th Bomb Group on 13 January 1945. The target was an important bridge near Maximiliansau, Germany, on the main route from Metz, France, to Munich, Germany. The mission narrative of the 457th Bomb Group as stated on the 457th web site at jttp://457thbombgroup.org is quoted as follows:

Six inches of snow fell the morning of this flight to Maximiliansau, Germany. The runways had to be plowed (mostly shoveled) before takeoff could occur. The Allied troops had reversed the German Advance in the Ardennes and it was now time for the 8th (8th U.S. Air Force) to assist in bombing supply routes to the German army. The 457th was assigned the bombing of a bridge on the main route from Metz to Munich. The group put up 36 planes. The bomb run was perfect and the bridge received direct hits in clear weather. Flak was moderate but accurate. Seventeen planes suffered damage and one plane s/n 43-38795 exploded in mid air over the target. There were reports that possibly another plane had dropped its bombs on the exploding plane, but it is more likely that it received a direct flak burst in the bombbay. Because of very bad weather in England the group landed at Woodbridge, an English base near the coast.

Plane s/n 43-38795, 751st Squadron, piloted by Lt. Irwin C. Popham, was hit directly by flak over the target at Maximiliansau and exploded after dropping its bombs. The explosion was described by others as "one big ball of fire." Several who witnessed this said they thought he still had bombs in the bomb bay when the plane exploded and others thought perhaps bombs from another plane in the squadron had hit him. It seems the explosion was that severe. There were no survivors. (Author's

Note: Spelling and grammatical errors are in the original report as seen on the web site.)

Counting Sergeant Hill's plane, which was lost, a total of eighteen of the thirty-six aircraft were hit by enemy fire of one kind or another for a lost/damaged total of 50 percent of the 457th Bomb Group aircraft which took part in the mission.

Keith Hill in front of Campbell's Drug Store, Wellston, OH

Keith W. Hill was born in Wellston, Ohio, on 12 August 1922, to George Harlan (Holly) Hill and Richie Merle Ervin Hill. Keith was the fourth of seven children; four boys and three girls. His early years were spent near Akron, Ohio, where he was the city marbles champion and he took part in the national marbles championship contest in New Jersey. The family later moved to the small town of Wellston in southeastern Ohio, and Keith graduated from Wellston High School in 1941. He worked at Campbell's Drug Store in Wellston while he was in high school.

Two brothers also served in the military during World War II. Ronald was in the Navy, and Cedric was a paratrooper in the 82d Airborne Division. Both brothers survived the war. A third brother, Ervin, had bad eyesight and was classified as 4F.

After volunteering for the Army Air Corps, Keith completed his basic training and advanced training as a radio operator (possibly at Scott Air Base in Illinois, but this could not be confirmed). After being sent overseas to England, Keith was assigned to the 457th Heavy Bomb Group in the 751st Bomber Squadron, where he stayed until his death.

Keith's only living sibling, Mrs. Dianne Hill Swingle, who still lives in Wellston, Ohio, told this author that the Hill family was a very close-knit group. During warm summer evenings the entire family would gather on their back porch and sing, harmonizing to the popular songs of the time. When he wrote home, Keith still called

Keith Hill with family dog

his father Daddy, as he had when a young boy. He frequently sent small gifts home to his younger sisters, and Dianne recalls that she and her older sister, Beverlee, each received seashell necklaces and matching pocketbooks from Keith before he was sent overseas.

T/Sgt. Keith W. Hill's name is inscribed on the Wall of the Missing at the Lorraine American Cemetery and Memorial near St. Avold, France. The other crew members of his aircraft are either listed as Missing in Action or are not listed at all on the American Battle Monuments Commission web site at www.abmc.gov. There is no indication that the other crew members' bodies were ever recovered. It is not known why the remaining crew members' names are not listed on one of the memorial walls at one of the American cemeteries in Europe.

None of Technical Sergeant Hill's family has been able to visit the St. Avold American Cemetery and Memorial.

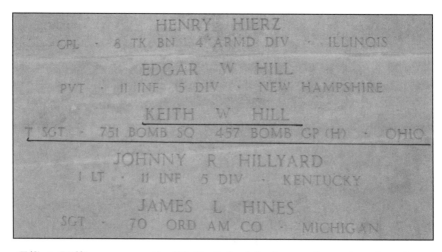

T/Sgt. Hill's name on the Wall of the Missing at Lorraine American Cemetery and Memorial near St. Avold, France. Photo by ABMC

Staff Sergeant Wilbur Ward[9]
Co. "B" 21st Infantry Regiment
24th Infantry Division

S/Sgt. Wilbur (Wib) Ward was killed in action on Lubang Island, the Philippines, on 2 March 1945, about five months before the Japanese surrendered, on the battleship USS *Missouri* in Tokyo Bay. Wib died as a result of a gunshot wound to the chest. S/Sgt. Ward's unit had been in almost constant combat against the Japanese since his regiment became engaged on Leyte Island in November 1944. One of the hundreds of hard fought, small unit battles on Leyte was that to push the Japanese troops off of what the Americans called "Breakneck

Wilbur Ward (left), his sister, Darlene, and best friend Dave Rose. Photo provided by Mrs. Dave Rose, Jackson, OH

Ridge," and the Japanese called the "Yamashita Line." Page 213 of the book *Children of Yesterday* by Jan Valtin, Readers' Press, New York, 1946, provides the following description of action in which Wib's company was involved during that battle:

> A company of Infantry was dispatched six-hundred yards to the rear of the Japanese defenses near Linon on a mission of disorganizing the retreat (of the Japanese). Led by Lieutenant Theodore Crouch of Owingsville, Kentucky, the company moved out stealthilly [*sic*] after sunset of November 15 in a forced march around hills and swamps. It circled the enemy flank and dug in astride the route of Japanese withdrawal. At noon November 16, falling back before the frontal attack, Japanese backed into Crouch's fire. The demoralized survivors fled into the bogs of the upper Naga River. The enemy had lost the passes over Breakneck Ridge. (Note: Lt. Crouch, S/Sgt. Ward's company commander, was later promoted to captain but was also killed.)

In a letter to this author's mother dated 16 August 1945, the 21st Infantry Regiment Chaplain, CPT H. R. Klann, stated:

> S/Sgt Ward went against an enemy position on Lubang Is, which is at the mouth of Manila Bay about 15 miles east of Corregidor, his platoon spearheading the attack. Heavy Jap fire met them in a narrow pass on a high hill. He was wounded four times, I believe, but before he died he gave the necessary orders to his men to withdraw, thus sparing further casualties. His Lieutenant and two other men died with him on that spot.
>
> I buried them all in temporary graves in the Lubang Municipal Cemetery. Later their caskets were removed and interred in the USAF Cemetery No. 1, San Jose, Mindanao Island.....I know that his company commander, Capt. Crouch, has written Wilbur's mother a few days after the conclusion of the Lubang Campaign. I'm sorry to say that Capt. Crouch has been killed two months ago in the Mindanao Campaign.

Why was it important to gain control of the small island of Lubang? It was only a little over 20 miles long and about 8 or 9 miles wide, but the island boasted of two airfields and a radio station, plus it provided an occupying force almost complete control of the essential route to Manila. Although the Americans knew that Japanese forces occupied Lubang, they did not know for sure how many Japanese were there or what the nature of any defensive positions might be. In the final accounting of action on Lubang Island, one source indicated that 8 Americans were killed and 18 wounded compared to over 200 Japanese killed and at least 6 Japanese prisoners.

After reading *Children of Yesterday*, it is this author's opinion that Chaplain Klann sanitized the facts of S/Sgt. Ward's death and burial to make Wib's death easier to accept by friends and family. This conclusion was reached based upon the following account of the action on Lubang Island as contained in the book:

> One patrol of four was lost in the mountains of Lubang. A rescue patrol of three set out to find them....One man of the rescue party was shot to death....The lost patrol of four was found days later, all four soldiers had been killed and mutilated beyond recognition.

If only eight Americans were killed on Lubang; and one of those was a member of the rescue party; and if S/Sgt. Ward's lieutenant and two other men were killed with him; then it stands to reason that S/Sgt. Ward, his lieutenant and the two other men killed with him must have been the "lost patrol," and their bodies were "mutilated beyond recognition." The chaplain did not disclose this information.

Also, the chaplain stated, as quoted above, "Later their caskets were removed and interred in the USAF Cemetery No.1, San Jose, Mindanao Island." This author requested and received from the Army Human Resources Command a copy of the Individual Deceased Personnel File (IDPF) pertaining to S/Sgt. Ward. Included in the file was QMC Form 1194 indicating that S/Sgt. Ward's remains were disinterred on 23 August 1948, that the remains were "skeletal" and the nature of burial had been "shelter half." (NOTE: Each infantryman carried one-half of a two-man "pup tent" called a shelter half.) Therefore, the facts do not support the chaplain's statement as to "their caskets" later being removed from Lubang. S/Sgt. Ward's skeletal remains were probably casketed for the first time when he was interred permanently in the Manila Cemetery. In fact, it appears that S/Sgt. Ward's remains were actually buried and reburied a total of four times as follows:

First: In the municipal cemetery on Lubang shortly after his death, as stated by the chaplain.

Second: In Plot 1, Row 13, Grave 184 at the San Jose Cemetery #1 on or about 17 March 1945, as stated in QMC Form 1194.

Third: In Plot 2, Row 8, Grave 976 at Manila Cemetery #2 on or about 10 December 1945, as stated in QMC Form 1194.

Fourth: In Plot F, Row 15, Grave 77 in the newly established Manila American Cemetery and Memorial sometime during 1948.

Should we fault the chaplain? Probably not. His letter served the purpose for which it was most likely intended. The letter informed people back home that S/Sgt. Ward had died while attempting to save other men in his unit, and he had received a Christian burial conducted by an Army Chaplain. Who would have benefited from the more gruesome facts that his body had been mutilated by the enemy and his remains buried in a piece of canvas?

Wilbur Ward was born on 25 August 1918, to Lot and Hope Rogers Ward. He had three brothers: Robert, who was wounded during World War II and discharged; Roger, who also served in the Army during World War II; and David, who was still in school when Wib was killed. He also had one married sister, Darlene Ward Crother.

After graduating from Oak Hill High School in 1936, Wib worked in Oak Hill until he enlisted in the National Guard on 15 October 1940. Following the sudden death of his father on 7 January 1941 at age 51, Wib received what was commonly called a "Hardship Discharge" as the sole means of support for his widowed mother and youngest brother. The record is not clear, but following that discharge he is believed to have worked as a bookkeeper for the Columbus and Southern Ohio Gas and Electric Company in Oak Hill until he reentered military service in 1943. He was accepted into the Naval Pre-Flight Cadet Program and was assigned to Wooster College, Wooster, Ohio, for ground school. Wooster College expected a peak enrollment of 600 Navy Aviation Cadets.

In a letter to his best friend's mother (this author's grandmother) Wib said:

> Speaking of classes or studies we really have plenty of them. For the dumb ones like myself they are really having a tough time getting their assignments. I failed almost all of my weekly tests last week, therefore, I am restricted from going on leave or liberty, as the Navy calls it, this weekend....I will probably be restricted again next week, but they can't keep you in more than 2 weeks in succession....Now don't get me wrong folks, it really isn't bad at all and the brighter side of it is that we get 8 hours of sleep every night, plenty of good food and a $40,000.00 education, that is if you get it all. Ha ha. I'm afraid I'll get kicked out before I get $40.00 worth of education if I don't started [*sic*] studying a little.

It is not known if Wib "washed out" of the Naval Pre-Flight Cadet Program or if the program was discontinued because of the extreme shortage of Infantry replacements for both the European and the Pacific Theaters of Operation in mid-1943. Regardless, Wilbur Ward ended up in the 21st Infantry Regiment of the 24th Infantry Division and achieved the rank of Staff Sergeant. The 24th Division was among the first divisions to face combat in World War II, and was also one of the last divisions to be engaged at the time the Japanese surrendered in August 1945. From the time the Japanese attacked Pearl Harbor on 7 December 1941, when three 24th Division men were killed and eight wounded, until the end of hostilities, over 1,300 24th Division men were killed in action and almost 4,900 were wounded, for a casualty total exceeding 6,200 men, not counting any men who may have been captured or were missing in action. Four 24th Division soldiers received the highest award the country had to offer, the Medal of Honor, all awarded posthumously.

In August 1945, Mrs. Ward received a government check for $44.50 representing the amount found in S/Sgt. Ward's personal effects following his death. She later received a small package containing the rest of his personal belongings: One cigarette lighter "Evans," five pictures, one driver's license, 4 Japanese Invasion Notes, one Franc [*sic*] note, and one wallet, brown leather, "poor." How must Mrs. Ward have felt as she held in her hands all that remained of her son?

When offered the choice in November 1947 of having S/Sgt. Ward's remains returned to the United States for burial in his home town or having him buried in the permanent American cemetery to be created in the Philippines, Mrs. Ward elected to have her son interred in the Manila American Cemetery and Memorial.

S/Sgt. Wilbur Ward is buried in Plot F, row 15, Grave 77.

S/Sgt. Ward's grave marker at the Manila American Cemetery and Memorial. Photo by MGT Bert Caloud, USMC (Retired)

Pfc. Coleman in uniform

Private First Class David D. Coleman[10]
383rd Infantry Regiment
96th Infantry Division

Pfc. David D. Coleman died on board a U.S. Navy hospital ship somewhere off the Coast of Okinawa Island in the Pacific on 11 April 1945. Pfc. Coleman was wounded 4 April while fighting to push the Japanese defenders off of Kamizama Ridge. His parents were later informed that Pfc. Coleman was buried at sea on 12 April according to the rites of his faith, and with full military honors.

The 96th Infantry Division previously participated in the invasion of Leyte Island in the Philippines on 20 October 1944. The division was engaged in almost continuous small unit actions until capturing the strongly defended Chalk Ridge on 12 December. The division then spent about ninety days clearing remaining pockets of Japanese troops and preparing for the next major combat action, the invasion of Okinawa.

The Okinawa invasion, code named Operation Iceberg, was to become the largest amphibious assault and the last major ground combat action in the Pacific Theater of Operations. It also involved the largest naval force utilized in the Pacific with well over 1,300 ships, including more than forty aircraft carriers. More than 182,000 ground troops from four Army infantry divisions and three Marine divisions made the assault on Easter Sunday, 1 April 1945. The immediate objective was the capture of Yontan and Kadena Airfields. The two airfields were captured very quickly. So quickly, in fact, that one Japanese pilot supposedly landed, exited his plane, and demanded to be refueled at once. He was killed before he could draw his weapon. For the first three days, little opposition was offered by the Japanese, allowing the Americans to establish the beachhead and land additional troops and supplies. The Japanese defenders, numbering about 100,000, elected not to oppose the beach landings, but had prepared a strong defense in depth consisting of an extensive tunnel system, artillery positions, and fortifications for machine guns and mortars.

On 4 April, while the 96th Infantry Division was moving inland, several hundred yards to the rear of the front line units, the Japanese suddenly launched an artillery barrage. It was during this heavy shelling that Pfc. Coleman was severely wounded and subsequently evacuated to an offshore hospital ship where he succumbed on 11 April 1945.

The fight to capture Okinawa and its several smaller offshore islands resulted in one of the bloodiest battles of World War II. After action reports indicate that almost 13,500 Army, Navy, and Marine troops were killed in action and more than 57,000 suffered wounds, combat fatigue, or accidental injury. The 96th Infantry Division alone suffered more than 1,600 killed or missing and over 5,600 wounded in action. Four 96th Division soldiers received the Medal of Honor for heroic action during the battle, two were awarded posthumously. A U.S. Army Okinawa Battle Monument was dedicated on 21 June 1995 at Torii Station, Okinawa. One of the plaques on the monument pertains to the 96th Infantry Division. That plaque reads as follows:

Deadeyes
Hereabouts, the 96th Infantry Division
Suffered over 10,000 casualties.
Their sacrifices testify to an
Unsurpassed measure of
Devotion, Pride and Courage.

David D. Coleman was one of ten children born to John and Sarah Leonard Coleman of Oak Hill, Ohio. There were seven boys and three girls, but one son died in infancy. (Author's Note: The one living Coleman sibling, Mrs. Gladys Hawkins, can recall seeing a photo of the dead infant in his tiny casket.) The Colemans lived on a small farm located on Rural Route 2 between the village of Oak Hill and what is now Lake Jackson. The farm house did not have electricity, running water or indoor plumbing. The family did not even have a well. Drinking and cooking water was carried in buckets from a nearby spring, and Mrs. Coleman collected rain water in barrels to use when washing the family's clothes. She had no washing machine, only a metal tub and a washboard. They did own one battery-powered radio which provided news and entertainment.

In addition to operating the small family farm and keeping cows, pigs and chickens, Mr. Coleman was employed by the Works Progress Administration (the WPA) during the Depression in order to earn cash money. It is not clear if David graduated from high school, but it is known that he joined the Civilian Conservation Corps (the CCC), as did thousands of other young men who could not find jobs during the Depression. Those young men lived in camps under Spartan conditions while working to build parks, lakes, roads and other public facilities. In addition to shelter and food, the men received a small stipend which most sent back home to their families.

Mrs. Hawkins recalls that shortly after the Japanese bombed Pearl Harbor, David and three of his brothers entered the military service. She feels sure they were drafted, but it is conceivable that one or more of the four may have enlisted. One of David's brothers, Charles, was wounded on Okinawa on 19 April 1945, only eight days after David died of his wounds. Mrs. Hawkins advised that David and Charles had seen each other briefly after the invasion and before David was wounded.

Pfc. David D. Coleman's name is inscribed on the Tablets of the Missing in the National Military Cemetery of the Pacific, Honolulu, Hawaii. No member of the Coleman family has been able to visit the cemetery.

*Pfc. Coleman's name on the Tablets of the Missing
at the "Punchbowl" Cemetery, Hawaii.
Photo by LTC H. J. Callahan, USAF (Retired)*

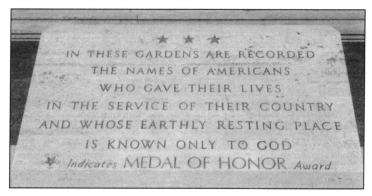

*Memorial stone to the missing at the "Punchbowl" Cemetery,
Hawaii. Photo by LTC H. J. Callahan, USAF (Retired)*

NOTES

[1] Information obtained from the Oak Hill, OH, Public Library microfilm files of the now defunct *Oak Hill Press* newspaper.

[2] Family information and photos related to Pvt. Staton provided by Ms. Linda Jones of Oak Hill, OH, niece of Pvt. Staton and by Mr. James Lloyd, also of Oak Hill, OH.

[3] Family information and photos obtained from booklet about 1LT Bicksler published by his father following 1LT Bicksler's death. The booklet was made available by Mr. James Lloyd, Oak Hill, OH, a friend of 1LT Bicksler.

[4] Family information related to 1LT Crick was provided by Mr. Carl Sears, Jackson, OH.

[5] Family information and photos related to Sgt. Ross provided by Mr. Bill Ross, Jackson, OH, brother of Sgt. Ross. (Note: Mr. Bill Ross is now deceased.)

[6] Family information and photos related to Cpl. Crace provided by Mrs. Opal Crabtree, Oak Hill, OH, sister of Cpl. Crace.

[7] Family information and photos related to Pvt. Swisher provided by Mr. James L. Sorrell, Wellston, OH, half-brother of Pvt. Swisher.

[8] Family information and photos related to T/Sgt. Hill provided by Mrs. Dean Swingle, Wellston, OH, sister of T/Sgt. Hill.

[9] Family information related to S/Sgt. Ward provided by Mr. James Lloyd, Oak Hill, OH, a friend of S/Sgt. Ward.

[10] Family information and photo related to Pfc. Coleman provided by Mrs. Gladys Coleman Hawkins, Columbus, OH, sister of Pfc. Coleman, and by Mrs. Charlene Wolford, Jackson, OH, niece of Pfc. Coleman.

Chapter Eight

THE AMERICAN BATTLE MONUMENTS COMMISSION[1]

"In peace, sons bury their fathers,
In war, fathers bury their sons."
Herodotus of Halicarnassus,
Greek researcher and storyteller.

The American Battle Monuments Commission (ABMC) was established by Congress in 1923. Congress recognized that a federal agency was needed to be responsible for the proper establishment, operation and maintenance of the various cemeteries, memorials, and monuments, which had been and would be established to honor the dead from World War I. At the end of the "War to End All Wars," eight permanent American cemeteries had been established on foreign soil by the War Department for the dead of that war. The ABMC, under its first chairman, General of the Armies John J. (Blackjack) Pershing, assumed the responsibility for a commemorative program to erect nonsectarian chapels in each of the eight cemeteries, landscape each cemetery, and erect eleven separate monuments and two tablets in Europe, as well as an American Expeditionary Forces Memorial in the United States. General Pershing was appointed to the Commission Board by President Warren G. Harding because of the general's reputation, his military background, and his deep personal interest in honoring the young men who served under him and lost their lives during the war. General Pershing was elected chairman by the other commission members. As a result of the outstanding accomplishments of the ABMC staff and personnel working in the overseas areas, a Presidential Executive Order was signed by President Roosevelt in 1934, formally transferring the eight cemeteries to the ABMC. The Presidential Executive Order also made the commission responsible for the design, construction, operation, and maintenance of future permanent American military cemeteries erected in foreign countries.

By the end of World War II, hundreds of temporary cemeteries had been established in Europe, the Mediterranean, North Africa and the Pacific. Some contained thousands of graves, while others contained less than 100. In addition, many remains were buried in remote towns and villages by the local residents. By 1947, the Secretary of the Army, in concert with the ABMC, designated fourteen locations in various foreign countries to become permanent cemeteries whereby next of kin could elect to have their loved ones buried with their comrades near the area in which they had been killed. Public Law 368, enacted by the 80th Congress of the United States, authorized the return and burial, at government expense, of American personnel who had been buried in temporary burial grounds. If the next of kin (normally either parents or spouses) elected to leave their loved ones overseas, that decision was final and could not be changed at a later date. A similar program was authorized by Public Law 389 of the 66th Congress of the United States after World War I. Following both wars, over 50 percent of the next of kin elected to have their loved ones returned to the United States for final burial. One very important difference between the two repatriation programs was that following World War I, mothers and wives who elected to have their loved ones buried in overseas cemeteries were offered a government-paid trip to visit the grave of their sons or husbands at the permanent overseas cemetery. Such a program was not deemed feasible following World War II. This was due to the larger number of service members who had been killed in action, the expense of such a program, and the fact that World War I American casualties had been limited, in the main, to Europe, while World War II casualties covered a large portion of the globe.

The mission of the ABMC, as stated in its Fiscal Year 2007 Annual Report, is to:

- Design, construct, operate, and maintain permanent American military burial grounds in foreign countries.
- Establish memorials outside the United States where American armed forces have served since April 6, 1917, the date of U.S.

entry into World War I, and within the U.S. when directed by public law.

- Control the design and construction on foreign soil of U.S. military monuments and markers by other U.S. citizens and organizations, both public and private.
- Encourage U.S. government agencies and private individuals and organizations to adequately maintain monuments and markers erected by them on foreign soils.

The Commission also administers trust funds to:

- Build memorials authorized by Congress, but financed primarily from private contributions, commemorative coin proceeds and investment earnings.
- Decorate grave sites with flowers from private contributions.
- Maintain and repair non-federal war memorials with private contributions.

The Commission's policies are established by the Board of Commissioners, composed of eleven members appointed by the President of the United States for an indefinite period. Members serve without pay. The chairmen of the commission, elected by the other commission members, have all been well-known military leaders whose own service to the United States was a testimonial to their abiding interest in the preservation of these cemeteries and memorials as a tribute to the young Americans who had sacrificed their lives in foreign lands. A listing of the past Commission Chairs amounts to a Whose Who of our military leadership for the past eighty-five years:

General of the Armies John J. Pershing........... 1923 to 1948
General George C. Marshall........................... 1948 to 1959
General Jacob L. Devers................................ 1959 to 1969
General Mark W. Clark................................. 1969 to 1985
General Andrew J. Goodpaster...................... 1985 to 1991
General P. X. Kelley .... 1991 to 1994
General Frederick F. Woerner........................ 1994 to 2001
General P. X. Kelley (second term)................ 2001 to 2005
General Frederick M. Franks Jr. .... 2005 to 2009

Members of the commission are listed on the commission web site at www.abmc.gov.

The ABMC currently manages a total of twenty-four cemeteries in foreign countries. In each case, the use of the land upon which the cemetery lies was granted in perpetuity to the United States by that country, and its use is free of charges or taxation. Therefore, each U.S. service member buried in a foreign country is actually interred on American soil. Of the twenty-four overseas cemeteries, there are eight World War I cemeteries of which one also has twenty-four World War II burials; fourteen World War II cemeteries; and two other cemeteries (one in Mexico City for deceased military from the Mexican War and one in Panama for American veterans and workers on the Panama Canal). Each permanent cemetery also has a memorial which lists the names of those Americans whose remains have not been found or who were buried at sea. In the event that remains are subsequently located, an appropriate designation is added to the memorial on which that person's name appears. Chapter Nine provides a complete listing of World War II cemeteries and the number of Americans interred or memorialized at that location. Total expenditures by the Commission in Fiscal Year 2007 amounted to $61,516,195.00.

The Commission also manages a total of twenty-five memorials, monuments or markers as well as four non-federal memorials. Although not commonly known, the ABMC also was responsible for the design and construction of the Korean War Memorial and the World War II Memorial, which are located on the National Mall in Washington, D.C. Both of those outstanding memorials are currently operated and maintained by the National Park Service.

As noted above, the ABMC maintains an excellent web site at www.abmc.gov. Many services are available to next of kin or other interested parties at the web site to include detailed information on each cemetery and memorial, as well as the names of all persons interred at each cemetery. By entering the ABMC web site, clicking on WWII, and then entering the name of a person thought to be buried overseas in the format described, one can locate the exact burial location, plot, row and grave of the person in question.

Upon request by next of kin or close family friends, the ABMC will provide a lithograph print of the cemetery in which their loved one is buried with a photo of that person's grave marker superimposed on the cemetery lithograph. Provided free of charge, the full color lithograph is suitable for framing. The ABMC will also obtain a floral display to place on individual grave sites upon submission of a simple request form and provision of the required funds. The author and his wife were present at the Epinal American Cemetery and Memorial in France when a family arrived to place a floral tribute on their loved one's grave site. We were impressed by the very high quality of the wreath and the personal services afforded the family by cemetery staff. A complete listing of all services available can be seen at the ABMC web site (www.abmc.gov), or you can call the ABMC office in Arlington, Virginia, at 703-696-6897.

NOTES

[1]   All information related to the American Battle Monuments Commission was obtained from the commission's annual reports, pamphlets available to the general public, and the commission's excellent web site, which contains detailed information as to the burials at each cemetery, descriptions of each cemetery or memorial, and a short video describing each cemetery.

Chapter Nine

PERMANENT CEMETERIES OF WORLD WAR II[1]

"What a cruel thing is war:
to separate and destroy families and friends,
and mar the purest joys and happiness
God has granted us in this world;
to fill our hearts with hatred
instead of love for our neighbors, and
to devastate the fair face of this beautiful world."
General Robert E. Lee

The American Battle Monuments Commission (ABMC) is responsible for the administration of fourteen World War II cemeteries and five memorials, which contain the remains of over 93,000 dead and recognizes the names of almost 79,000 missing. An additional 13,000 World War II dead are buried in the National Memorial Cemetery of the Pacific in Honolulu, Hawaii, which is administered by the Department of Veterans Affairs (the VA). The ABMC web site at www.abmc.gov contains both general and detailed descriptions of each cemetery, cemetery photos, and a short video describing each cemetery. The cemetery descriptions can be downloaded or interested parties can request copies from the ABMC Headquarters in Washington, D.C.

The following points of general interest relate to the World War II cemeteries and memorials:

• The Manila Cemetery has the largest number of burials (17,202), the largest number of missing (36,285), and the largest combined total of dead and missing (53,487). The number of missing cited at the Manila Cemetery is almost one-half of the total still listed as missing at all World War II Cemeteries.

• The Normandy Cemetery has the largest land area (172 ½ acres).

- Three cemeteries have a larger number of missing than burials:
    Manila with 36,285 missing and 17,202 dead
    Cambridge with 5,127 missing and 3,812 dead
    North Africa with 3,724 missing and 2,841 dead

- The Rhone Cemetery is the smallest cemetery in acreage (12 ½ acres), the number of burials (861), the number of missing (294), and the combined number of dead and missing (1,155).

- The Cambridge Cemetery has the largest number of missing (5,127) of any of the European cemeteries. It includes naval losses during the Battle of the Atlantic and air crew losses from the European bombing campaign.

- The Lorraine Cemetery has the largest number of burials in Europe (10,489).

- The total acreage of all World War II cemeteries under the administration of the American Battle Monuments Commission is 894.6 acres.

- The American Battle Monuments Commission Memorial at the National Memorial Cemetery of the Pacific in Honolulu contains the names of 18,096 World War II missing, as well as 8,200 missing from the Korean War and 2,504 missing from the Vietnam War.

- If remains of those listed as Missing in Action are subsequently identified, a small brass rosette is placed beside that person's name on the Walls of the Missing.

The names, locations, and a basic description of each of the fourteen World War II cemeteries and four separate memorials follow in alphabetical order:

The Ardennes American Cemetery and Memorial

Located near the southeast edge of Neupre, about twelve miles southeast of Liege, Belgium, the cemetery covers ninety acres and contains the burial locations for over 5,300 persons. Many of the dead were killed in the fierce fighting that took place in December 1944 and January 1945 during the last-gasp German offensive which came to be known as the Battle of the Bulge. The memorial is one of the more imposing of all World War II overseas cemetery memorials. It is a massive square stone structure with a large American Eagle facing visitors as they approach the cemetery. A chapel, with three large wall maps inside, is contained within the memorial. On the outside of the memorial are granite slabs on which are listed the names of 462 missing. On the side of the memorial facing the graves are the very colorful insignia of the major U.S. units that operated in this region during the war. The headstones are arranged to form a Greek cross when seen from the air.

The Brittany American Cemetery and Memorial

Located roughly 220 miles from Paris, this cemetery is about 1 ½ miles southeast of St. James, 12 miles south of the city of Avranches. The cemetery, which occupies 28 acres of what was once rolling farm lands, contains the graves of over 4,400 dead, many of whom were killed during the fight to expel the Germans from Normandy and Brittany during the summer of 1944. The somewhat drab-looking memorial/chapel is constructed of gray granite and is typical of the construction found throughout Brittany. The chapel's bell tower rises about 100 feet, and its lookout area offers a panoramic view of the Brittany countryside, as well as a full sweep of the more than 4,400 headstones. Outside the chapel is a memorial terrace whose retaining walls list the names of 498 missing. Only a short distance north of the cemetery is one of the iconic structures in France, Mont St. Michel.

The Cambridge American Cemetery and Memorial

This cemetery is located 60 miles north of London, and about 3 miles west of historic Cambridge, England, home to the famed university of the same name, which donated the property for use as an American cemetery. The cemetery is about 60 miles north of London. Over 3,800 graves are arranged in long, sweeping curves along the sloping grounds which cover a total of 30 ½ acres. Tablets of the Missing list the names of 5,127 personnel whose remains were not recovered, or, if recovered, could not be identified. Most of the missing lost their lives during naval action in the Atlantic Ocean or during the bombing campaigns over northeast Europe. The large memorial itself contains a chapel, two large maps that depict the actions that took place, beautiful stained glass windows, and a mosaic ceiling which honors the dead. The western and southern edges of the cemetery are still bordered by typical British woodlands.

The Epinal American Cemetery and Memorial

About four miles southeast of Epinal, France, and about 230 miles southeast of Paris, the cemetery is situated on over forty-eight acres of land on a plateau roughly 100 feet above the Moselle River. Established in October 1944, in support of the U.S. Seventh Army during the thrust from the Rhone River valley of France toward Germany, Epinal is located in the foothills of the Vosges Mountains, the location for some of the heaviest fighting that occurred in late 1944 and early 1945 as American forces were attempting to push the Germans back across the Rhine into the German homeland. Over 5,200 graves are situated in two large plots in a beautiful tree-lined mall. The memorial itself is a large rectangular structure containing a chapel, a portico, and a museum room with mosaic maps of the operations that took place over northeastern France and across the Rhine River into Germany itself. The walls of a Court of Honor list the names of 424 missing. It was from this cemetery in May of 1958 that thirteen unknown remains were selected, from which the Commanding General of the U.S. Army Communications Zone,

Europe, chose one casket to represent the European Theater in the process by which the World War II Unknown Soldier was selected. Near the northernmost part of the cemetery mall is a raised circular plaza over which flies the American flag. From this plaza one has an excellent view of the beautiful Moselle River valley.

The Florence American Cemetery and Memorial

This cemetery is located along the Via Cassia, a roadway used by the Romans, and near the Rome-Milan Autostrada about 7 1/2 miles south of Florence. Wooded hills frame most of the 70 acres of cemetery area with a small stream flowing past the main entrance. The headstones of over 4,400 honored dead are arranged in rows seeming to "march" up the gradual slope toward the memorial. In the center of the memorial is one tall stone pylon with a sculpture on top. Two open court areas flank the pylon and are joined by the Tablets of the Missing, listing the names of 1,409 Americans whose remains are still missing or could not be identified. Many of those buried here died during the fighting that took place between the Alps and Rome. Others died during the heavy fighting in the Apenine Mountains not long before the war ended. As in all overseas American cemeteries, there is a small chapel decorated with marble and a beautiful mosaic.

The Henri-Chapelle American Cemetery and Memorial

Located about two miles northwest of the village of Henri-Chapelle, Belgium, and only about seven miles from the border with Germany, the cemetery contains the graves of almost 8,000 Americans. Most were killed during efforts to force the Germans back into Germany and during the fierce battle to capture the town of Aachen. Other honored dead buried here lost their lives during the Battle of the Bulge. Entering the burial area through the long colonnade memorial structure, visitors see the headstones arranged in a gentle curve and sloping downhill across fifty-seven acres of beautifully manicured fields. Within the colonnade itself are a small chapel and a map room. The vertical slabs of the colonnade list the names of 450 missing in action. In 1947, the first American dead from World War II were disinterred from Henri-Chapelle and taken to the port city of Antwerp, Belgium, for return by ship to the United States and burial in cemeteries of their loved ones' choosing.

The Lorraine American Cemetery and Memorial

This cemetery is located less than a mile north of St. Avold, France, and about 220 miles east of Paris. About 10,500 U.S. dead, the largest number of graves of any single U.S. Cemetery in Europe, are buried in over 113 acres. The headstones occupy seven different plots sloping downward from the tall memorial structure. The memorial has a large carved stone relief of the Roman soldier, St. Nabor, seemingly keeping watch over the headstones in the cemetery. Inside the memorial is a small chapel and ceramic military operations maps showing the actions that took place in the area. Outside the memorial and parallel to the front of the structure are the Tablets of the Missing with the names of 444 Americans inscribed.

The Luxembourg American Cemetery and Memorial

The small Principality of Luxembourg is tucked in an area adjacent to Belgium, France and Germany. Within the cemetery, located only three miles east of historic Luxembourg City, over 5,000 Americans are buried on the 50 ½ acres surrounded by densely wooded areas. Near the main entrance to the cemetery is a white stone chapel sited on a raised circular base. The chapel's stained glass window depicts the various unit insignia of the American units that fought in the area. Outside the chapel, on a lower plot of ground, are two big pylons made of stone, with inlays of various shades of granite showing the actions of the American forces that fought through this area. Also inscribed on the same pylons are the names of 371 missing Americans. Many of the dead and missing memorialized here were killed during the Battle of the Bulge. Although general officers are buried in a number of U.S. overseas cemeteries, one of the more famous of our World War II generals, GEN George S. Patton Jr, is buried in this cemetery. The headquarters for General Patton's Third U.S. Army was located in Luxembourg City in December 1944, when Hitler launched the surprise attack that came to be known as the Battle of the Bulge. Patton quickly directed an armored thrust aimed at the southern flank of the German forces in the bulge and fought his way to relieve the 101st Airborne Division which had been holding against heavy odds in the vital Belgium crossroads town of Bastogne. General Patton died almost a year to the day later in 1945, as a result of injuries suffered when his staff car was hit by a U.S. army truck. General Patton was initially buried among all the other graves, but his remains were later moved to an area near the entrance to the burial plots. He now rests in a location overlooking all the other marble crosses and Stars of David, much like a general reviewing his troops.

The Manila American Cemetery and Memorial

Located near the Philippine capital city within what was once Fort William McKinley, the cemetery grounds cover 152 acres and are situated on top of a plateau, visible from all four points of the compass. More than 17,200 graves are sited in eleven plots among tropical shrubs and trees. The eleven plots form a rough circular pattern when viewed from the air. Many of those buried here were killed while serving under Gen. Douglas MacArthur as he drove the Japanese from New Guinea and the Philippines. A chapel is located approximately in the center of the cemetery. On a terrace in front of the chapel are two large hemicycles (semicircles) which contain twenty-five mosaic maps of the battles fought in the Pacific, India, China, and Burma. Inside the semicircle of battle maps are located rectangular limestone piers on which are recorded the names of 36,285 of the missing. In total, the Manila Cemetery contains the remains or names of almost 53,500 Americans killed in the Pacific area. No other overseas cemetery comes close to this number of dead and missing.

The Netherlands American Cemetery and Memorial

Located in the village of Margraten, the Netherlands, six miles east of Maastricht and about 250 miles from Paris, the tall memorial tower is visible before reaching the entrance to the cemetery. Upon entering the 65 acres of cemetery grounds, visitors see a beautiful Court of Honor with a pool reflecting the memorial tower. To the right of the tower is a museum with three engraved maps of the military operations of American forces in this area of the Netherlands, Belgium and Germany. Alongside the Court of Honor are two Tablets of the Missing which list 1,722 names. Inside the memorial tower itself is a small chapel which contains a beautiful light fixture, altar candelabra, and a flower bowl, all presented by the government of the Netherlands and local provincial governing bodies. The cemetery is divided into sixteen separate plots, which hold the graves of more than 8,300 Americans arranged in long, gentle curves, with a wide, tree-lined mall leading to an American flag.

The Normandy American Cemetery and Memorial

Originally designated as the St. Laurent Cemetery, a temporary cemetery established by the U.S. First Army days after U.S. troops landed on Omaha Beach, this cemetery became one of the permanent cemeteries following the end of hostilities. Visitors can see the D-Day landing beaches at the foot of the bluff on which the permanent cemetery is now located. The cemetery lies just east of the village of St. Laurent-sur-Mer and about 170 miles west of Paris. Occupying 172 1/2 acres, it has the largest ground area of any World War II overseas cemetery. Almost 9,400 Americans are buried here, and the names of an additional 1,557 are listed on the Walls of the Missing in a small garden just to the rear of the memorial. The memorial structure is a semicircular colonnade with huge engraved maps on each end. In the center of the colonnade is a striking bronze statue of a young man titled "Spirit of American Youth." In front of the statue, as one looks out on the marble crosses and Stars of David, is a reflecting pool, and beyond the pool, about in the middle of all of the grave markers, is a small circular chapel. Although the Lorraine Cemetery has the largest number of burials of all the World War II European cemeteries (almost 10,500), the Normandy Cemetery has the largest total number of dead and missing combined (10,944). The Normandy Cemetery contains the remains of two sons of the American President, Theodore Roosevelt: Brig. Gen. Theodore J. Roosevelt (Teddy), recipient of the Medal of Honor for his heroic actions on the beach during the D-Day landings on 6 June of 1944, who died of a heart attack on 12 July 1944; and Quentin Roosevelt, the older brother of Teddy, who was killed during World War I when his plane crashed in eastern France. At the request of his father, the former president, Quentin was buried on the same field where he had died in 1918, but his remains were reburied next to his younger brother following World War II. Also buried side by side in the Normandy Cemetery are the two Niland brothers, Sgt. Robert J. Niland, killed on 6 June 1944, and his brother, 2LT Preston T. Niland, killed on 7 June 1944, about whom the movie, "Saving Private Ryan" was loosely based. Because of its location on one of the D-Day beaches, its proximity to Paris, and the ease of access by plane or ferry from Great Britain, the Normandy Cemetery probably has more visitors each year than any cemetery administered by the American Battle Monuments Commission.

The North Africa American Cemetery and Memorial

Situated on ground that was once part of the Roman city of Carthage and about ten miles from the city of Tunis, the capital of the Tunisian Republic, the cemetery occupies twenty-seven acres of land and contains the remains of more than 2,800 honored dead in nine rectangular plots. Decorative pools are located at the intersections of the plots. In addition to a small chapel and a memorial court containing mosaic maps of operations from North Africa and as far away as the Persian Gulf, there is a long Wall of the Missing on which are inscribed the names of 3,724 missing.

The Rhone American Cemetery and Memorial

This cemetery is inside the city limits of the city of Draguignan, France, only forty miles from Cannes on the French Riviera. Although the smallest cemetery administered by the American Battle Monuments Commission in terms of land occupied (twelve and a half acres), the number of burials (861), and the number of missing (294), the Rhone Cemetery is as well maintained and as beautiful as any of the larger cemeteries. Within the cemetery and adjacent to it are small olive trees, tall cypress trees, and flowering oleanders so typical of southern France. From the entrance gates, the cemetery's four plots slope gently upward toward a beautiful sculptured figure on the outer wall of the chapel. The retaining walls contain the names of the 294 missing. In front of the chapel, level with the burial sites, is a large bronze relief map depicting the military actions in this region starting with Operation Dragoon, the invasion of southern France by the U.S. Seventh Army in July 1944. Although the Rhone Cemetery is small, it is visited by many tourists each year because of its close proximity to Cannes and Nice and the famous Provence Region of France.

The Sicily-Rome American Cemetery and Memorial

Located on the north side of the town of Nettuno, Italy, about thirty-eight miles south of Rome, it is also just east of Anzio, where American forces were pinned down for months by savage German attempts to force the Americans back into the Mediterranean Sea. The cemetery consists of seventy-seven acres of gently sloping land that holds the remains of almost 7,900 military dead. The graves are arranged in sweeping arcs among row upon row of Roman pine trees. There is a wide mall leading to the memorial with its tall white columns. The memorial houses a chapel and a museum room. The chapel's beautiful, white marble walls record the names of 3,095 of the missing. Inside the museum are four fresco maps showing the military operations which took place in both Sicily and Italy, as well as a bronze relief map of the combat areas.

The Suresnes American Cemetery and Memorial

This cemetery, located outside of Paris, is actually a World War I cemetery and memorial. However, there is one small area in the cemetery with twenty-four white marble crosses, beneath which lie the remains of World War II unknowns. These men presumably died of wounds while being treated in hospitals in or near Paris, but did not have the identification tags or other personal belongings such as rings or watches to permit proper identification. They may also have been so badly wounded as to preclude recognition.

World War II Memorials

East Coast Memorial: This memorial is located in Battery Park in New York City, New York. The memorial commemorates over 4,600 missing soldiers, sailors, marines, airmen, coast guardsmen, and merchant marines who lost their lives in the western Atlantic. Included among the names of the missing are the four chaplains whose heroic deaths are described in Chapter Two.

West Coast Memorial: Located on the grounds of the Presidio of San Francisco not far from the Golden Gate Bridge, the memorial wall lists the names of 412 missing in action whose remains were either never recovered or could not be positively identified.

The Honolulu Memorial: This memorial is located on the grounds of the National Memorial Cemetery of the Pacific in what was once an active volcano. The huge memorial consists of a large staircase leading up to a chapel. The staircase is flanked on each side by four Courts of the Missing listing the names of 18,096 missing in the Pacific during World War II, 8,200 missing during the Korean War and 2,504 missing during the Vietnam War.

The Cabanatuan Memorial: On the site of the notorious Japanese Prison Camp where about 20,000 Americans, both military and civilian, were held captive for over three years under inhumane conditions, this memorial is located eighty-five miles north of Manila, the Philippines. The memorial also honors the sacrifices made by Filipino servicemen and civilians. The Wall of Honor lists the names of close to 3,000 Americans who died while imprisoned here.

The Guadalcanal American Memorial: Located on a hill overlooking the town of Honiara, Guadalcanal, the Solomon Islands, this memorial was erected to honor American and Allied servicemen of all branches who lost their lives during the extended fight (August 1942-February 1943) to defeat the Japanese who defended the island. The invasion of Guadalcanal was one of the first offensive actions against the Japanese by American forces after the bombing of Pearl Harbor and the invasion of the Philippines in December 1944.

NOTES

[1] All information related to the permanent cemeteries of World War II was obtained from the American Battle Monuments Commission's annual reports, pamphlets available to the general public, and the commission's excellent web site, which contains detailed information as to the burials at each cemetery, descriptions of each cemetery or memorial, and a short video describing each cemetery.

Chapter Ten

IN THE WORDS OF THE POET

"Mankind must put an end to war
before war puts an end to mankind."
John F. Kennedy

How many funerals have you attended? Most people in their fifties, sixties or seventies have probably attended at least a dozen or more funerals, while those in their teens may either not have attended a funeral yet or perhaps only those of their grandparents. The majority of funeral homes normally provide a small pamphlet, which describes, in brief terms, the life of the deceased. That pamphlet usually contains either a religious verse or a poem, possibly both. Poems, in the Western tradition, seem to be appropriate at the time of death and mourning. It only seems fitting, as a closing chapter to this book, that several poems related to the death of those killed in battle should be included.

The first poem, titled *Bivouac of the Dead*, was written by Theodore O'Hara (1820-1867) in memory of troops from the state of Kentucky who had been killed during the Mexican War. Mr. O'Hara was born in Danville, Kentucky, and died in Bullock County, Alabama, at the young age of forty-seven. Entering the Mexican War as a captain of volunteers, he was appointed to the temporary rank of major for gallantry during combat in Mexico and was discharged in 1848. Later, he was appointed a captain of cavalry in 1855 but resigned the commission in 1856. He was appointed a colonel in the 12th Alabama Regiment during the Civil War and served on the staffs of both Gen. Albert Sidney Johnston and Gen. John C. Breckinridge. Deeply moved by the tragedies of war, he wrote the poem, *Bivouac of the Dead*, in honor of Kentucky soldiers whose remains were re-

turned to Kentucky for burial some years after the Mexican War.
Lines from this poem have been used at several national cemeteries.

The Bivouac of the Dead

The muffled drum's sad roll has beat
The soldier's last tattoo;
No more on Life's parade shall meet
That brave and fallen few.
On fame's eternal camping ground
Their silent tents to spread,
And glory guards, with solemn round
The bivouac of the dead.

No rumor of the foe's advance
Now swells upon the wind;
Nor troubled thought at midnight haunts
Of loved ones left behind;
No vision of the morrow's strife
The warrior's dream alarms;
No braying horn or screaming fife
At dawn shall call to arms.

Their shriveled swords are red with rust,
Their plumed heads are bowed,
Their haughty banner, trailed in dust,
Is now their martial shroud.
And plenteous funeral tears have washed
The red stains from each brow,
And the proud forms, by battle gashed
Are free from anguish now.

The neighing troop, the flashing blade,
The bugle's stirring blast,
The charge, the dreadful cannonade,
The din and shout, are past;
Nor war's wild note, nor glory's peal
Shall thrill with fierce delight
Those breasts that nevermore may feel
The rapture of the fight.

Let the fierce Northern hurricane
That sweeps the great plateau,
Flushed with triumph, yet to gain,
Come down the serried foe,
Who heard the thunder of the fray
Break o'er the field beneath,
Knew the watchword of the day
Was "Victory or death!"

Long had the doubtful conflict raged
O'er all that stricken plain,
For never fiercer fight had waged
The vengeful blood of Spain.
And still the storm of battle blew,
Still swelled the glory tide,
Not long, our stout old Chieftain knew,
Such odds his strength could bide.

Twas in that hour his stern command
Called to a martyr's grave
The flower of his beloved land,
The nation's flag to save.
By rivers of their father's gore
His first-born laurels grew,
And well he deemed the sons would pour
Their lives for glory too.

For many a mother's breath has swept
O'er Angostura's plain,
And long the pitying sky has wept
Above its moldered slain.
The raven's scream, or eagle's flight,
Or shepherd's pensive lay,
Alone awakes each sullen height
That frowned o'er that dread fray.

Sons of the Dark and Bloody Ground
Ye must not slumber there,
Where stranger steps and tongues resound
Along the heedless air.
Your own proud land's heroic soil

Shall be your fitter grave;
She claims from war his richest spoil—
The ashes of her brave.

Thus 'neath their parent turf they rest,
Far from the gory field,
Borne to a Spartan mother's breast
On many a bloody shield;
The sunshine of their native sky
Smiles sadly on them here,
And kindred eyes and hearts watch by
The heroes sepulcher.

Rest on embalmed and sainted dead!
Dear as the blood ye gave;
No impious footstep here shall tread
The herbage of your grave;
Nor shall your glory be forgot
While Fame her record keeps,
For honor points the hallowed spot
Where valor proudly sleeps.

Yon marble minstrel's voiceless stone
In deathless song shall tell,
When many a vanquished ago has flown,
The story how ye fell;
Nor wreck, nor change, nor winter's blight,
Nor time's remorseless doom,
Can dim one ray of glory's light
That gilds your deathless tomb.

The Bivouac of the Dead was written by a former soldier in honor of fallen comrades some time after the conflict ended. The next poem, *Peace*, was written by a young American infantryman, Pfc. Morris B. Redmann Jr., while he was still engaged in combat as a member of the 376th Infantry Regiment, 94th Infantry Division. Morris was the oldest of ten children of Morris B. Redmann and Esther Alice Joyce Redmann. His father was a successful attorney in New Orleans, and his mother was a schoolteacher with a love for music. Morris was an exceptional young man who had a strong interest in and talent for learning. A graduate of New Orleans' Jesuit High School at the age of fourteen, he entered Loyola University from which he graduated in 1943 at age eighteen, when other boys his age were just entering college. He then entered Loyola University School of Law and had completed most of his first semester when he was drafted. The book, *Unfinished Journey*, by his brother, Kerry P. Redmann, is a compilation of Morris's letters to and from his family and friends from the time he entered service in September 1943, until he was killed in Germany on Sunday, 15 January 1945, shortly after his 19th birthday. Morris was killed instantly by an artillery shell from a German 88mm gun, one of the most accurate and most feared of the German weapons.

Private First Class Redmann is buried in the Luxembourg American Cemetery at Hamm, a suburb of Luxembourg City. Morris wrote his poem, *Peace*, on 30 October 1944 at a time when many Americans felt that the war in Europe would be over before Christmas. This was before the famous Battle of the Bulge which the Germans initiated on 16 December 1944. Morris must have been thinking of an early reunion with his parents and nine siblings when he wrote this poem.

Peace[1]

Ring out, ring out ye chapel bells
For peace is here once more.
Sing loud, sing loud ye birds of the sea,
Come rest upon the shore.

The trees shall blossom forth in green
The sun shall shine today
The people of the hamlet towns
Shall sing their grief away.

No more shall vultures rule the air
Nor seek a fallen prey
No more will men be at other throats
For all is peace today.

Bring out the aged, crippled, maimed
For these will smile anew
On English boys from English towns
Passing in review.

They've just got back from over there,
From the trenches and the gore.
But some there are that march not here
They're gone forevermore.

The cathedral bells do peal the joy
Upon this happy day
As happy tears and joyous kisses
Chase the fears away.

But some there are that stand and wait
And clench their throats with fear
And choke themselves with muffled sobs—
They dare not shed a tear.

They are the mothers of the boys
Whose places go unfilled
Whose names appear on lengthy lists
Of the missing and the killed.

And as I stood there waving, waiting
Watching the troops go by,
I noticed a lady standing there
I heard her sniff and sigh.

"I guess wilna be home today,"
She said as she crossed the street
My heart beat hard in quickened time—
In time with the marching feet.

And a sadness crept into my soul
As the soldiers marched away
But the bells pealed forth their joyous songs
For all is peace today.

But many a wreck lies on the beach
And many a heart is torn
And upon the breast of many a mother
The golden star is worn.

Oh, the crosses gleam white on Belgian fields
And they mark the shallow graves
Of those who fell on Belgian fields—
They will never be slaves.

The churches stand as hollow shells
Their bells shall ring no more
And many a boy sleeps in the ground
At peace forevermore.

But from these battle graves
They all must rise some day
But, forget, forget them now
For all is peace today.

"Ah, peace, peace," the nation sighs
Forgets the things it said
Forgets the pledges made to God
Forgets, forgets – the dead.

The following poem, a tribute to Pfc. Morris Redmann Jr., was written by his brother Kerry P. Redmann, author of the book, *Unfinished Journey*, mentioned earlier. This poem can almost be viewed as counterpoint to his brother's poem, *Peace,* since it educes the mental picture of a mud-caked body, the "screeching fire" of the German 88mm guns, and the burial of the dead "gently bagged."

A Combat Infantryman's Burial[2]

Not midst tolling dirge of church bells,
Not with solemn prayers and Requiem mass,
'Neath misty shadows emerging through stained glass windows,
And air so filled with scent of incense was he interred;

But in the subtle stillness of after battle,
In dawn's first light that quietly ushers in the day,
We carried his body all caked with mud,
And placed it, gently bagged, into the clay.

Yet who shall say that he was not content,
Or missed the incessant prayers and chanting choir,
He who had heard all day the battle anthems,
Echoed a thousand times by the 88's screeching fire.

What oriel glass can lovelier images cast,
Than those the evening skies majestically unfold,
Their mingling light creating magic colors o'er the dead,
Softly illuminating the spangled banner for which he died.

The next poem was written by the great American poet, Walt Whitman, during the Civil War. In the book, *God Rest Ye Merry Soldiers: A True Civil War Christmas Story*, the author, James McIvor, states:

> The poet Walt Whitman offered another expression of faith as he struggled to find meaning in so much death. It was a faith that tied the war to the most basic meaning of Christmas. But it was shocking nonetheless. Abandoning all high-minded pretense of martial glory and romance, shunning even the sentimental Christmas associations of home and boyhood nostalgia, Whitman looked death in the face in a way that would have seemed indelicate, even callous, a year earlier. But in confronting himself with the martyrdom of innocence that the war now daily brought, Whitman was led to think of Christ himself:

A Sight in Camp in the Daybreak Gray and Dim

A sight in camp in the daybreak gray and dim,
As from my tent I emerge so early sleepless,
As slow I walk in the cool fresh air the path nearby the hospital tent,
Three forms I see on stretchers lying, brought out there untended lying,
Over each the blanket spread, ample brownish woolen blanket,
Gray and heavy blanket, folding, covering all.

Curious I halt and silent stand,
Then with light fingers I from the face of the nearest the first
just lift the blanket;
Who are you elderly man so gaunt and grim, with well-gray'd hair,
and flesh all sunken about the eyes?
Who are you my dear comrade?
Then to the second I step- and who are you my child and darling?
Who are you sweet boy with cheeks yet blooming?
Then to the third—a face nor child nor old, very calm, as of
beautiful yellow-white ivory;
Young man I think I know you – I think this face is the face of the
Christ himself,
Dead and divine and brother of all, and here again he lies.

Many books have been written about the exploits, both good and bad, of GEN George S. Patton Jr. during both World War I and World War II. One of the most viewed of all World War II movies is *Patton*. The movie has even been very popular in China. However, few people know that Patton read and wrote poetry. The following poem by General Patton would seem to belie the view that his only interest was in killing the enemy.

A Soldier's Burial
George S. Patton

> Not midst the chanting of the Requiem Hymn,
> Nor with the solemn ritual of prayer,
> Neath misty shadows from the oriel glass,
> And dreamy perfume of the incensed air
> Was he interred.
> But the subtle stillness after fight,
> And the half light between the night and the day,
> We dragged his body all besmeared with mud,
> And dropped it, clod-like, back into the clay.
> Yet who shall say that he was not content,
> Or missed the prayers, or drone of chanting choir,
> He who had heard all day the Battle Hymn
> Sung on all sides by a thousand throats of fire.
> What painted glass can lovelier shadows cast
> Than those the evening skies shall ever shed,

While, mingled with their light, Red Battle's Sun
Completes in magic colors o'er our dead
The Flag for which they died.

Chapter six of this book described the American World War II Orphans Network (AWON). The following poem was written by AWON member Elaine Ricketson Danks in memory of her father, AMM3C Jacob Elijah Ricketson. AMM3C Ricketson, a member of the Torpedo Bomber Squadron, Air Group 17, assigned to the aircraft carrier USS *Hornet*, was killed in action on 7 April 1945, during combat operations against the Japanese in the East China Sea near Kyushu, Japan. After learning the details of her father's death some fifty-four years later, Ms. Danks was able to retrace the route of his last voyage and have a headstone placed in Arlington Cemetery, as well as a memorial service for AMM3C Ricketson.

In His Memory[3]

Hush, hush...the word goes out across the land–
A fallen hero comes this way!
Be still, O seas! Be silent, wind!
All creatures in a solemn vigil stand.
Their whispered cries swell and wing into space,
Past far-flung stars that gaze, forlorn;
While in somber clouds, puffed with tears,
An ashen sun sinks to bury its face.

Though monuments be raised and tributes paid,
Such meager words offend the deed
Of him whose youth, and dreams, and life
On Freedom's altar were so early laid.

Hush, hush...with humble reverence we meet this day
His death to mourn, his life to bless.
Hearts beat the cadence of his name.
Take heed,
A fallen hero comes this way.

Tombstone epitaphs are frequently borrowed from poems. The following epitaph found on page 107 of the book, *The Bottom Line on Tombstones, That is, In Western Kentucky Cemeteries,* by

Walter Beasley, and published by McClanahan Publishing Company with a 1999 copyright, is one such epitaph.

> He shall not grow old,
> As we who are left grow old,
> Age shall not weary him
> Nor the years condemn:
> In the glory of his youth
> We shall remember him.

The epitaph quoted above, which was actually found in a cemetery in Cincinnati, Ohio, was lifted from the fourth stanza of the poem, *For the Fallen,* by Laurence Binyon. Mr. Binyon was born in England in 1869 and died there in 1943. A book of his works, *Collected Poems,* was published in 1931. The complete poem follows:

For the Fallen
Laurence Binyon

> With proud thanksgiving, a mother for her children,
> England mourns for her dead across the sea.
> Flesh of her flesh they were, spirit of her spirit,
> Fallen in the cause of the free.
>
> Solemn the drums thrill; Death august and royal
> Sings sorrow up into immortal spheres,
> There is music in the midst of desolation
> And a glory that shines upon our tears.
>
> They went with songs to the battle, they were young,
> Straight of limb, true of eye, steady and aglow.
> They were staunch to the end against odds uncounted;
> They fell with their faces to the foe.
>
> They shall grow not old, as we that are left grow old:
> Age shall not weary them, nor the years condemn.
> At the going down of the sun and in the morning
> We will remember them.
>
> They mingle not with their laughing comrades again;
> They sit no more at familiar tables of home;
> They have no lot in our labour of the day-time;
> They sleep beyond England's foam.

But where our desires are and our hopes profound,
Felt as a well-spring that is hidden from sight,
To the innermost heart of their own land they are known
As the stars are known to the night.

As the stars that shall be bright when we are dust,
Moving in marches upon the heavenly plain;
As the stars that are starry in the time of our darkness,
To the end, to the end, they remain.

George Henry Boker, 1823-1889, was a noted dramatist who also served President Ulysses S. Grant as the U.S. Minister to Constantinople, Turkey, from 1871 to 1875 and in Russia from 1875 to 1878. In addition to his many plays, Boker was also a poet of some acclaim. His book of poetry, *Poems of the War,* was published in 1864. The following poem is taken from that book.

Dirge for a Soldier
George H. Boker

Close his eyes; his work is done!
What to him is friend or foeman,
Rise of moon, or set of sun,
Hand of man, or kiss of woman?
Lay him low, lay him low,
In the clover or in the snow!
What cares he? He can not know;
Lay him low!

As man may, he fought his fight,
Proved his truth by his endeavor.
Let him sleep in solemn night,
Sleep forever and forever.
Lay him low, lay him low,
In the clover or the snow!
What cares he? He can not know;
Lay him low!

Fold him in his country's stars,
Roll the drum and fire the volley!
What to him are all our wars,
What but death be mocking folly?
Lay him low, lay him low,

In the clover or the snow!
What cares he? He can not know;
Lay him low!

Leave him in God's watching eye,
Trust him to the hand that made him.
Mortal love weeps idly by;
God alone has power to aid him.
Lay him low, lay him low,
In the clover or the snow!
What cares he? He can not know;
Lay him low!

The poem which follows was written by Miss Angela Morgan, an American poet who lived from 1873 to 1957. Miss Morgan, never financially secure, had to declare bankruptcy in 1935 and died in 1957 while living with friends. Her poem, *The Unknown Soldier,* could apply equally well to either of the two Unknown Soldiers in Arlington Cemetery in Virginia, as well as the thousands of unknowns buried in the World War I and World War II cemeteries described in this book.

The Unknown Soldier
Angela Morgan

He is known to the sun-white Majesties
Who stand at the gates of dawn.
He is known to the cloud-borne company
Whose souls but late have gone.
Like wind-flung stars through lattice bars
They throng to greet their own.
With voice of flame they sound his name
Who died to us unknown.

He is hailed by the time-crowned brotherhood,
By the Dauntless of Marathon,
By Raymond, Godfrey, and Lion Heart
Whose dreams he carried on.
His name they call through the heavenly hall
Unheard by earthly ear.
He is claimed by the famed in Arcady
Who knew no title here.

Oh faint was the lamp of Sirius
And dim was the Milky Way.
Oh far was the floor of Paradise
From the soil where the soldier lay.
Oh chill and stark was the crimson dark
Where huddled men lay deep;
His comrades all denied his call
Long had they lain in sleep.

Oh strange how the lamp of Sirius
Drops low to the dazzled eyes,
Oh strange how the steel-red battlefields
Are floors of Paradise.
Oh strange how the ground with never a sound
Swings open, tier on tier,
And standing there in the shining air
Are the friends he cherished here.

They are known to the sun-shod sentinels
Who circle the morning's door,
They are led by the cloud-bright company
Through paths unseen before.
Like blossoms blown, their souls have flown
Past war and reeking sod,
In the book unbound their names are found
They are known in the Courts of God!

For the last poem I have selected a poet who may not be as well known in the United States as in his native England. Wilfred Edward Salter Owen was born in Oswestry, Shropshire, England in 1893. He was deeply impressed as a youth by the poets Keats and Shelly, and, by age nineteen, decided to become a poet himself. His poems did not attract much attention until his military service during World War I. He volunteered for military service and was assigned to duty in the trenches of France. After recovering from a near death experience and shell shock, he was again assigned to the trenches where he was killed on 4 November 1918, when he was barely 25 years old, only 7 days before the Armistice. In fact, his parent learned of his death while hearing the bells of victory ring out from all of the local churches. Owen wrote over forty war poems, but perhaps his most famous is the one that follows.

DULCE ET DECORUM EST
Wilfrid Owen (1917)

Bent double, like old beggars under sacks,
Knock-kneed, coughing like hags, we cursed through sludge,
Till on the haunting flares we turned our backs
And towards our distant rest began to trudge.
Men marched asleep. Many had lost their boots
But limped on, blood-shod. All went lame; all blind;
Drunk with fatigue; deaf even to the hoots
Of tired, outstripped Five-Nines that dropped behind.

Gas! Gas! Quick, boys! – An ecstasy of fumbling,
Fitting the clumsy helmets just in time;
But someone still was yelling out and stumbling,
And flound'ring like a man in fire or lime . . .
Dim, through the misty panes and thick green light,
As under a green sea, I saw him drowning.

In all my dreams, before my helpless sight,
He plunges at me, guttering, choking, drowning.
If in sonic smothering dreams you too could pace
Behind the wagon that we flung him in,
And watch the white eyes writhing in his face,
His hanging face, like a devil's sick of sin;
If you could hear, at every jolt, the blood
Come gargling from the froth-corrupted lungs,
Obscene as cancer, bitter as the cud
Of vile, incurable sores on innocent tongues, –
My friend, you would not tell with such high zest
To children ardent for some desperate glory,
The old Lie: Dulce et decorum est
Pro patria mori.

(Author's Note: Quoted from Horace and translated as "It is sweet to die for one's country.")

CONCLUSION

For the families of those young Americans whose last resting place is in a foreign land, you can take solace knowing that those whom you loved are buried among thousands upon thousands of other young Americans, who, like your own beloved, died at a tender age to help bring peace to a troubled world. Some died upon the beaches of previously unknown Pacific islands and atolls, while others died on land where their ancestors may have been born or lived before journeying to the "new world." A few may even have died on ground near where their fathers or grandfathers died in the "Great War." Regardless, the families of those buried in foreign countries can rest assured that the monuments to their sacrifices are among the most beautiful in the world, and that the ground in which they lie will be maintained to the highest standards for so long as our great nation may exist. Some family members may never have had the opportunity to personally journey to the site where their loved one rests. However, through the good works of the staff of the American Battle Monuments Commission, they can obtain a color print of that special cemetery with a photo of their loved one's own marker. Others may have made one or more visits to the location where their loved one is buried or remembered on the Wall of the Missing and personally laid flowers at the foot of the marker or tablet which defines their final resting place. It is hoped that through the pages of this book the reader may now have a better understanding of the hopes and aspirations of those thousands of young Americans who now lie beneath those white marble crosses or Stars of David or whose names are inscribed on the Walls of the Missing.

I can think of no better way to end this book than by quoting from the last paragraph of President Abraham Lincoln's Gettysburg Address:

> From these honored dead we take increased devotion to that cause for which they gave the last full measure of devotion – that we here highly resolve that these dead shall not have died in vain – that this nation, under God, shall have a new birth of freedom – and that government of the people, by the people, for the people, shall not perish from the earth.

NOTES

[1]   Redmann, Kerry P., *Unfinished Journey: A World War II Remembrance*, (Guilford, CT: Lyons Press, 2006), PP. 217-219. Used by permission of Lyons Press.

[2]   Ibid, p. 255. Used by permission of Lyons Press.

[3]   Poem copyrighted by the author. Used by permission of the author.

ACKNOWLEDGMENTS

As noted in the introduction, the genesis for this book was my first visit to the American Cemetery on Omaha Beach in October of 2003. That very emotional experience led me to undertake the telling of the stories of some small number of the young men and women buried in our overseas cemeteries. Subsequently, my wife and I spent a month in France in 2005, and drove to eight of the nine World War II American Cemeteries located in France, Belgium, Holland and Luxembourg. At each of these cemeteries we were assisted by the resident staff. In some cases the superintendent or assistant superintendent took time from their own busy schedules to help. In other cases the capable staff provided the assistance required. Without fail, each member of the cemetery staff with whom we came in contact was anxious to show us "their" cemetery and tell us its history, as well as tell us some of the individual stories about the brave young men and women buried there. In one case our visit was on a Sunday morning, and the young local intern volunteered to call the superintendent from his nearby home. The two of them spent over an hour helping to identify burials that might best result in my being able to contact family members or friends on my return to the United States. In each and every case the staff members were first very careful to explain that they *could not* violate the confidentiality of the family members by giving me their names, addresses, and phone numbers. I could not have asked for more gracious assistance.

During our month in France, LTC Margaret Flott, USA (Retired), who was assigned to the American Battle Monuments Commission Staff in Paris, was only a phone call away when assistance was needed to vouch for my visits to each cemetery and the taking of photographs. Margaret and her staff also assisted in recommending hotels/motels for our stay in the vicinity of each cemetery. Ms. Martha Sell, deputy public relations officer of the American Battle Monuments Commission in Washington, D.C., took time from her own busy schedule in the midst of moving from one office complex to another to spend most of one morning in October 2006, answering my questions and providing direction in my quest for sources of personal information about the men and women buried overseas.

Mr. Luther D. Hanson, Curator at the Quartermaster Museum at Fort Lee, Virginia, and Mr. Douglas L. Howard (now deceased), Deputy Director of the Mortuary Affairs Center at Fort Lee, were most helpful in making available information related to the Graves Registration Services provided during WWII as well as information related to the numerous temporary cemeteries established during that period. Mr. Hanson was gracious enough to make available copies of articles related to Graves Registration during World War II, which had appeared in various Quartermaster publications over the past sixty years. Dr. Steven Anders, Quartermaster Center Historian, was most helpful in tracking down information on temporary cemeteries in the Pacific Theater of Operations, as well as providing guidance on a number of questions that surfaced during my research.

One of my most fortunate contacts was with the American World War II Orphans Network (AWON). Several of the cemetery superintendents, LTC Flott, and Ms. Sell recommended that I contact the orphans' network. When I did so by e-mail, the response was virtually instantaneous and most helpful. Not only was I provided a copy of their newsletter, but the nature of my project was posted on their Internet bulletin board and I immediately started receiving e-mail from AWON members anxious to help with my project and to ensure the sacrifices made by their parent or other loved one were not forgotten. Of special note among the many AWON members must be Mr. James Gregory, who managed their web site at that time; Ms. Judy Hoffman, who wrote the chapter which describes AWON; and Ms. Ann Mix, who has published several books to assist family members and friends who are searching for information pertaining to their World War II relatives and friends. Ms. Mix was the originator of the concept which led to the establishment of AWON while attempting to learn more about her own father, who was killed in Italy.

Ms. Shannon Brooks, Associate for Research and Publications, the National D-Day Memorial Foundation in Bedford, Virginia, was most helpful. She made available to the author all of the foundation's extensive archives related to the Bedford Boys and the National

D-Day Memorial. She answered numerous questions by telephone or by e-mail, and proofed aspects of the book and a supplemental magazine article related to those subjects, while carrying on her own important duties with the help of a very small staff.

Mr. James Lloyd of Oak Hill, Ohio, contributed significantly to the chapter on Jackson County Men. He tracked down living relatives of several of the men whose vignettes appear in that chapter, and he found one of the last copies of the booklet about First Lieutenant Bicksler that had been prepared by his father following his death over sixty years ago. He proofed several vignettes and his suggestions were always valuable and appreciated. His knowledge of the Oak Hill, Ohio, community and its citizens added significantly to elements of those vignettes related to men from the Oak Hill area.

Mr. Willard Davis, also of Oak Hill, Ohio, provided valuable information, which enabled me to contact family members of several Oak Hill men.

Ms. Pam Rhodes, of the Oak Hill, Ohio, Public Library, assisted materially by culling through old micro-film records of issues of the now defunct Oak Hill Press while attempting to locate information about the Oak Hill men who are included in the chapter on "Jackson County Men." I feel certain that her efforts were over and above the position description for which she is paid. The small donation I made to the library in her name does not come close to recognition of her assistance to the author.

Ms. Jane Yates, Archivist and Director of The Citadel Museum at The Citadel, the Military College of South Carolina, was of great assistance in locating information about Major Thomas Dry Howie, "the Major of Saint-Lo." She took time from her busy schedule to collect pertinent files and photos in advance of the author's visit to The Citadel, and then explained each file or photo to ensure that the author understood how much cadet life at The Citadel had impacted Major Howie's later life and the preparation for the key leadership position he subsequently occupied during the battle for Saint-Lo. Ms. Yates made available in digital format and copies of printed matter, the background information from which the author was able to develop the Howie vignette.

Mrs. Meredith Yates of Mt. Pleasant, SC, graciously agreed to read a very rough first draft of the manuscript and edit it with an eye not only for spelling, punctuation, and grammar errors, but also for sentence structure, repetitive use of words or phrases, and "readability." Mrs. Yates developed her editing skills while serving in various administrative positions at The Citadel, the Military College of South Carolina. She not only assisted professors by editing research papers and book drafts, but also proofed the college alumni magazine on a regular basis. Mrs. Yates served as my administrative assistant during the last half of my fifteen plus years in the position of Vice President for Finance and Business Affairs at The Citadel. She not only managed to keep me on schedule for important meetings and committee sessions, but she displayed an unusual degree of patience and humor while doing it. She was recognized campus-wide as one of the most knowledgeable and professional administrative assistants at the college.

Ms. Kristin Williams, owner of Kristin Designs, Inc., Knoxville, TN, was invaluable as she developed and presented concepts for the book jacket. She very courteously and professionally explained why my original concept for the book jacket would not help attract potential buyers. This was not an easy task, since my concept involved the use of a photo I had taken and felt was at least worthy of the front page of any major news magazine. The final result speaks for itself.

Ms. Joyce W. Maddox of Warwick House Publishing Co., Lynchburg, VA, was extremely patient and professional as she walked this first-time author through the ins and outs of the book publishing business. She spent much time on the phone, and more time replying to e-mail queries while answering numerous questions that she must have answered hundreds of times for other authors. Not once did she appear to lose patience! Without her assistance and encouragement, this book would most likely never have made it to fruition.

Ms. Amy Moore, also of Warwick House Publishing, worked wonders in order to scan over 100 photos of different sizes, colors and quality and integrate them in the proper location within the text of the book. She also is responsible for converting hundreds of pages of manuscript into a format acceptable to the printer.

My thanks to Mr. Lester V. Horwitz, author of *The Longest Raid of the Civil War*, one of the best Civil War books I have read, for his wise and patient counsel throughout the process of researching and writing this book.

Thanks must also go to many friends and family members whom I "encouraged" to read various drafts and outlines. Without exception, their comments and suggestions have added to the readability and cohesiveness of the finished project.

I owe a deep debt of gratitude to my wife of over fifty-two years, Helen Beckley Lyons, for her support and help throughout this project. She not only encouraged me from day one when I first broached the concept, but she served as my secretary when I was taking hundreds of photos at the cemetery locations in Europe. She made note of the personal information from each grave marker and numbered the photos so that we had the correct name to go with each photo. She spent many evenings alone, reading in bed, while I "played" (her words, not mine) on the computer searching for references and sources, verifying information, drafting and redrafting vignettes, sorting photos, etc. She accompanied me on my visits to the American Battle Monuments Commission offices in Washington, D.C., as well as to the Quartermaster Museum at Fort Lee, Virginia, and she made the necessary adjustments in our household budgets from month to month as I incurred out-of-pocket expenses related to the "project." Over fifty-two years, two children, and four grandchildren later, she is still my best friend, my number one supporter, and a role model for our whole family.

Finally, as with any author, I must reserve for myself any criticism for errors of fact or other mistakes which may have found their way into the finished product. I accept full responsibility for all errors, and I can only hope that the acceptance of the book is such that I may have a chance to correct such errors in a second edition. Please feel free to send any comments, recommended corrections, or suggestions to me at cglyons34@tds.net.

Calvin G. (Jerry) Lyons
Colonel U.S. Army (Retired)

PERMANENT CEMETERIES OF WORLD WAR I[1]

"We make war that we may live in peace."
Aristotle

The American Battle Monuments Commission (ABMC) is responsible for the administration of eight World War I Cemeteries in Europe. One cemetery is located in Great Britain, one is located in Belgium and the remaining six are in France. These eight cemeteries contain a total of 30,421 U.S. World War I dead and the names of 4,452 missing. In addition, one World War I cemetery also contains the remains of twenty-four World War II unknowns. The ABMC web site at www.abmc.gov contains both general and detailed descriptions of each cemetery, cemetery photos, and a short video describing each cemetery. The cemetery descriptions can be downloaded, if desired, or interested parties can request copies from the ABMC headquarters in Washington, D.C.

The names, locations, and a basic description of each of the eight World War I cemeteries follow in alphabetical order.:

The Aisne-Marne Cemetery

South of the village of Belleau, France, and about 6 ½ miles northwest of Chateau-Thierry, the Aisne-Marne Cemetery is about one hour from Paris by train. Occupying 42 ½ acres at the foot of a Belleau Wood hill, the cemetery contains the graves of 2,289 deceased veterans of the Marne Valley battles in the summer of 1918. The memorial chapel, situated on a hillside within the cemetery, has stained glass details of personnel, equipment and insignia. On the interior walls of the chapel are the names of 1,060 missing.

The Brookwood Cemetery

This cemetery is the only American World War I cemetery in Great Britain. Located south of the town of Brookwood, England,

and 28 miles from London, Brookwood consists of 4 ½ acres and is near a larger civilian cemetery. The Brookwood Cemetery contains the graves of 468 U.S. military dead. The chapel, a classic white stone building, has small stained glass windows which light the altar, flags, and a carved cross. The walls of the chapel are inscribed with the names of 563 of the missing, most of whom lost their lives at sea.

The Flanders Field Cemetery

Near the small town of Waregem, Belgium, 175 miles north of Paris and 52 miles west of Brussels, Flanders Field contains the fewest remains of any U.S. World War I cemetery. The cemetery is comprised of 6.2 acres with graceful trees and shrubs shielding the burial area from passing traffic. Three hundred sixty-eight American dead from World War I are buried here. Among those buried at Flanders Field is Lt. Kenneth A. MacLeish, brother of the famous American poet, Archibald MacLeish. One of the early group of Naval aviators, he was killed less than one month prior to the Armistice that ended World War I. A white stone chapel is at the center of the cemetery, and above the altar of the chapel is a crusader's sword outlined in gold. The side walls of the chapel contain the names of forty-three of the missing.

The Meuse–Argonne Cemetery

Nearly 150 miles from Paris, this cemetery is located east of the small village of Romagne-sous-Montfaucon, about 26 miles southwest of Verdun. The largest World War I cemetery in numbers of dead and in land area, it is also the largest American cemetery in Europe in terms of the numbers of burials for either World War I or World War II. The cemetery occupies 130 ½ acres of land and has 14,246 World War I dead buried there. Most of the soldiers buried in this cemetery lost their lives during the Meuse-Argonne Offensive of 1918. The cemetery contains the remains of nine recipients of the Medal of Honor. The chapel has memorial loggia on either side with the names of 954 Americans whose remains were never recovered. Included also are the names of the missing from a United States expedition to northern Russia during the period 1918–1919.

The Oise–Aisne Cemetery

This beautiful cemetery, consisting of 36 ½ acres, is located about 1 ½ miles east of the small French village of Fere-en-Tardenois, about 14 miles northeast of Chateau-Thierry, and less than 75 miles from Paris. From the entry gate along the highway, the cemetery grounds sweep up a slight incline with grave sites along each side of a walkway. At the top of the incline stands the curving colonnade memorial. The cemetery contains the remains of 6,012 military dead, most of whom lost their lives during fighting nearby in 1918. Among those buried here is Sgt. Joyce Kilmer, the noted American poet and author of the poem, *Trees*. Sergeant Kilmer was killed only 800 yards from the cemetery on 30 July 1918, while assigned to the 165th Infantry Regiment of the 42[d] Division. One end of the memorial has a room devoted to maps depicting the battles in this area during 1918. The other end houses the small chapel which contains a carved stone altar. On the walls of the chapel are listed the names of 241 of the missing.

The Somme Cemetery

The Somme Cemetery is about ½ mile southwest of the small village of Bony, France, and lies about 98 miles northeast of Paris. The cemetery is located on 14.3 acres of gently sloping, rolling country, typical of the Picardy area. It contains 1,844 World War I U.S. soldiers who lost their lives in this area while their units were serving with elements of the British Army. A small chapel at the eastern end of the cemetery has a beautiful bronze door with an imposing American eagle overhead. Inside the chapel the altar benefits from light streaming through a cross-shaped crystal window. On the walls of the chapel are inscribed the names of 333 of the missing.

The St. Mihiel Cemetery

Near the western edge of Thiaucourt, France, the St. Mihiel Cemetery is about 190 miles from Paris and only 23 miles from Metz, France. The cemetery, on 40 ½ acres of land, has 4,153 World War I American dead buried there. Most of the soldiers buried here were killed during the Allied attempt to push the Germans back from what became known as the St. Mihiel Salient–much like the Battle of the Bulge during World War II. The cemetery is divided into four equal plots and has a large sundial in the center. The sundial has an American eagle mounted on it. To the south of the burial sites is a white stone memorial comprised of a small chapel, a peristyle with a funeral urn at the center, and a museum building. Inside the chapel is a beautiful mosaic of an angel sheathing its sword. Two walls of the museum contain the names of 284 of the missing.

The Suresnes Cemetery

The Suresnes Cemetery is neither the largest nor the smallest World War I cemetery in Europe, but it certainly is in one of the most spectacular locations. Located near the top of a very high hill in the Paris suburban town of Suresnes, it is about five miles from the very center of Paris. Across the street from the cemetery is a small park with a beautiful view of much of the city of Paris, to include the Eiffel Tower and the Sacre-Coeur. The cemetery consists of seven and a half acres of gently sloping grounds and contains the remains of 1,541 World War I dead, as well as the graves of twenty-four unknowns from World War II. These twenty-four WWII dead are located in a small plot near the foot of the cemetery. Most of these twenty-four men died in Paris military hospitals after being evacuated from front-line combat areas, but their identities could not be established. On the walls of the chapel are bronze tablets listing the names of 974 men who were either missing in action or buried at sea. The World War I memorial chapel was enlarged by adding two loggias dedicated to the dead of both wars. On one wall of the visitors' center is a plaque presented by President Woodrow Wilson during a visit to the cemetery following the end of World War I.

NOTES

[1]   All information related to the permanent cemeteries of World War I was obtained from the American Battle Monuments Commission's annual reports, pamphlets available to the general public, and the commission's excellent web site, which contains detailed information as to the burials at each cemetery, descriptions of each cemetery or memorial, and a short video describing each cemetery.

Appendix II

RECOMMENDED READING

I have only just a minute,
Only sixty seconds in it,
Forced upon me, can't refuse it.
Didn't seek it, didn't choose it,
But it's up to me to use it.
I must suffer if I lose it,
Just a tiny little minute—
But eternity is in it.
From the *Service Prayer Book of WWII*

This appendix is NOT a bibliography of references used during the writing of *If These Stones Could Talk*. Instead, it is a somewhat random listing of the books which the author has found to be some of the most interesting reading about World War II that he has enjoyed during almost sixty years of reading about that war. Some of the books listed are recent while others are quite old. Regardless of the date of publication, the books recommended in this appendix are all well written and tell a story about the events, the men and women who took part in those events, the political, strategic and tactical ins and outs of decisions made during the conflict, and the results of those decisions. The listing will not be in typical "footnote" format. Nor will the titles be collected in logical groupings as editors and publishers might prefer. Rather, this is a somewhat helter-skelter listing of books that the author feels the typical reader of World War II history will find to be a "good read." Some of the books listed may well be out of print by now, but even out of print books can many times be found through your local library by using the inter-library loan system. Also, many of the books listed may be found at very reasonable cost on eBay, at abebooks.com, or at amazon.com. That is, if you don't mind not having the feel and smell of a crisp new book.

GOOD READING!

A Bridge Too Far by Cornelius Ryan.

Americans at War by Stephen E. Ambrose.

Band of Brothers, E Company, 506th Regiment, 101st Airborne from Normandy to Hitler's Eagle's Nest by Stephen E. Ambrose.

Bedford Goes to War: The Heroic Story of a Small Virginia Community in World War II by James W. Morrison.

Brave Men by Ernie Pyle.

Children of Yesterday by Jan Valtin.

Crosses in the Wind by Joseph James Shomon.

Eisenhower's Lieutenants, the Campaigns of France and Germany, 1944-1945 by Russell F. Weigley.

Ernie's War: The Best of Ernie Pyle's World War II Dispatches edited by David Nichols.

G.I.: The American Soldier in World War II by Lee Kennett.

Here is Your War by Ernie Pyle.

Last Chapter by Ernie Pyle.

Lost in the Victory: Reflections of American War Orphans of World War II by Susan Johnson Hadler and Ann Bennett Mix, edited by Calvin L. Christman.

No Greater Glory: The Four Immortal Chaplains and the Sinking of the Dorchester in World War II by Dan Kurzman.

Pearl Harbor Ghosts: The Legacy of December 7, 1941 by Thurston Clarke.

Safely Rest by David P. Colley.

Serenade to the Big Bird by Bert Stiles.

Soldiers and Slaves: American POWs Trapped by the Nazis' Final Gamble by Roger Cohen.

Stalingrad: The Fateful Siege 1942-1943 by Antony Beevor.

The Bedford Boys by Alex Kershaw.

The Dead of Winter: How Battlefield Investigators, WWII Veterans, and Forensic Scientists Solved the Mystery of the Bulge's Lost Soldiers by Bill Warnock.

The Eagles' War by Vern Haugland.

The Good War: An Oral History of World War II by Studs Terkel.

The Pacific War 1941-1945 by John Costello.

The Path to Victory: The Mediterranean Theater in World War II by Douglas Porch.

The Story of the Second World War by Henry Steele Commager.

The Victors, Eisenhower and His Boys: the Men of World War II by Stephen E. Ambrose.

They Were on Omaha Beach (The Story of D-Day, Told by Veterans) by Laurent Lefebvre.

U.S. Army in World War II (A series of volumes covering all phases of the U.S. Army's actions during WWII) written and published by the Office of the Chief of Military History, Department of the Army.

Unfinished Journey: A World War II Remembrance by Kerry P. Redmann.

Voices of Valor D-Day: June 6, 1944 by Douglas Brinkley and Ronald J. Drez.

For those readers with access to a computer, there are two excellent web sites for information about many of the individual Army divisions which fought during WWII:

    a. www.lonesentry.com

    b. www.army.mil.cmh

INDEX